MW01292626

PSYCHOANALYSIS, IDENTITY, AND IDEOLOGY
Critical Essays on the Israel/Palestine Case

PSYCHOANALYSIS, IDENTITY, AND IDEOLOGY
Critical Essays on the Israel/Palestine Case

edited by

John Bunzl
University of Vienna

and

Benjamin Beit-Hallahmi
University of Haifa

KLUWER ACADEMIC PUBLISHERS
Boston / Dordrecht / New York / London

Distributors for North, Central and South America:
Kluwer Academic Publishers
101 Philip Drive
Assinippi Park
Norwell, Massachusetts 02061 USA
Telephone (781) 871-6600
Fax (781) 681-9045
E-Mail: kluwer@wkap.com

Distributors for all other countries:
Kluwer Academic Publishers Group
Post Office Box 322
3300 AH Dordrecht, THE NETHERLANDS
Telephone 31 786 576 000
Fax 31 786 576 474
E-Mail: services@wkap.nl

 Electronic Services < http://www.wkap.nl >

Library of Congress Cataloging-in-Publication Data
1-4020-7155-8
PSYCHOANALYSIS, IDENTITY, AND IDEOLOGY:
Critical Essays on the Israel / Palestine Case
Edited by John Bunzl and Benjamin Beit-Hallahmi

A C.I.P. Catalogue record for this book is available
from the Library of Congress.

Copyright © 2002 by Kluwer Academic Publishers

All rights reserved. No part of this work may be reproduced, stored in a retrieval system, or transmitted in any form or by any means, electronic, mechanical, photocopying, microfilming, recording, or otherwise, without the written permission from the Publisher, with the exception of any material supplied specifically for the purpose of being entered and executed on a computer system, for exclusive use by the purchaser of the work.

Permission for books published in Europe: permissions@wkap.nl
Permission for books published in the United States of America: permissions@wkap.com

Printed on acid-free paper.

Printed in the United States of America.

The Publisher offers discounts on this book for course use and bulk purchases. For further information, send an email to <michael.williams@wkap.com>.

To the memory of

Rafael Moses

(1924-2001)

Contents

CONTRIBUTORS

Benjamin Beit-Hallahmi – Professor, Department of Psychology, University of Haifa, Haifa 31905, Israel

Emanuel Berman – Professor, Department of Psychology, University of Haifa, Haifa 31905 Israel; Training Analyst, Israel Psychoanalytic Institute, Jerusalem

José Brunner – The Cohn Institute for the History and Philosophy of Science and Ideas, and The Buchmann Faculty of Law, Tel-Aviv University

John Bunzl – Senior Research Fellow, Austrian Institute for International Affairs, Vienna, Austria; Lecturer, Department of Political Science, University of Vienna

Dan Diner – Professor, Department of History, The Hebrew University, Jerusalem 91905 Israel; Director, The Simon Dubnow Institute for Jewish History and Culture, University of Leipzig, Germany

Yolanda Gampel – Professor, Department of Psychology, Tel-Aviv University, Tel-Aviv 69978, Israel; Training Analyst, Israel Psychoanalytic Institute, Jerusalem

Rafael Moses (deceased) – Emeritus Professor of Psychoanalysis, The Hebrew University; Training Analyst, Israel Psychoanalytic Institute, Jerusalem

Eran J. Rolnik – Department of Psychiatry, Tel-Aviv Suraski Medical Center; The Cohn Institute for the History and Philosophy of Science and Ideas, Tel-Aviv University

Ramzi Suleiman – Senior Lecturer, Department of Psychology, University of Haifa, Haifa 31905 Israel; President, The Galilee Center for Social Research, Haifa, Israel

Moshe Zuckerman – The Cohn Institute of the History and Philosophy of Science and Ideas; Director of the Institute for German History, Tel-Aviv University, Tel-Aviv 69978 Israel

Preface

LOOKING BACKWARD

John Bunzl
University of Vienna

This book is a collection of dialogues with psychoanalytic ideas and critical readings of such ideas, in an attempt to meet the challenges of history, ideology, and politics, as they unfold before us. A series of dialogues then became a multilogue, conversations among various approaches to the interpretation of collective behavior, including psychoanalysis, social psychology, literature, political science, and history, as well as a conversation among various theoretical schools in psychoanalysis, and among different stages in the history of psychoanalysis itself. All these dialogues are united by the questions of the psychological structure of identities and ideologies. How has this series of dialogues ever gotten started?

Having observed the perseverance of the Israeli-Palestinian drama from Vienna for almost forty years, I could not disregard the fact that this was the city not only of Theodor Herzl and Adolph Hitler, but also of Sigmund Freud. While it turned out that a clear and direct relationship existed between the disastrous tradition of Central European anti-Semitism on the one hand, and the Zionist response to it on the other, it was less clear that this response would itself not only transfer old Jewish dilemmas of identity to the shores of West Asia, but, in addition, would create new, and severe, problems resulting from a colonial encounter with Arab reality inside and outside of Palestine. However one might interpret the political origins and causes of this one-hundred-year-old conflict, one of its results was obviously the formation of new individual and collective forms of consciousness and unconsciousness.

Our conference was convened under the heading of 'Identity and Trauma', and not much needs to be said to justify that. Anyone barely familiar with current events in West Asia would see this heading as natural, almost self-evident. The combination of a traumatic history with the necessity of developing a discourse of rationalizations, within the framework of an ongoing colonial encounter, made the construction of myths about oneself and the Other ostensibly unavoidable. As long as there was no movement towards change in the reality of the conflict and the confrontation remained rigid and relentless, only marginal voices were able to question conventional myths and apparent certainties. But historical events of major proportions, starting with the Lebanon War of 1982, did contribute to the erosion of traditional stereotypes and the questioning of conventional narratives on a large scale. The formal mutual recognition between Israel and the PLO (in 1993), which followed the First Palestinian *Intifada*, eventually could not but affect identity and image of both collectives. What the "New Historians" had painfully uncovered in their research seemed to transcend academic barriers and become part of the heated public discourse within Israeli society, revolving around identity and narcissism (Brunner, 2002).

Observing the years since the Oslo Accords of 1993, however, one could not fail to notice the contradictions between official recognition of the Other and the constant de-legitimation of that Other as a real partner, between intentions and results, between the elites and the masses. It became obvious that in order to overcome the conflict it was not sufficient to conclude formal agreements between the leaderships on both sides. Unless there was a socially relevant minimal understanding of one's own traumata and those of the other side, no enduring mutual confidence seemed possible, or relevant, despite a variety of "confidence building measures". In cases where more or less recent catastrophes have an obvious impact on political behavior, a psycho-political dimension has to be added to the study of conflict. The group dynamics resulting from past traumata have to be added to the tensions resulting from an ongoing quasi-colonial situation in order to explain their impact on current perceptions, and the resulting demonization of the other.

In the case before us it is important to stress that we are not dealing with two equal communities; although both were or are traumatized at some point in time, no symmetry exists between them regarding the present relationship of forces and the colonial dimension of their mutual embrace, and this means historical traumata and memory.

> Even if oppression took place decades or centuries past, if the grievances of the ethnic group have not been acknowledged by outsiders, particularly by the oppressor nation …and the losses resulting from oppression unmourned, then the sense of ethnic victimhood thus engendered can be passed from generation to generation (Volkan, 1990, p. 34).

In the Israeli-Palestinian case, both the oppressors and the oppressed cultivate an identity of victimhood. The presently and actually strong had been, historically speaking, extremely weak and feels so potentially within an Arab-Moslem ocean. The presently and actually weak have a more immediate and more realistic sense of victimization. But a century of lethal encounter has also created a host of projections, distortions, rationalizations and instrumentalizations of one's own, and the other's, real experiences of suffering.

This brings us back to the psycho-political relevance of Zionist discourse on Jewish existence in the Diaspora. The "Negation of Exile" is/was obviously associated with the Zionist rejection of "Jewish" qualities that had become the rationalizations of anti-Semitic hostility. Accordingly the Zionist role model of a "new Jew" coincided, not by chance, with the "*völkisch*" stereotype that haunted (mainly Central) Europe: strong, beautiful, manly, anti-urban, rooted in the soil, and being part of the (ethnic) "community" (*Gemeinschaft*), and not of just a society (*Gesellscha*ft). These were the conscious and unconscious ideals of the "Negation of Exile".

This ideological predisposition could not pass the "test" of the Holocaust; it also impeded a genuine empathy with its victims and survivors. Instead of adequate mourning, shame, contempt, and even disgust pervaded the public discourse of the *Yishuv*, the Jewish community of Palestine during the Second World War (Segev, 1994). On the other hand survivors were, of course, relatives, and represented in one way or the other, a part of one's own pre-history; so the Jews of Palestine also experienced a "return of the repressed", because, as Idith Zertal (1988) quotes Freud: "Das Unheimliche war einmal heimlich" [What is uncanny was once canny](Freud, 1918, p. 250).

While an appropriate coping with the recent past was prevented by the enormity of the event, there were also mental pre-dispositions and circumstances of the struggle in Palestine contributed to a selective appropriation of the tragedy. By "adopting" instances of Jewish resistance, heroism, and uprisings, a link could be established to one's own fight against the British Mandate regime and the Palestinian Arabs. Thus the Holocaust was taken out of its historical context, and resistance was "Zionized" a posteriori. Both events became rationalizations for Jewish nation-state building and could not be dealt with as tragedies in their own right, an occurrence that Zertal defines as "collective defense mechanisms".

Obviously, the perception of Israel's confrontation with the Palestinians could not remain unaffected by the Zionist modes of dealing with the Holocaust; and it is apparently no accident that a critical re-evaluation of relations with the Palestinians happened at about the same time as new approaches to mourning the Jewish catastrophe of the twentieth century appeared.

Two of our psychoanalytic colleagues pointed out a few years ago that one's own traumatization in general does not increase the sensitivity toward the traumatization of others; however, if the traumatization of the other is to be perceived as a consequence of one's own doing, this mechanism is vastly intensified (Moses & Moses-Hrushovski, 1996). In such a context of denial of, and defense against, responsibility and guilt, a fetishization of the Holocaust occurred, and in this form the *Shoah* memory could be instrumentalized for diverse purposes, including an identification of the Palestinian resistance with Nazism, thus often legitimizing the use of disproportional violence against Arab opponents (see Zuckerman, 2002). Moses (2002) reminds us that defending against guilt feelings often (especially with children) takes the form of outbursts of anger, extreme self-righteousness, or "punishment" of victims.

This is not to say that Israeli society only deals in such ways with its traumata. There can be no doubt that the Holocaust and the wars since 1948 left deep marks on individual and collective psyches. Even without the Holocaust the Israeli-Palestinian conflict would have been antagonistic enough to produce and re-produce corresponding attitudes. Enemy images, anxiety, and distrust do conform to the violent character of a colonial encounter. However, they are overdetermined by the memory of real mass-extermination in the twentieth century.

As mentioned above, the Lebanon War of 1982 signified a breach in the Israeli denial of the Palestinian Other, while the First Palestinian

Intifada (1987-1993) widened this breach; it shook up, even more forcefully, the repression of the inevitable victimization caused by Zionist colonization. The Oslo Agreements of 1993 represented a qualitative change insofar as they led to an official mutual recognition. This could not but affect the narratives of both sides. As the conflict had mobilized the emotional, cognitive, and practical behavior of Israeli society for a very long time, it was no wonder that a relativization of enemy images would cause an identity crisis (Bar-On,1997). Israeli-Jewish identity was, to a large extent, determined through external hostility; how could it be defined anew? If previous self-images were a construct based on narcissistic clichés (Brunner, 2002) and (necessary) myths, what should an improved narrative of oneself and the (demonized) Other look like? Does admitting guilt and/or responsibility conjure up dangers of punishment and revenge? And if does, what practical steps could be taken to lessen their impact? (Beit-Hallahmi, 1993).

And what about the consequences of any revisions in images and myths for the "lessons" to be drawn from the Holocaust? A specific interpretation of the Holocaust had been an important argument for the policy of strength and mistrust vis-à-vis the "world" (Zuckerman, 2002). Organized large-group visits of Israeli high school students to Auschwitz and Treblinka had consolidated this attitude. However, if one's own victimhood in relation to the Palestinians is being re-considered, the relevance of the Holocaust for the conflict then changes. A different lesson of a more universalist kind would allow for the integration of *al-nakba* (the Palestinian trauma of 1948) into Israeli-Jewish memory.

Having such considerations in mind we (at the Austrian Institute for International Affairs) thought that psychoanalytic concepts could contribute to an explanation of psychodynamic processes going on within Israeli society. Thus a conference was designed to further explore these and related issues. And so, in June 1999, a group of psychoanalysts, psychologists, and historians, gathered in Sigmund Freud's home in 19 Berggasse , Vienna (now the Freud Museum) for a two-day conference, where presentations were given before an attentive audience of European, Israeli, and Palestinian scholars and mental health practitioners. Its focus was the possible connections (including the application) of psychoanalytic interpretations to Jewish history of the past 100 years, and in particular to Zionism and Israel.

Psychoanalysis, ever since its beginnings in the same location, 19 Berggasse, more than one hundred years ago, has been the focus of contention, controversy, and debate. What is psychoanalysis? Beyond its theoretical and technical boundaries, it is first and foremost a special mode of critical thinking and demystification. It looks at the past as the key to all observable behaviors, and seeks to uncover the hidden aspects of our lives, where the more important unconscious motives rule unchallenged. You can try to ignore the past which has become unseen and invisible, but not its memory and representations. Psychoanalysis in this volume is a system of interpretation as well as an object of interpretation. What this book embodies is this tradition of critical thinking, examining closely ideologies and identities, in particular Zionism, and relying, but not exclusively, on several psychoanalytic traditions .

The 1999 conference was unique not only because the participants included both (a majority of) Israelis and (a minority of) Palestinians. Among the participants were some of the leading psychoanalysts in Israel, and, contrary to common stereotypes, these psychoanalysts, as demonstrated in some of our chapters, did not shy away from discussing both sensitive professional dilemmas and sensitive historical issues. The book is only one product of this conference. It is our hope that it will lead to more fruitful discussions and even some concrete outcomes.

References

Bar-On, D. (1997). Israeli society between the culture of death and the culture of life. *Israel Studies, 2*, 88-112.

Beit-Hallahmi, B. (1993). *Original Sins: Reflections on the History of Zionism and Israel*. New York: Interlink.

Brunner, J. (2002). Contentious origins: Psychoanalytic comments on the debate over Israel's creation. In this volume.

Freud, S. (1919). The 'Uncanny. In *The Standard Edition of the Complete Psychological Works of Sigmund Freud*, 24 vols. Vol. 17. pp. 217-252. Hogarth Press: London

Moses, R. & Moses-Hrushovski, R. (1996). Some Social and Psychological Perspectives on the Meaning of the Holocaust: A View from Israel. Unpublished.

Moses, R. (2002) Unconscious defense mechanisms and social mechanisms used in national and political conflicts . In this volume.

Segev, T. (1994). *The Seventh Million: The Israelis and the Holocaust*. New York: Hill & Wang.

Volkan, V.D. An Overview of Psychological Concepts. In Volkan, V.D., Julius, D.A. & Montville, J.V. (1990-1991). *The Psychodynamics of International Relationships*. Vol. 1. Lexington, Mass: Lexington Books.

Zertal, I. (1988). *From Catastrophe to Power: Holocaust Survivors and the Emergence of Israel*. Berkeley: University of California Press.

Zuckerman, M (2002). Towards an Analysis of Israeli Political Culture. In this volume.

ACKNOWLEDGEMENTS

The preparation of the 1999 conference on Identity and Trauma, held at the Freud Museum in Vienna, and the publication of this volume, based on the conference presentations, have been made possible through the help and support of numerous organizations and individuals.

We would like to express our gratitude and appreciation to the Austrian Institute for International Affairs and especially to Angelika Theurl, Gabriele Reinharter and Otmar Häll, and to the staff of the Freud Museum, and especially Katharina Murschetz and Harald Leupold-Löwenthal. The Identity and Trauma conference was also sponsored by the Austrian Ministry of Science, the Jewish Museum in Vienna, and the City of Vienna .

The Austrian Ministry of Science supported the final preparation of this volume for publication. We would also like to thank the University of Haifa Research Authority and its staff, especially Patrick Maestracci.

Part I

Identity, Ideology, and History

Simply defining psychoanalysis has sometimes been regarded as an unmet challenge. What has been clear, despite all controversies, is that the psychoanalytic tradition created and inspired special modes of critical thinking, which have been used to examine both human behavior and corresponding social ideologies. What we can observe in this tradition in action is a unique way of deconstructing human behavior, which is a tradition of asking some rarely asked questions. Sigmund Freud has served as the great cultural and academic stimulus, whether you liked or did not like his ideas. In this book he serves as a source of inspiration or opposition, but never as a source of dogma.

The following six chapters constitute six variations on a theme, with each expressing a unique perspective. Psychoanalysis serves as an inspiration for the analysis of history and culture, as the processes involving culture and politics are examined through a broad view. This is the red thread running through all contributions.

Part I displays both the advantages and the disadvantages of hindsight; it's great to look at others with such an advantage, but rather difficult to be looked at. As we stand almost helpless before the enormous tragedies and disasters of history, reading these chapters is a sobering experience, forcing us to recognize once again our enormous limitations. The dilemmas of Jewish identity at the end of the nineteenth century could not have been better expressed than through the case of Sigmund Freud himself. In the first chapter, Freud is compared to other Europeans of his time, and that is the way he had wished to be looked at.

The Zionist dream, which Freud was not ready to embrace, had become a reality. Dan Diner and Moshe Zuckerman offer two highly original surveys of the realization of this dream, in the history of the State of Israel, presenting a model of critical thinking and a dialogue with psychoanalytic ideas. Rafael Moses and José Brunner present two kinds of psychoanalytic interpretations for the passions of political struggles, while Ramzi Suleiman looks at the those who are left out of the Zionist dream. His chapter is based on social psychological theories, in a dialogue with psychoanalysis.

Chapter 1

Political and Literary Answers to Some 'Jewish Questions': Proust, Joyce, Freud, and Herzl

Benjamin Beit-Hallahmi
University of Haifa

How did Europeans of the early twentieth century look at the questions of Jewish identity and Zionism? Jews in the European world, whose lives were being shaped by European traditions of anti-Semitism on the one hand and the recent coming of the Enlightenment and capitalism on the other, had to re-define their identity. The struggles with Jewish identity, as it became separated from Judaism, are examined through the writings and the lives of Marcel Proust, James Joyce, Sigmund Freud, and Theodor Herzl. What we find is that European social realities are faithfully reflected in two great modern novels. The failure of assimilation, which led Herzl to Zionism, is thoroughly documented by the novelists, who show us that a racial conception of Jews dooms assimilation to failure. Could Europe be trusted? That was the question. Herzl was the most pessimistic, and called for desperate action; Freud was stoically optimistic, as were Proust and Joyce.

1. Introduction

The past two hundred years have seen a total revolution in Jewish existence, with the almost complete disappearance of historical Judaism and the traditional Jewish way of life except as a minority option. Today, there is a minority of less than 10 percent of world Jewry that still preserves historical Judaism. Through modernization, Jews have changed from an obscure, backward tribe, to a community involved in all the great advances of humanity in culture, science, arts and politics. Two hundred years ago European Jews were a small, marginal group, completely outside the mainstream of social and cultural developments, a minority of outsiders. In 1800, there were 1.5 million Jews in Europe, out of a European population of 100 million, and a world Jewish population of 2.5 million. Not only were the Jews a small minority in Europe, but most Jewish communities had fewer than 300 members (see Goldscheider & Zuckerman, 1984). The modernization of European Jews, which took place between 1780 and 1880, involved physical, social, and cultural dislocations on a massive scale. It took another one hundred years, between 1880 and 1980, for another cycle of political and geographical dislocations.

Emancipation for the Jews, the granting of normal citizenship and political rights, came against the background of the decline of religion and feudalism and the coming of secular nationalism, democracy, and socialism. The rise of the new bourgeoisie and the appearance of the ideals of equality, popular representation, and pluralism, which ran counter to religious traditions, made emancipation for oppressed and excluded groups possible. The decline of religion also meant a decrease in anti-Semitic prejudice. Entering the modern world via the grace of emancipation meant the collapse of the Jewish consensus and society. It was nothing less than a complete overturn of the Jewish world, which until then could be regarded as medieval. Tearing down the figurative walls of the ghetto and the concrete limitations on full participation in society brought about not just the weakening, but the destruction, of historical community structure. The Jewish community might have been a ghetto, but it offered a home. Now Jews lost it.

Gustav Mahler (who met Freud once for a famous consultation; see Jones, 1957; Reik, 1953) described himself as thrice homeless, as a native of Bohemia among Austrians, as an Austrian among Germans, and as a Jew throughout the world (Schorske, 1998). This complaint may sound rather strange today, but undoubtedly reflects real pain, alienation, and even humiliation. We all want to be unconditionally accepted and loved and to belong, and we all carry within us the fantasy of a happy family, where we find love and unconditional acceptance. Can such a happy human family become a reality? And if we cannot believe in the reality of unconditional and universal love, we may hope to find it at least within the bosom of our own tribe. Homelessness might have meant also the ambition and freedom from tradition that enabled Jews to become so successful under capitalism (Beit-Hallahmi, 1993).

The breakdown of both consciousness and institutions and the consequent crisis of homelessness, are still felt today through the movements it gave birth to, including Zionism, which are all reactions to the decline of the old Jewish community system. Zionism has been an attempt to re-invent and reconstruct the lost Jewish community. The secularization of the Jews has been one of the main factors in their accommodation to the modern world. The religious idea of a Jewish mission construes Judaism as God's pilot project, carried on by world Jewry. Jews were the chosen few, who, when the Messiah comes, would lead the rest of the world towards global salvation (Marmorstein, 1969). This notion is clearly not unique to Judaism, and is central to most, if not all, religious communities. A belief in the group's superiority and election may be found in many secular groupings as well. A gap between a group's hopes for itself and its objective conditions may be attenuated by the belief in mission and superiority. Believing in a collective mission for the Jewish people has made it easier for individual Jews to understand, or at least accept, their individual destinies. Most modern Jews have rejected the idea of a special mission for the Jewish people, either a religious or a secular one.

The emancipation of Jews as individuals and citizens offered a new solution to the social problem of Jews as a group: integration into society or assimilation. If Jews were indeed accepted as individuals in the modern state, and invited to share in the duties and responsibilities of normal citizens, then a collective problem had been solved. Emancipation, and then assimilation, were the two stages of a great dream, which was about the integration of Jews into Western society. The assimilationist movement encouraged Jews to become integrated in their surrounding society. A new world opened up before the denizens of the ghetto as Jews were entering the mainstream of liberal society and presumably losing their marginality. This was the logic of the assimilation process. It involved a complete change in the traditional

Jewish attitude towards gentiles, from contempt for the out-group culture to respect and emulation.

The most direct form of assimilation was a formal conversion to Christianity, an admission ticket to mainstream European society and national cultures. Jews were baptized as a matter of convenience, not because of some profound religious change. The prevalence of conversions to Christianity was significant among the well-educated and wealthy, who formalized their entrance into the ranks of the bourgeoisie, but it was rare among the Jewish masses. According to some estimates, a quarter of a million Jews (about 5 per cent of the total number of Jews in the world by mid-century) were converted during the nineteenth century (see Marmorstein, 1969). The assimilation process still did not eliminate "sociological Jews": the vast majority of individuals who wanted to preserve their groups identity, but were not sure what content they were going to put into it.

Secularization meant thus that Jewishness has been separated from Judaism, and most Jews today are such only in a sociological sense. They are "assimilated" and far removed from historical traditions. In most cases, they have no idea what those traditions are. Alfred Kazin described them at the end of the twentieth century as "Jews who no longer know what they stand for and can't believe that Judaism once postulated the immortality of the soul" (Kazin, 1998, p. 5). They cannot believe that their identity is tied to a religion which in its essence, belief in the world of the spirits, is just like all other religions. This is, of course, the final outcome of a long historical process.

> From the beginning of Jewish modernity, Jews have had three choices: to be Jews, to be Christians, to be secularists. Many have decided that they cannot conscientiously be Jews because they cannot believe what Judaism requires them to believe: that there is a God, the Creator who revealed himself as Lawgiver to the patriarchs and the prophets (Himmelfarb, 1967, p. 226).

Jewish secularization has been vigorous and thorough ever since it started in the eighteenth century. It meant that Jewish identity was being maintained by individuals who completely stopped the observance of Jewish religious practices. Indeed, the absence of any religious practices is the most prominent characteristic of modern Jews, who are among the most secularized groups anywhere. Jewish identity was still there, because the world defined them as Jewish, but Judaism had gone from their lives. Secularized Jews were a European reality by the early nineteenth century, and a significant majority in Western Europe by its end. By the same time the process of secularization was making significant inroads into Jewish communities in Eastern Europe. Since, for most Jews, Jewishness and Judaism became separated in the nineteenth century, and the Jewish caste weakened its hold on its members and then disintegrated (except for the Orthodox minority), the need arose for a new definition (and self-definition) of Jewish identity.

Zionism was one of several responses to the process of secularization among Jews, which has been more thorough and more radical than in any similar group. The Zionist definition of world Jewry stated that Jews were members of a national group, deserving its own nation-state. Israel is that nation-state, aiming at providing as home for all Jews. Israel is clearly not just another ordinary, normal, nation-state but a revolutionary experiment devoted to creating an ideological state, a state with a mission.

Zionism aims at preserving Jewish identity (for reasons that are not always spelled out clearly, and possibly resulting from external pressures), but rejects its historical forms, wanting to leave behind Diaspora culture in all its manifestations. What we see in Israel, and in the Zionist movement, which created it, is a deliberate attempt, at this point far from being successful, to create a secular nationalism and a secular identity out of a collective history which used to be totally marked and dominated by religion.

Modernization, not only among Jews, but in all traditional cultures, means the rejection of the past. It is tied to private and public shame about one's cultural history and identity. What to do about the Jewish past? How to read it? This shame is added to the wounds of powerlessness and humiliation. The constant pain of homelessness and rejection, the pain of being a Jew, is expressed in Sigmund Freud's own emblematic story of his father's all-too routine encounter with an anti-Semitic thug.

> At that point I was brought up against the event in my youth whose power was still being shown in all these emotions and dreams. I may have been ten or twelve years old, when my father began to take his views upon things in the world we live in. Thus it was, on one such

occasion, that he told me a story to show me how much better things were now than they had been in his days. When I was a young man, he said, I went for a walk one Saturday in the streets of your birthplace. I was well dressed, and had a new fur cap on my head. A Christian came up to me and with a single blow knocked off my cap into the mud and shouted: 'Jew! get off the pavement!' 'And what did you do?' I with the victims forever, and contribute, as in Freud's case asked. 'I went into the roadway and picked up my cap,' was the quiet reply. This struck me as unheroic conduct of the part of the big strong man who was holding the little boy by the hand. I contrasted this situation with another which fitted my feelings better: the scene in which Hanninbal's father Hamilcar Barca, made his boy swear before the household altar to take vengeance on the Romans. Ever since that time Hannibal had had a place in my phantasies. (Freud, 1900, p. 197).

The scars of alienation and rejection stay, to dreams of revenge and liberation.

The Jewish Question put itself on Europe's agenda in the nineteenth century. The assimilation project, which many Jews embraced, was tied to the rise of liberal politics, as Europe was becoming more secular, less prejudiced, and more democratic, promising all citizens equal protection. Moreover, this revolutionary, or mostly evolutionary, assimilation program invited Jews, or so they thought, to take part in it. Zionism, on the other hand, invited them to worry first about themselves, rather than put the least bit of trust in universal progress which might benefit Jews among the whole of humanity.

2. Some Jewish questions

Why and how to be Jewish, that is the first Jewish Question, one that Jews had to deal with individually and communally, and we have looked at that question above. There were really two additional Jewish questions I want to touch on, one practical and the other psychological. Freud wrote clearly about the second Jewish Question. In response to Herzl's play, *The New Ghetto*, Freud had a dream about "the Jewish question, the worry about the future of one's children, whom one could not give a homeland" (Freud, 1900, p. 442). So the second (or first?) Jewish Question is that of the basic responsibility of a parent to his children, the duty of securing a future. This is a feeling we can all identify with, and it is both pragmatic and emotional. It is a truly human question.

The third Jewish Question we are going to deal with had to do with Jewish masculinity (Gilman, 1991, 1993; Mosse, 1985). Were Jewish men real men? Freud touched on this issue when discussing the views of non-Jews, especially in relation to the Jewish practice of circumcision. Freud stated that the castration complex was the most important source of anti-Semitism, because of circumcision, just as the absence of a penis is the source of contempt for women (Freud, 1905). It is small wonder that the circumcision ritual has been regarded as symbolic castration.

In Europe through the ages, Jews, that is Jewish males, were (quite correctly) perceived as genitally mutilated, and this made them less than full men. It was not just a matter of genital mutilation, which was psychologically the most significant. It was a question of masculine identity and behavior. There was a socially defined "effeminacy of the male Jewish body" (Bunzl, 1997, p. 74). There was a medieval tradition that claimed that Jewish males menstruated, and it was Carl Gustav Jung, among others in modern times, who discussed openly the femininity of Jewish males (Gilman, 1993).

This was tied to the racial-biological conception of Jews in the nineteenth century (Gilman, 1991, 1993) which dictated use of the term Jew as noun, rather than Jewish as adjective. This racialism was possibly tied to popular ideas about evolution, as promoted by so-called social Darwinists. Races were not just different; they were also inferior, or superior, to others. Zionism has accepted the racial-tribal view, projecting the family structure onto the world.

Parenthetically, I should add that the emasculation metaphor has been used and is being used in connection with many oppressed groups, including women (Greer, 1971). It reflects our male-dominated thinking, which seems quite universal. While the feminine is judged to be weak and deficient, manliness images are everywhere tied to political and psychological empowerment. Masculinity remains not only a universal human ideal, but also a focus of many rituals, most of them highly destructive.

Every national revival movement offers a way of erasing the memory of an imagined experience of deficient manhood. Zionism offered a dream of the New Jew, who would be strongly and clearly masculine. Jewish sovereignty was to create a new human type: in touch with nature, working on the land, productive, physical, renewed by the Hebrew language and by the encounter with pre-Diaspora geography, in short, the anti-Jew. Jabotinsky wrote about the new Hebrew as follows:

> Because the Jid [Russian derogatory term for Jew] is ugly sickly, and lacks decorum, we shall endow the ideal image of the Hebrew with masculine beauty, tall stature, mighty shoulders, vigorous movement, radiance of colors and complexion (Beit-Hallahmi, 1993, pp. 130-131).

What comes to mind here is Alfred Adler's concept of the masculine protest (Adler, 1956). In the case of Jews in Europe, it was circumcision that made the metaphor of deficient masculinity more vivid. Zionist writers did not refer to genital mutilation, but described Jews as being physically and mentally crippled by Diaspora existence. This idea was expressed by sympathetic non-Jews as well. John Adams, second president of the United States, wrote in 1825 : "I really wish the Jews back in Judea, an independent nation...once restored to an independent government, and no longer persecuted, they would soon wear away some of the asperities and peculiarities of their character" (Beit-Hallahmi, 1993, p. 39). All ideological varieties of Zionism, from right to left, were united in claiming that a territorial concentration of the Jewish people in Palestine would cure the anomalies of Jewish existence in the Diaspora. Thus, Ber Borochov, the founder of Marxist Zionism in the early twentieth century, suggested that there were in the world some abnormal nations which need a "therapeutic movement" to achieve normalcy. "This kind of movement possesses the abilities to normalize disharmonies rooted in the pathological situations of a social organism" (Yassour, 1986, p. 10).

What Zionism was proposing was not only national liberation and human renewal, but a complete physical and psychic changeover and regeneration for both the collectivity and the individual. Herzl's dream of the *Judenstaat* included an element of physical rehabilitation and regeneration as well. In an interview about his political program, given in 1898, he says: "We have stepped in as such a volunteer corps of nurses, and we want, as patients, the poor sick Jewish nation which we wish to restore to a healthful mode of life on the soil of our fathers" (Herzl, 1898). On another occasion, Herzl wrote: "We believe that all [the nation's] illnesses, both physical and moral, may be cured, if it is returned to a natural course of life" (1899, p. 7).

Beyond the male physique, there are masculine behaviors and attributes, such as assertiveness, energy, power, and success. Nationalism needs masculine heroes, symbols and myths as it engages in a process of selective glorification. If you want to create a secular Jewish national mythology, modeled after that of the Hungarians or Italians, basing it on exemplary stories of physical courage is a real problem. For Zionism, manly heroes were sorely needed. Rabbinical Judaism is not a good source for finding such heroes. Its huge literature of rituals and legalisms does not exalt the devotion to a homeland or the courage in battle. Jewish history in the Diaspora is not a source of stories about valor and victory. Even using a steamroller, squeezing one drop of admirable muscular and secular nationalism out of Diaspora chronicles would be practically impossible. The common store of memories was filled with massacres and victimization, with Jews dying out of devotion to the ancient faith, slaughtered by gentiles who stood for military prowess and manly bearing. There were countless Jewish martyrs, slaughtered in countless massacres, sanctifying the Holy Name in their martyrdom, but dying passively.

For Zionism, these were ignominious deaths, not to be commemorated but to be forgotten and lost. Proving one's real devotion to the faith by dying had no real value for the secular Zionist vision. Diaspora Jews died for their religious faith, not for secular nationalism. Religious martyrdom was seen as not just shameful, but purposeless and wasteful. It had never contributed to the cause of sovereignty and national separatism. The only honorable death was fighting, with weapon in hand, while promoting national goals. The only heroic death could be death for the sake of an existing nation, not for a non-existent God. This death would follow a life in which the new masculinity would be proudly and fully displayed. Freud's fantasies about Hamilcar Barca, the Semitic hero, cited above, fit right in with the idea of true manhood expressed in all rising nationalisms.

3. Methodology

In seeking new vantage points on the Zionist project and some of its psychological aspects, I decided to turn to texts by those who were able to witness the Zionist dream as it was taking form in Europe, long before it became a great success story. Let us go back to the stage where Zionism was just a possibility, not an accomplished historical fact. History is often written backwards, as an inevitable process of change, but we can at least imagine what it was like to observe the uncertain process in the making.

I am going to present two literary case studies, which is methodologically quite suspect, as it should be. In my defense I will claim that these case studies are indeed representative of broader historical realities. Freud has taught us that art means first and foremost pleasure and beauty, but behind the immense pleasures created by the two great novelists, we can discern pain and conflict.

The novelists we are dealing with quite clearly reflected the zeitgeist, in which the Jewish Questions were close to center stage and Zionism a real option, or at least a real fantasy, for many. These artistic renderings should be treated today as historical texts, produced by the special European sensibilities of that period. An encounter with these artistic sensibilities should be not just fascinating, but instructive. My reading of the novels is not, of course, that of an expert on literature but that of a consumer of art.

4. Literary Materials

The literary materials I am using here consist of what are widely considered the two greatest modern and modernist novels, authored by James Joyce and Marcel Proust. It is interesting to note that at least one of the two concurred with the judgment of their common greatness. This is supported by one report of their only meeting. Joyce and Proust met just once, on May 18, 1922, in Paris, at a midnight dinner party in the Ritz Hotel, which was also attended by Igor Stravinsky, Serge Diaghilev, and Pablo Picasso. But the meeting was far from memorable. According to one account, Joyce said "Here are the two greatest literary figures of our time meeting and asking each other whether they like truffles" (Hayman, 1990, pp. 483-484).

The stature of both literary works is beyond any doubt. In 1998, a list of the 100 most important English-language novels was published in New York (Ilnytzky, 1998). If we examine the list, we note that Jews are less than prominent, either as characters or as authors, and

Jewishness is not a common topic or trait. And on this list *Ulysses*, by James Joyce, was number one. In addition to *Ulysses*, only one other book on the list of 100 can be, called Jewish, and that is *Portnoy's Complaint*, by Philip Roth, listed as number 52. The other work I would like to examine, *A la Recherche du Temps Perdu*, is widely considered to be among the masterpieces of modern French literature, as well as among the greatest literary achievement of all time.

Both books were written during the same period, approximately 1905 to 1922, roughly the first quarter of the twentieth century. The two novelists were selected to serve as observers of the history and politics of modern Europe. What we realize is that both novels deal seriously with the Jewish Questions listed above and take a stand on Zionism as the answer to these Questions. In both novels, Jewishness as a phenomenon and the personal struggle with the terrible burden of a Jewish heritage are major themes. A Jewish heritage as described in both texts, is something you must cope with, like an inherited disease, an affliction to be healed or exorcised. Zionism in both novels is a reality as an ideological movement and as a real option for Jews, who may or may not choose to espouse it.

5. Jewishness and Zionism in Proust: *A La Recherche Du Temps Perdu*

Marcel Proust is the more original (or perverse) of the two authors, and his observations on Jews and Zionism are more likely to shock the reader. Himself born to a Jewish mother, and thus sharing in the Jewish condition, he described being Jewish as a burden, an incurable inherited illness. Marcel Proust identified with French Catholicism, and regarded Jews as a race. In 1896, Proust wrote: " ...I am a Catholic, like my father and my brother, my mother is Jewish" (cited in Hayman, 1990, p. 108). This self-definition of Proust as a Catholic was never accepted by any of his contemporaries. His outstanding dark looks marked him immediately and he was always regarded as a Jew, despite his Roman Catholic baptism as a baby. Wilson (1928) described Proust as "half-Jewish" and claimed that two central elements in *A La Recherche* were the moral indignation "of the classical Jewish prophet" and "a certain Jewish family piety". Two other contemporaries, the writers Collette and Francois Mauriac, expressed in writing their revulsion at his 'Jewish' physical appearance, something which did not prevent them from recognizing his literary genius. Actually, this universal recognition of a giant who is handicapped by both ancestry and sexual proclivities (while, as we will see, denying both) is evidence of a victory of art over all prejudice.

Marcel Proust and his great work present us with an ideal case for psychoanalytic interpretations. We might claim that Proust, expressing himself through the fictional Marcel, the narrator of *A La Recherche*, was denying his true identity. His narrator is a heterosexual gentile, and not a homosexual Jew. The author has chosen a narrator very different than himself. Not just that, but in a predictable manner, the narrator is developed as a mirror-image of the real Marcel Proust. Moreover, this heterosexual gentile narrator is quite preoccupied with homosexuality, and not much less concerned about Jewishness. Marcel, the narrator, encounters throughout his life instances of homosexual behavior in both women and men, and reacts to both in horror. First, he discovers that the women he is in love with are actually lesbians. Then, much later in life, he discovers male homosexuality, which he finds even more shocking. This horror of sexual perversion creates a major source of tension in *A la Recherche* and adds to our pleasure as readers. There are other sources of tension and interest as well. Marcel, the arch-insider, keeps running into both homosexuals and Jews every turn, and gives us fascinating portraits which are always critical and judgmental, keeping his distance from those outsiders.

One might say that Proust's efforts at denial, undoing, and reversal are the real source of his greatness. But is Proust denying his identity? As readers, we must separate narrator and author (Shattuck, 1974). We decided that Proust is denying because of extra-textual information. For us as readers in this case, a text can be enjoyed, and perhaps analyzed, on its own merits, without references to extra-textual knowledge and biographical information, so let us go back to the text, and to the Jewish Questions.

For Proust, Jewishness (and anti-Semitism) were a major theme because his work expressed a preoccupation with social acceptance and social exclusion, and so the practice of rejection, directed at Jews and other social inferiors, is a frequent topic. No matter how hard they try by changing their names and converting to Christianity, society will always recognize Jews as outsiders, "Orientals" in European drawing rooms. As we know, Marcel Proust himself was a living example.

The reality which Proust both lived and faithfully chronicled meant that even successful Jews could not escape rejection by polite society and would never be truly accepted. Because of social rejection, Jews must hide their identity, a preoccupation which affects their character and develops a new kind of personality. Proust paints cruel caricatures of Jews who try to climb up and be accepted into society. The portrayal of Jews are often so critical that one can see why Proust has been accused of anti-Semitism. Bloch (the prototypical French-Jewish name) is one of the most negative characters in *A La Recherche*. White (1999) judges Proust to be a normal anti-Semite for his time, while still being puzzled by the co-existence of such feelings with an uncommon love for his Jewish mother.

Proust's narrator looks at the Jews from a distance in disdain, the way he looks at homosexuals. Discovering the reality of both Jews and homosexuals is a major shock for Marcel. Jews and homosexuals were two kinds of pariahs, but they might have themselves to blame for their status. Members of both groups were less than real men, and both wanted to hide that. Both groups try to escape their bitter fate, to no avail. Jews to Marcel, like homosexuals, are a race, a biological species of men-women, not real men. They are like homosexuals who also must hide their true identity, and Jewishness, like homosexuality, is an incurable disease. The narrator mocks Jews and homosexuals who claim Jesus and Socrates as their own. Despite the mockery, some readers may feel pity for both Jews and homosexuals as victims. The description of both groups is quite unsympathetic, but in the case of Jews readers can be more compassionate because it is cruel fate that corrupted and bent them into their present ugly shape.

Proust would let us have some compassion for Jews, but not for homosexuals, who are innately and essentially evil. In the case of homosexuals, there is no room for compassion. Some of the individual wandering Jews in *A La Recherche* are described by the narrator as not without saving graces. One of them, Swann, is even a role model, and Proust cannot resist telling the reader about the real Jewish businessman, Charles Haas, who served as the inspiration for the fictional Swann.

While anti-Semitism is a major theme in the novel, the only explicit references to Zionism as its solution in *A la Recherche* appear in the context of the fictional discovery of male homosexuality, described in the *Sodome et Gomorrhe* volume of the work. And when it comes to Zionism, Proust is more critical and more mocking than ever. He considers any separatism impossible, because it goes against the real nature of both Jewishness and homosexuality (Sprinker, 1994).

And here is his fantastic warning:

> ...mais on a voulu provisoirement prévenir l'erreur funeste qui consisterait, de même qu'on a encouragé un mouvement sioniste, à créer un mouvement sodomiste et à rebâtir Sodome. Or, à peine arrivés, les Sodomistes quitteraient la ville pour ne pas avoir l'air d'en être, prendraient femme, entretiendraient des maîtresses dans l'autres cités où ils trouveraient d'ailleurs toutes les distractions convenables. Ils n'iraient à Sodome que les jours de suprême nécessité, quand leur ville sera vide, pas ces temps où la faim fait sortir le loup du bois. C'est dire que tout se passerait en somme comme à Londres, à Berlin, à Rome, à Petrograd, ou à Paris. (Proust, 1954, p. 42).

> [I have thought it as well to utter here a provisional warning against the lamentable error of proposing (just as people have encouraged a Zionist movement) to create a Sodomist movement and to rebuild Sodom. For, no sooner had they arrived there than the Sodomites would leave the town so as not to have the appearance of belonging to it, would take wives, keep mistresses in other cities where they would find, incidentally, every diversion that appealed to them...In other words, everything would go on very much as it does today in London, Berlin, Rome, Petrograd or Paris (Proust, 1992, pp. 37-38).]

The idea of regeneration for either Jews or homosexuals is out of the question. Jews will never change and their rehabilitation is impossible. The idea of rebirth through national revival is an illusion, and it is not only implausible, but simply ridiculous. Zionism is simply an unnatural idea, destined to fail.

Proust accepts the social definition which does not let Jews escape their ancestry, but is slightly optimistic about eventual (relative) assimilation for Jews. The evidence for change in European society is found in the outcome of the Dreyfus Affair, which is part of the history covered by *A la Recherche*, and in which Proust was actively involved when it erupted in 1897. Rather uncharacteristically, the twenty-six years old Marcel Proust took a very public stand. He was active in getting Anatole France to support Dreyfus, and attended every session of the Zola trial. This put him on a collision course with most of his family and alienated him from the high society hostesses he so actively courted (Shattuck, 1974). How could this outburst of uncharacteristic commitment and action be explained? According to one interpretation (Recanati, 1979), Proust's identification with Dreyfus was based not on any feelings about the Jewishness of the victim, but on an automatic leaning towards the outsider, the proscribed, the powerless victim. And, when the powerless outsider won his case, this was a cause for some cautious hope about the future. But integration, or assimilation, depends on Jews and not on the society in which they live. They must be realistic and adopt the majority's social definitions of identity and acceptance.

6. Jewishness and Zionism in *Ulysses*

James Joyce himself described *Ulysses* as "...the epic of two races (Israel-Ireland) and at the same time the cycle of the human body" (Joyce, 1975, p. 271). And this is a truly remarkable way of how things evolved and revolved in the author's mind. Not only are two *races* involved, but they are chosen to represent themselves, as well as humanity in its essence and the cycle of life, in an epic. The term 'epic' represents an ancient tradition of long narrative poems relating the deeds of legendary heroes. The ancient Greek epos was a long poem in dactylic hexameter telling the story of gods and heroic warriors. A modern author who seeks to compose such a work is not only ambitious, but clearly megalomaniac (Burgess, 1965). Ulysses leaves on a trip in search of universal truth, meaning, and identity (and so does Marcel, Proust's hero in *A La Recherche*). James Joyce seeks to create a hero who will represent not only exceptional deeds, but each one of us, for better or worse. Fictional biographies make much sense and reflect social realities, and *Ulysses* turns out to be a fictional biography of an assimilated Jew (cf. Costello, 1981). While Marcel Proust chose a gentile hero for an autobiographical novel based on the unique experience of a socially-defined Jew, Joyce selected such a Jew as his hero and his model for humanity in *Ulysses*.

When Joyce wanted to portray the human condition in modern times, or in all times, in *Ulysses*, he selected Leopold Bloom. Modern, alienated, humanity in search of a home for its soul on the road to redemption is naturally represented by a (twice baptized and uncircumcised) Jew. Actually, Bloom is only half-Jewish by European standards, and a real gentile by Orthodox Jewish standards. His mother, Ellen Higgins, was not Jewish. His maternal grandfather, Julius Higgins (Karoly), who was presumably a Jew, married an Irish woman named Fanny Hegarty, making his daughter Ellen half-Jewish by European standards and non-Jewish by Jewish Law. At birth, Leopold was not circumcised, but baptized in a Protestant church, the Church of Ireland, which his father, Rudolph Bloom (Virag) joined in 1865. Rudolph Bloom (Virag), Leopold's father, wandered all over Europe from his Hungarian birthplace, Szombathely to Vienna, and then to Budapest, Milan, London, and Dublin. Still, The wandering Virag family, after moving all over Europe, as a result of a accursed fate, culture, or character, does find a home in Ireland.

Rudolph was received to the Church of Ireland by the Society for Promoting Christianity among the Jews. In his old age he reverted back to Jewish customs and celebrated Jewish holidays. His son Leopold scoffed at this return to childhood ways. Leopold Bloom himself, "The Jewish Hungarian Irish Protestant Masonic freethinker" converted to Roman Catholicism to marry Molly (Costello, 1981, p. 36). Nevertheless, Bloom is recognized by the surrounding Irish society as a Jew, and no act of his will ever change that. He remains a Jew because Jews are considered a racial group. In addition to his baptism as an infant, Bloom has converted, and has switched from Protestantism to Roman Catholicism, thus expressing a renewed commitment to Christianity, but for society around him, this will not do. He remains a Jew and an outsider to the nth degree. As Gershom Scholem, one of the greatest historians of Judaism, put it:

> This hero is a Jew "only" in the consciousness of his author, in the consciousness of his Irish environment, and in the consciousness of all the book's readers (including myself)...while the book emphasizes, from beginning to end, that the hero is the son of a Jew and a gentile woman, brought up as a perfect gentile and living as a perfect gentile. And despite that he is universally regarded as a Jew (Scholem, 1959/1989, p. 501).

The fictional Leopold Bloom was just like the real Marcel Proust. A touch of Jewishness was enough to keep them marked off, or stigmatized.

Bloom is not only Everyman, but also Every Jew. *Ulysses* turns out to be, quite clearly, a Jewish novel, or rather a Jewish symphony. Its hero, the modern Odysseus, Leopold Bloom, "despite his Protestant past and Catholic present, is forever a Jew" (Nadel, 1989, p. 13). "He is the eternal exile, the universalized victim-hero...wants to liberate himself from those inauthentic identities of the "sheeny, "ikey", "Jew Bug", imposed on him by the anti-Semites" (Simon, 1996, pp. 139-140). There is a parallel between the alienated, introverted modernist artist and the Jewish outsider (Davidson, 1996; Fiedler, 1991). "Always seeking resemblances, Joyce found the Jew a fitting analogy not only for Ulysses but for himself...for himself as exile, seeking home. As Joyce's image, Bloom is fittingly Jewish" (Tindall, 1959, p. 131).

Of our two literary observers, Joyce is the more analytical in attitude as well as quite well-informed. James Joyce identified strongly with everything Jewish. At least once in his life, not long before his death in 1941, he was officially identified as a Jew. The Swiss *Fremdenpolizei* refused Joyce an entry permit in September 1940 because he was considered a Jew (Nadel, 1989). Joyce had done an impressive amount of reading on Zionism, and we know that he bought a copy of Herzl's *Der Judenstaat* in Zurich in 1915. Joyce also knew quite a bit about psychoanalysis, not only when he refers to "the new Viennese school", which studies incest. In Chapter 9 of *Ulysses* (known as "Scylla and Charybdis"), and devoted to literature, Stephen Dedalus expounds his theory of literary creation, which shows a thorough familiarity with psychoanalytic writings on literature. Joyce is well-read, a collector of linguistic music, and a polyglot who switches between languages in his infinite puns and associations. Hebrew, however, is not something that Joyce really knew, but he managed to find the right Hebrew words to express the major issues of Bloom's Jewishness. Leopold Bloom's knowledge of Judaic traditions and the Hebrew language is quite limited, and Joyce expresses this both wittingly and unwittingly, as when the inconsistent transliterations of Hebrew words demonstrate Joyce's own limits. But in Joyce's symphony what matters is the music, and not any single word, and this Jewish-Irish epic mesmerizes every reader with its elegiac tunes.

Leopold Bloom is not a victim of any pogroms, and is not confined to a Pale of Settlement, like Jews in Czarist Russia in his time.

Actually, there was a case in modern Ireland, in the fictional Bloom's lifetime, of what has become known as a pogrom, though it does not really fit this term. It was in the year 1904, in the city of Limerick, that Father John Creagh, a priest of the Redemptorist order, incited the local population against 'blood-sucking' Jewish merchants. John Creagh received his theological training in France at the time of the Dreyfus affair, which had probably much to do with his anti-Semitic campaign. His sermons led to a two-year trade boycott of Jewish businesses which was accompanied by harassment and physical attacks and resulted in the almost total departure of the 150-strong Limerick Jewish community. Today this incident, as well as some others, are remembered only by historians (cf. Keogh, 1998). Joyce undoubtedly was well aware of it.

Anti-Semitism is a major topic in *Ulysses*, first because Christianity is a major theme. And the way Christianity looks at the Jews is one starting point: "They sinned against the light, Mr. Deasy said gravely. And you can see the darkness in their eyes. And that is why they are wanderers on the earth to this day" (Joyce, 1986, p. 28). In *A La Recherche du Temps Perdu*, the narrator Marcel ridicules Jews who claim Jesus, the mythological founder of Christianity, as one of their own. In *Ulysses*, we see Leopold Bloom doing just that: "Mendelsson was a Jew and Karl Marx and Mercadante and Spinoza. And the Saviour was a Jew...Christ was a Jew like me" (1986, p. 280). This takes place after Bloom's attempt to define himself as being Irish fail to persuade his companions.

Vladimir Nabokov sums up the book as "Bloom and fate in the hopeless past, the ridiculous and tragic present, and the pathetic future" (1980, p. 295). Bloom constantly dwells on his son's death, his father's suicide, and his own failures in every facet of life. Beyond the personal struggle with Fate, we can observe here the collective Jewish past and the miserable present, represented by Bloom's life, not only affected by cruel Fate, but cursed with dead words and with the burden of history. "History, said Stephen, is the nightmare from which I am trying to wake up" (Joyce, 1986, p. 28). Can we all wake up? Can there be a rebirth or a future, collectively or individually?

A man who is not Jewish in any tangible way, but still a socially-defined Jew, Leopold Bloom is exactly the Jew that Zionism wants to redeem. Bloom's is Herzl's Jew, or maybe even Theodor Herzl himself.

Jewish identity, the identity of the circumcised, keeps haunting Bloom, who is caught chanting an ancient Judaic prayer, "Shema Israel Adonai Elohenu" (p. 444). *Ulysses* sometimes reads like a wild Jewish opera, as when Leopold Bloom recites all the Hebrew words he knows (p. 397):

> (The rams' horns sound for silence. The standard of Zion is hoisted.)
> BLOOM (uncloaks impressively, revealing obesity, unrolls a paper and reads solemnly) Aleph Beth Ghimel Daleth Hagadah Tephilim Kosher Yom Kippur Hanukah Roschaschana Beni Brith Bar Mitzvah Mazzoth Askenazim Meshuggah Talith. (An official translation is read by Jimmy Henry, assistant town clerk.).

This brief paragraph summarizes the content of modern Jewish identity, as experienced by most modern Jews. Joyce correctly selects every remnant of past traditions, still vaguely remembered, but not really lived or understood. This short recitation of key words becomes a magical experience for those who crave for lost home and lost memories.

As is well known even to those who have never opened the actual book, *Ulysses* tells the story of Bloom's Odyssey through just one day of his life, June 16, 1904, in Dublin. And this modern Odyssey involves also a walk through the day with a concrete and invitation to join the Zionist. Early in the day, Bloom is presented with an invitation to join in the efforts of practical Zionism. When he goes to his favorite butcher he finds on one of the wrapping papers an advertisement for a model farm at Kinnereth on the Sea of Galilee. Walking home from the butcher-shop, he reads on his sausage-wrapper about another Zionist project, known as 'Agendath Netaim' (this is undoubtedly an error, and should be Agudat Netaim), a planting company seeking investors who would like to own a dunam of land planted with 'olives, oranges, almonds or citrons'. "To purchase waste sandy tracts from Turkish government and plant with eucalyptus trees. Excellent for shade, fuel, and construction. Orangegroves and immense melonfields north of Jaffa" (p. 49). This is an attractive dream of new life, and the of wastelands redeemed, but he rejects this investment opportunity, as well as the whole Zionist idea. What follow throughout the day are Bloom's free associations around the images of Zionist revival.

Through an amazing distortion by Bloom (and by Joyce), the sea of Galilee, with its promise of new life, is turned into the Dead Sea. Joyce uses stunning metaphors in expressing Bloom's rejection: "...a dead sea in a dead land, grey and old... the oldest people. Wandered far away over all the earth, captivity to captivity, multiplying, dying, being born everywhere... Dead; an old woman's: the grey sunken cunt of the world" (1986, p. 50). There is no chance for the Zionist dream, because the Dead Sea can never be brought to life.

Joyce has done his homework and was quite familiar with the reality of Zionist enterprises. Eucalyptus trees had been for many decades the true botanical marker of Zionist settlements. The two settlement schemes advertised in fictional Dublin were actually started around 1905, and we should mention that while Agudat Netaim is recalled today only in specialized historical monographs (Katz, 1989), the model farm at Kinneret went on to play a major role in Zionist settlement history. It was the place where in 1910 a small group of workers decided to start the first *kibbutz*, a unique communal settlement, very close to the farm on the lake. The real locale around the model farm on the southwestern edge of the Sea of Galilee has become an Israeli cultural symbol of the early pristine days of the Zionist enterprise, celebrated in countless romantic songs. The main farm house is preserved today as a shrine.

In the fictional case of Leopold Bloom, alienation and weakness are expressed through allusions to deficient manliness. Bloom's masculinity is a major topic in the novel, and a sore point. His full name is Leopold Paula Bloom, tying him to the founder of Christianity, but in a feminine version. He is described as bisexual, effeminate, and always less than a real man. "Professor Bloom is a finished example of the new womanly man" (Joyce, 1986, p. 403). Offenses against his manhood, like this one, abound in *Ulysses* (French, 1982; Zimmerman, 1979).

Could Zionism offer a symbolic cure to this problem? We have seen how he was carrying with him, throughout his Odyssey this invitation to be born again as a real man, who lives close to nature and works the land. The dream of Kinneret is a Zionist collective fantasy which became reality, as settlers found their way back to nature and real manhood on the shores of the Sea of Galilee.The invitation to be reborn as a New Man in the Old New Homeland, through the story of the new

Zionist agriculture in Palestine keeps haunting Bloom all through the book, despite his overt disdain. It seems to haunt him, becoming an obsessional refrain. He carries the folded prospectus of the model farm and the plantation with him during the day of June 16, and ends up burning it, and then smelling the "aromatic oriental incense".

Joyce has researched what was then the developing Zionist culture, and has Bloom singing (in a strange Polish-German transcription) "Kolod Balejwaw pnimah Nefesch, jehudi, homijah" (p. 564). Bloom in 1904 could already sing *Hatikva*, "The Hope", a Zionist anthem which since 1948 is considered the official anthem of the State of Israel (It is the Israeli national anthem according to custom, but not by law, in part due to opposition from Orthodox Jews). But Bloom, the wandering Jew, will go on wandering, coping as best as he can with life which is the lot of all modern humanity, without any real hope for rebirth. Joyce demonstrates here, with Bloom as case study, the utter failure of the assimilation of Jews into European society, as well as the inevitability of alienated Jewish existence in Europe. This stoic solution, as we will see, is quite Freudian. Bloom, and possibly Joyce, is quite skeptical, or pessimistic, about the salvation of Jews as he is about the salvation of the Irish through nationalism (Nolan, 1995). The Irish tragedy, as bad as it is, will not equal the Jewish one, for not all Irish are exiles, but all Jews are and shall ever be.

We can observe that in the case of James Joyce, identification with Jews did not lead to identification with Zionism, always regarded as both unwelcome and unnatural. We know that Joyce was also highly critical of Irish nationalism and separatism. In the writings of both Proust and Joyce, we can find much ambivalence in the way Jews are described, but no ambivalence in the treatment of Zionism. Both Proust and Joyce agree that Jewish rebirth is simply impossible.

7. Herzl's National Revival Project

As is universally recognized, Theodor Herzl did not start Zionism either as an ideology or as an actual movement. The idea of creating a nation-state for the Jews had been a part of European political consciousness for a hundred years before he ever started thinking about it, and Zionist colonies were founded in Palestine almost twenty years before he became a committed Zionist. But Herzl was among the first to propose a global political strategy, allying Zionism with big-power imperialism. He was not interested in small-scale settlements, which were started by others long before he appeared on the scene. He wanted a large scale strategic effort, in alliance with world powers. Thus, he rightly came to embody political Zionism and its practical achievements. And Herzl made his diagnosis and proposed his cure in the world that the novelists portrayed so accurately.

What both Proust and Joyce proved was that the separation between Judaism and Jewishness did not help individual Jews in assimilating. Leopold Bloom, while not being Jewish, is still the Jew, just like Bloch and Swann in *A La Recherche du Temps Perdu*. The novelists provide us with an accurate description of the reality of assimilation and its failures, and point to the coming of the racial definition, which eventually was to destroy six million European Jews. Towards the end of the nineteenth century it was clear that Jewish readiness for assimilation or integration was not enough. The appearance of modern anti-Semitism made integration difficult, or even impossible. The rise of anti-Semitic parties, pogroms, blood libels, and the Dreyfus Affair in France impressed upon European Jews a new reality. The problem was not social acceptance, but a real threat. Jews were in danger again. It was not a matter of choice. Jews may try to integrate, but were not only socially rejected, but seriously threatened. Could Europe ever be trusted? Faced with the uncertain success of the integration (or assimilation) project, the issue of a future for Jews in Europe had to be addressed. This was neither an abstract nor a personal matter, a question of an identity choice, but a political issue. All Europeans and all Jews had to take a stand on various options. Did Jews have a future in Europe? If not, where should they go?

> We should realize that in the book of our tragic history Chapter II is about to start, titled 'National Extremism', and the relative ease in recent times has been only like the blank page between two book chapters...None of us know in advance how many blood-written pages the new chapter will have, and what chapters will follow. So we should make an effort to settle Palestine by Jewish farmers, so that in the next 100 years our brethren will be able to leave Europe, which has turned on them, and settle in the nearby land of our ancestors, to which we have a historical right (in Beit-Hallahmi, 1993, pp. 40-41).

This was written in 1881 by Moshe Leib Lilienblum, and reflected the Zionist diagnosis of the future of European Jewry, made when Herzl was still totally oblivious to any Jewish Questions.

We have to recall that conversion to Christianity was a real option for many European Jews. Millions of Jews did just that. In 1893 Herzl was planning an answer to the Jewish Question through mass conversion to Catholicism. The conversion option was the option of first resort not only for Herzl, but did not easily work, as we see in the writings of Proust and Joyce. Herzl realized that nationalism was becoming a force, and a threat, all over Europe (Pawel, 1989). Both the Austro-Hungarian and the Russian empires were facing increasingly powerful movements for self-determination, by Poles, Hungarians, Slovaks, and Croats, to name a few. These inherently justified claims for self-determination would make life for Jews in Europe harder. Separatism for Herzl was a defensive response, and it was both necessary and possible. Herzl's prediction was that Jews who would not join the Zionist project would be assimilated, and was probably correct, with the exception of those Jews who still stick to Orthodoxy.

8. Freud, Jewishness and Zionism

Sigmund Freud (1856-1939) can serve as an example of the new secular Jew, who was already in evidence in the middle of the nineteenth century. The question of Freud's Jewishness and the question of Freud's own religious identity as he was growing up have been discussed quite widely, but often without much real knowledge of its historical context (Beit-Hallahmi, 1989, 1996). Over the past 50 years, a long bookshelf has been produced around this issue, which as been framed along two parallel, but related lines. The first has to do with Freud's attitude towards being born Jewish, and the second with the question of the impact of Jewish culture on psychoanalysis itself. We will deal only with the first issue. There are at least 10 major books and about thirty published articles touching on the question of Freud's personal attitude towards Judaism and Jewishness (e.g. Bakan, 1965; Rizzuto, 1998; Robert, 1977; Rothman & Isenberg, 1974).

Some of the most crucial decisions about Freud's Jewish identity were made by his parents, and this is usually the case (Beit-Hallahmi &

Argyle, 1997). In his case, as in the case of Albert Einstein, the secularization process started with his father, Jacob, who did not go as far as his illustrious son, but left ancient traditions behind (See Krull, 1986). Sigmund Freud's parents, and especially his father, made the crucial decisions in terms of education and practice that determined the development of his religious identity. Jakob Freud (1815-1896) was a literate man with some traditional Jewish upbringing, but he was no Talmudic scholar and already quite secularized before his son Sigmund was born in 1856. The famous story about Freud's Roman Catholic nanny, who took him regularly to church with her is an indication of relative secularization. A truly Orthodox family would not have allowed that to happen.

The question before Jakob Freud, as his son Sigmund was reaching school age, was that of deciding on which school and what kind of schooling to choose for his son. Jakob's decision was to send his son to a state school, where the curriculum was dictated by the gentile authorities. It also specified the study of religion. This meant that Jewish pupils received lessons in the Jewish tradition and the Old Testament. Jakob's decision was an example of the new Jewish identity being formed in Europe. Jakob Freud had an illustrated bi-lingual Old Testament, in both Hebrew and German, which Sigmund enjoyed reading. For a Jew in the 1860s, having your son read an illustrated version of the Old Testament is evidence of secularization rather than a mark of Orthodoxy. Orthodox Jewish education is not based on the Old Testament but on the Talmud. It has been the Talmud that informed and formed Judaism since the eighth century. For a thousand years, Jewish identity and Jewish culture were totally Talmudic, and every Jew had to learn at least some of it. Much is made in some studies (Rizzuto, 1998) of the famous dedication in Hebrew written by Jakob Freud on Sigmund's 35th birthday. As Bergmann (1995) correctly pointed out, that fact that it was in Hebrew does not prove that Sigmund could read it. This brief paragraph, written in literate Hebrew with allusions to the Old Testament, is interpreted as expressing a wish for Sigmund to become a devout Jew, but was too little, too late when Sigmund was 35 years old!

The so-called "return" to studying the Old Testament has been part of Jewish secularization in Europe, the Jewish Enlightenment, and of the new Zionist culture. If Jakob had been truly committed to Orthodox Judaism, he could have sent his son at age four to get a thorough Orthodox education, meaning a Talmudic training, and could have insisted on real observance of ritual purity at home. He never did any of that.

Was there a turning point, an identity crisis in the life of young Sigmund? Were there sleepless nights during which Freud was agonizing over his religious faith or his Jewish identity? There is no evidence of that. Young Sigmund was no rebel and became exactly what his parents had wanted. There was no struggle with a tradition-bound father, and if Sigmund Freud experienced personal secularization, it was Jakob Freud that engineered it. We know that mothers play a vital role in forming their children's religious identity. What about Amalia Freud? What was her contribution? As Rizzuto (1998) reports, Freud's mother instituted family reunions on Christmas Day, another clear sign of leaving Jewish tradition and the sacred calendar far behind.

The Freud family was not unique and Sigmund Freud's rejection of religion, any religion, was typical of his generation. The rejection of large parts of the Jewish tradition and most Jewish observances appeared already in Jakob's generation and even earlier. Jakob Freud passed on to all of his children (not just Sigmund) his own deeply felt ambivalence about Judaism and Jewish identity. This same ambivalence has been felt by millions of Jews and was not unique to the Freud family. Likewise, millions of Jews took part in the radical secularization process that changed the Jewish world since the beginning of the nineteenth century. The secularization of the Jews was not unrelated to a less radical secularization and de-Christianization of Europe. Franz Brentano's philosophy lectures of 1874 in defense of theism, which Freud attended and liked were also part of unfolding secularization. And this process was directly related to the weakening of father's authority everywhere. The decline of religion is tied to the decline in the status of the fathers, the waning of absolute monarchy and absolute patriarchy.

Peter Gay calls Freud's choice of self-definition "Defiance as Identity", and indeed defiance, oppositionalism, and counter-dependence are the hallmarks of Freud's mature personality. "I... never pretended to be anything but what I am: A Jew from Moravia whose parents come from Austrian Galicia" (Gay, 1988, p. 597). Faced with the dilemmas of the real Marcel Proust and the fictional Leopold Bloom, Freud insists on not playing any social games and reporting the facts of his not only stigmatized, but also lowly, origins. He hides nothing, and admits that he is not only a Jew, but an *ostjude*. But still, as Gay put it in another context, Freud "was not very Jewish" (Gay, 1985, p. 81; cf. Gay, 1987).

Was there nevertheless any special meaning to Jewishness?

> And beyond this there was a perception that it was to my Jewish nature alone that I owed two characteristics that had become indispensable to me in the difficult course of my life. Because I was a Jew I found myself free from many prejudices which restricted others in the use of their intellect; and as a Jew I was prepared to join the Opposition and to do without agreement with the "compact majority" (Freud, 1926, p. 274).

But if this was the case, there was really no need to remain Jewish. Some non-Jews could, and did, act in the same way. The values expressed in the Bnai-Brith address could be preserved and promoted without the excess baggage of Jewishness. There were many other ideological frameworks that could sustain them, from socialism to psychoanalysis itself.

Freud represented the new generation of Jews who had little familiarity with Jewish law, as expressed in the Talmud, and with Jewish ritual practices, which defined Jewish communal life and the daily life of every Orthodox Jew for a thousand years. The coming of Jewish Enlightenment (known as the *Haskala)* and of Zionism meant the return to the texts of Old Testament, which for children meant an exposure to Jewish mythology, as well as to legends of past glory and Jewish sovereignty. This was meant to replace the direct experience of religious practices and commandments. At the end of his life, Freud went back to Jewish mythology in *Moses and Monotheism* (Freud, 1939). This work turns out to be a strange combination of useful insights about religion and an embarrassing, bizarre, attempt by Freud to escape the burden of historical Judaism by putting his a mark on Jewish mythology.

What is Jewishness in European history if not a pattern of

despised Otherness? Jewish descent and heritage have been perceived as a burden, if not a disaster. Jews were not free to make choices as long as Anti-Semites and anti-Semitism were major forces in society, and even when only the cultural residues of anti-Semitism lingered on. To cite one observer of modern anti-Semitism,

> It is society, not the decree of God, that has made him a Jew and brought the Jewish problem into being. As he is forced to make his choices entirely within the perspective set by his problem, it is in and through the social that he chooses even his own existence. His constructive effort to integrate himself in the national community is social; social is the effort he makes to think of himself, that is to situate himself, among other men; his joys and sorrows are social; but all this is because the curse that rests upon him is social (Sartre, 1965, pp. 134-135; cf. Charmé, 1986, 1991).

As Charmé (1991, p. 117) put it "neither Freud nor Sartre understood Jewish identity to stem from some inherent spiritual message in Judaism".

Freud inherited from his parents a Jewish identity which was mostly cultural, the identity of a typical sociological Jew. Like most sociological Jews in the world today, he had only a limited experience of historical Judaism. Sigmund Freud grew up indeed to be what we should call a sociological Jew, and what Heilman (1998) called a "heritage Jew", someone who recognizes Jewish ancestry. However, beyond this recognition there was no room for any traditional practices. "Freud's rigorous secularism did not permit the slightest trace of religious observance to survive in his domestic life" (Gay, 1988, p. 600). This meant that no Jewish holidays or rites of passage were ever celebrated. While Freud both defiantly and pragmatically was ready to accept Jewish identity as his reality and as social reality, he was not ready to promote and preserve Jewish identity for his children and for future generations. He did find a homeland for his children, and that was Britain, where most of his descendants live today.

Freud did not think that it made any sense to resist the social definition followed by non-Jews and Jews alike. Freud's solution consisted of accepting the internal and external social definition of Jews, together with total contempt for anti-Semitism and other conventions, and with movement towards cultural and personal integration (or assimilation). Freud's authenticity is expressed in his opposition to playacting (cf. Charmé, 1986, 1991). He could not change his own social identity, because you cannot escape reality, but you can still change your descendants' fate. Then they will face less of a stigma.

Jewishness as reality was expressed in jokes, social contacts with mostly Jewish friends, the reality of family and tribe. The expression of Jewish identity could take only a private, personal form in the shape of an independent, defiant, character, and a preference for intimate ties with kinfolk. As the twentieth century renowned art critic Clement Greenberg put it: "Jewishness, in so far as it has to be asserted in a predominantly Gentile world, should be a personal rather than a mass manifestation, and more a matter of individual self-reliance" (Greenberg, 1950/1995, p. 53; cf. Steyn, 1999). Writing fifty years later, Cohen & Eisen (2000, p. 184) reported that Greenberg's vision has won the day in North America: "American Jews have drawn the activity and significance of their group identity into the subjectivity of the individual".

Handling Jewishness in Freud's stoic manner meant the readiness to carry the burden of being socially identified as a Jew, but avoiding any investment in either religious tradition, or in the modern incarnation of Jewishness as nationalism. Jewishness was a social fact, not something to be kept and preserved The problem with being Jewish was twofold. First, Jewish identity was a stigma and a misfortune. Beyond that, it was a religious identity, tied to rituals which Freud considered barbaric. Regarding the role of religion in his identity, Freud was clear when he described himself as "an infidel Jew" (Freud, 1928, p. 170). He was an atheist, contemptuous of religion in general, and the Jewish case, which touched him personally, aroused aversion. For modern Jews distance from the past was measured by adherence to the rites of passage and to the sacred calendar. For Freud the mere content of beliefs and rituals, which for some Jews has been associated with to warm feelings of ties to home and ancestry was only a source of alienation. There was nothing attractive about them.

He could analyze them as an observer, but not take part in any of them. Jewish rites of passage were for Freud something he could not tolerate. In 1886, "Freud thought of joining the Protestant 'Confession' so as to be able to marry without having the complicated Jewish ceremonies he hated so much" (Jones, 1957, Vol. 1, p. 167). Then, when he had three sons, he did not have them circumcised. And when the time came, Freud's funeral ceremony, at Golders Green Crematorium in North London, was devoid of anything Jewish or religious.

The model Sigmund Freud presented at his home was one of total secularity, which means giving up any vestiges of Jewishness, because those were bound to be of a religious nature. Even the most minimally defined Jewish identity meant, for most individuals, some traces of religion. Among relatively secularized Jews, those who want to convey a symbolic sense of Jewish identity to the next generation still celebrate major holidays and some rites of passage, especially circumcision. Freud was quite strict in staying away from such symbolic gestures. Cutting off all ties to Jewish tradition was the only way to create a better world, with as little religion as possible. The humanist, stoic, way was not just a matter of ideals, but of everyday practice. This clearly could lead only to total assimilation.

The message Freud passed on to his children and descendants was unmistakable: Don't be Jewish! This message was conveyed through daily life and explicit enough words. And so, within three generations, the distance from tradition has grown and the descendants of Jakob and Amalia Freud became non-Jews. Most of Sigmund Freud's descendants today are clearly not Jewish in any discernible way. Europe has changed and has become more secular. Anti-Semitism has declined, otherwise integration could not have been possible. The case of the Freud family (or clan) is a good one to look at in assessing the success of integration into European society, as envisioned by Sigmund Freud. His descendants, most of whom live in Britain, are well-integrated Europeans, indifferent to either Jewishness or Zionism. They are members in good standing of the First World elite. We don't know much about many of them, and do not wish to invade their privacy, but some of them are public personalities. The best known among the descendants of Sigmund and Martha Freud are the brothers Lucian and Clement Freud. Like most of the clan, they embody the contempt for conventions and creativity tied to the family name. When it comes to Jewishness, the two brothers (who have not exchanged a word since 1954) chose separate, but equally distant paths. Lucian, whose identity is clearly tied to art, denies any connection to Jewishness. And when Sir Clement Freud (knighted in 1987) was once listed among the Jewish members of the House of Commons, where he served 1973-1983, he was quick to correct the error. He has been a member of the Anglican Church since his marriage (Grunberger, 2001). His parents, Ernst and Lucie Freud, as atheists, refused to attend the church wedding , but did attend the reception that followed (Freud, 2001).

Freud's message of avoiding Jewishness was not rare among intellectuals of Jewish descent. If we look at the list of prominent psychoanalytic thinkers since Freud, we discover that those of Jewish descent expressed the same message. They did not want to be known as Jews, and did not want their children to be known as Jews. If we look at the life of Melanie Klein (Grosskurth, 1986), Erik Erikson (Falk, 1975-76; Friedman, 2000), or Heinz Kohut (Strozier, 2001), the picture is identical. All these great theoreticians of psychoanalysis wanted to cleanse their lives from any traces of Jewish identity. It is not a matter of ambivalence, but of total aversion. In this context we should mention that Alfred Adler, an early disciple of Freud and a leader of another Viennese school, chose to convert to Christianity, not because of religious faith, but as a public repudiation of Jewish tribalism and in defiance of dominant social boundaries.

If we examine Freud 's writings, published and unpublished, we can immediately recognize an attitude of deep ambivalence about being Jewish, and later on his characteristic stoicism and even disdain regarding nationalism as a solution to the "Jewish question" and Zionism as a political movement. In this complex of attitudes Freud is not unique; he is rather representative of his generation and of several generation of European Jews. Freud represents the whole population of modern secular Jews, as they faced the dilemma of accepting the social definition of their identity. He is only unique in being so articulate and supplying us with so much material for interpretation and understanding.

Sigmund Freud was quite representative of his generation not only in regard to both Jewish identity, but also in regard to Zionism. He was not the only prominent Jew who has responded to anti-Semitism through defiance, and this without showing much enthusiasm for Jewish nationalism. Albert Einstein is another example that readily comes to mind. If a Jewish heritage meant affliction and misfortune, Sigmund Freud handled them realistically and stoically. He was not only stoic, but conservative, realistic, and courageous (Gay, 1978, 1988).

Freud's feelings about the ancient homeland of the Jews were far from positive. In a personal letter in 1932, he wrote: "Palestine has never produced anything but religious, sacred frenzies, presumptuous attempts to overcome the outer world of appearance by means of the inner world of wishful thinking" (Freud, 1970, p. 40). His attitude towards the ideas of Jewish nationalism was quite critical, linking Zionism to religion. In a letter to Albert Einstein, of February 26, 1930, Freud wrote: "I can muster no sympathy whatever for the misguided piety that makes a national religion from a piece of the wall of Herod, and for its sake challenge the feelings of the local natives" (Gay, 1988, p. 598; cf. Rolnik, 2002). As spelled out in this letter, he was more than skeptical about Zionism. He is doubtful about the possibility of a real revival, has reservations about the symbols used by the reviving national movement, and is critical of the way the indigenous population is being treated. Here Freud seems to be critical of colonialism, which ignores the natural rights of the natives, as well as irritated by the connection between nationalism and religion. While both Proust and Joyce seem to be unaware of the natives, who were never considered in fantasies of the Zionist utopia, Freud, writing at least a decade later than both, seems to be familiar with press reports of the 1929 riots in Palestine. The 1929 events were one of the first expressions of Palestinian resistance to Zionism, foreshadowing developments in the following eight decades.

Freud, the uncanny observer and diagnostician of others' problems, is in this case personally involved, like Leopold Bloom, and must respond to the invitation, coming from Zionism, to be reborn. Freud in his mature years did not think he had to be reborn as a New Jew. It is possible that he wanted all of humanity to be reborn as realistic, moral, human beings without neurotic practices and religious illusions, but then he was wishing for a human liberation, rather than Jewish liberation.

9. Conclusion: Integration or Separatism

Both Joyce and Proust regarded the dry bones of European Jewish existence as beyond redemption. The literary imagination, as represented here by two great novelists, regarded Zionism as an absurdity, and the idea of Jewish regeneration as an illusion. They were also opposed to Jewish national separatism. Freud and Herzl (1860-1894) were members of the same generation and were exposed to a variety of utopian movements in Vienna before the turn of the century. In some ways, Freud was closer to the novelists than to the his neighbor, the Viennese author Theodor Herzl (Falk, 1978).

While Proust, Joyce, and Freud were witnesses, Herzl was the protagonist who acted in full sight of both a global audience and other actors. It was Herzl who overcame the seeming absurdity of the Zionist idea by devising a great political strategy. While the artist's only commitment is to pleasure and beauty, both Freud and Herzl had other commitments. Herzl was not just a witness to history, he stepped into it and his strategy keeps working even today.

Both Herzl and Freud proposed ways of improving humanity's lot. Herzl, as a political leader, had a commitment to his followers, and offered them a practical dream. Freud was offering a vision of a liberated, supra-national humanity. We find Freud in surprising (or not so surprising) agreement with the two novelists, and his attitude of suspicion and criticism is something we might well adopt.

Could Jews share in the dream of a united, liberal, Europe? Despite the continuing de-Christianization of Europe, the Jewish characters created by Proust and Joyce still lived in the shadow of an ever-present cross, experiencing alienation and insecurity. Was true integration of the Jews in Europe possible? Could Europe be trusted to integrate the Jews?

The answers to these questions were No, according to Herzl, because it is anti-Semitism, and not Jewishness, which is an incurable disease. Separatism for European Jews is a necessity, not a choice. Herzl's political approach reflected a bitter disappointment and much personal pain. The answers were Yes, according to Proust, because Dreyfus has been exonerated and anti-Semitism has lost a decisive battle. And so Zionism is a regressive, perverse, fantasy. Proust said yes to liberal Europe, which could be trusted because Dreyfus won his case.

His reading of the Affair is the opposite of Herzl's. For Marcel Proust and for Theodor Herzl, the Dreyfus Affair carried diametrically opposed lessons. For Proust it was the victory of progressive forces in French society, and the beginning of a new Europe. For Herzl it was clear evidence of recurring dangers. And the answer to the question of integration into Europe was Yes, according to Joyce, because Zionism, and all nationalisms, are retrograde.

Another affirmative reply was offered by Freud, because, in terms of psychoanalytic personality theory, the mature ego can overcome unrealistic fantasies and control the frustration which may lead to impulsive actions. Zionism, viewed in these terms, is only a temporary regression. Freud is among the naysayers to Herzl, and seems more than critical of Jewish separatism. Freud and Herzl, of course, were similar in terms of background, and were members of the same generation, but chose opposing paths. Herzl gave up on the dream of liberal Europe, while Freud did not.

What could can we learn from Freud, if we wished to follow his example? First and foremost, to be realistic and stoic and to discuss openly the real but unpleasant facts of life. Freud is opposed to any false consolations in the face of bitter reality. He is skeptical about the national revival project, just like Proust and Joyce. All of them want to be part of the uniting new liberal Europe. Freud explicitly stood for faith in the modern liberal state.

The majority of Diaspora Jews were quite indifferent to Zionism, and most of those few, like Leopold Bloom, who were ready to consider its promise could not gather up any real enthusiasm. They had seen much in their lives that made them skeptical, pessimistic, and stoic. Like Freud, Proust and Joyce, they were less than sure about the success of this "therapeutic movement".

Actually, the indifference of most Diaspora Jews to its cause was Zionism's first and possibly most serious failure, always undermining its claim to be the national liberation movement of the Jewish people. Most Jews, when encountering the Zionist idea, were less than certain that they needed liberation, or if they needed one, like Leopold Bloom, they were not sure whether it was the national kind that was in order.

Being a Jew in Europe (and in the First World in general) today is much less of a misfortune, and the conversion option has almost disappeared because of Christianity's decline, but the European dream of integration and full citizenship is still on the agenda more than one hundred years later. Actually, Jews in the First World today enjoy a reality of acceptance and integration, which seemed like a dream only a short time ago. Despite the relics of cultural anti-Semitism, secularized Jews have been very successful in modern times, and among those cases of remarkable success we may count Theodor Herzl, Sigmund Freud, and Marcel Proust. And that is perhaps why contemporary First World Jews, just like Leopold Bloom, are still so reluctant to accept the sentimental invitations calling them to settle on the shores of the Sea of Galilee.

References

Adler, A. (1956). *The Individual Psychology of Alfred Adler*. New York: Harper & Row.

Bakan, D. (1965). *Sigmund Freud And The Jewish Mystical Tradition*. New York: Schocken.

Beit-Hallahmi, B. (1989). *Prolegomena to the Psychological Study of Religion*. Lewisburg, PA: Bucknell University Press.

Beit-Hallahmi, B. (1993). *Original Sins: Reflections on the History of Zionism and Israel*. New York: Interlink.

Beit-Hallahmi, B. *Psychoanalytic Studies of Religion: Critical Assessment and Annotated Bibliography*. Westport, CT: Greenwood Press, 1996.

Beit-Hallahmi, B. & Argyle, M. (1997). *The Psychology of Religious Behaviour, Belief, and Experience*. London: Routledge.

Bergmann, M.S. (1995). The Jewish and German roots of psychoanalysis and the impact of the Holocaust. *American Imago, 52*, 243-259.

Bunzl, M. (1997). Theodor Herzl's Zionism as gendered discourse. In R. Robertson & E. Timms (Eds.) *Theodor Herzl and the Origins of Zionism*. Edinburgh: Edinburgh University Press.

Burgess, A. (1965). *Re Joyce*. New York: Norton.

Charmé, S.L. (1986). 'A Ticket to Ride': Bourgeois Civility, Jewish Marginality, and Existential Authenticity in the Lives of Freud and Sartre. *Review of Existential Psychology & Psychiatry, 19*, 143-159.

Charmé, S.L. (1991). *Vulgarity and Authenticity: Dimensions of Otherness in the World of Jean-Paul* Sartre. University of Massachusetts Press,

Cohen, S.M. & Eisen, A.M.(2000). *The Jew Within: Self, Family and Community in America.* Bloomington: Indiana University Press.

Costello, P. (1981). *Leopold Bloom: A Biography.* London: Gill and Macmillan.

Davidson, N.R. (1996). *James Joyce, "Ulysses", and the Construction of Jewish Identity: Culture, Identity, and "the Jew" in Modernist Europe.* New York: Cambridge University Press.

Falk, A. (1975-1976). Identity and Name Changes. *The Psychoanalytic Review, 62*, 647–657.

Falk, A. (1978). Freud and Herzl. *Contemporary Psychoanalysis, 14*, 357-387.

Fiedler, L.A. (1991). *Fiedler on the Roof: Essays on Literature and Jewish Identity.* Boston: D.R. Godine.

French, M. (1982). *The Book as World: James Joyce's* Ulysses. London: Abacus.

Friedman, L.J. 2000). *Identity's Architect: A Biography of Erik Erikson.* Cambridge, MA: Harvard University Press.

Freud, C. (2001). *Freud Ego.* London: BBC Consumer Publishing.

Freud, S. (1900). *Interpretation of Dreams.* In *The Standard Edition of the Complete Psychological Writings of Sigmund Freud.* Vol. *5.* London: Hogarth Press.

Freud, S. (1905). An analysis of phobia in a five-year-old boy. In *The Standard Edition of the Complete Psychological Writings of Sigmund Freud. Vol.* 10, 3-149. London: Hogarth Press

Freud, S. (1926) Address to the society of Bnai-Brith. In *The Standard Edition of the Complete Psychological Writings of Sigmund Freud. Vol. 20*, 271-276. London: Hogarth Press

Freud, S. (1928). A religious experience. . In *The Standard Edition of the Complete Psychological Writings of Sigmund Freud. Vol.* 21, 167-174. London: Hogarth Press

Freud, S (1939). *Moses and Monotheism.* In *The Standard Edition of the Complete Psychological Writings of Sigmund Freud .* Vol. *23*. London: Hogarth Press

Freud, S. (1970). *The Letters of Sigmund Freud and Arnold Zweig.* New York: Harvest.

Gay, P. (1978). *Freud, Jews and Other Germans.* New York: Oxford University Press.

Gay, P. (1985). *Freud for Historians.* New York: Oxford University Press.

Gay, P. (1987). *A Godless Jew: Freud, Atheism and the Making of Psychoanalysis.* New Haven, CT: Yale University Press.

Gay, P. (1988). *Freud: A Life for Our Time.* New York: Norton.

Gilman, S. (1991). *The Jew's Body.* London: Routledge.

Gilman, S. (1993). *Freud, Race, and Gender.* Princeton: Princeton University Press.

Goldscheider, C. & Zuckerman, A.S. *The Transformation Of the Jews.* Chicago: University of Chicago Press, 1984.

Greer, G. (1971). *The Female Eunuch.* New York: McGraw-Hill.

Greenberg, C. (1950/1995). Self-hatred and Jewish chauvinism: Some reflections on "positive Jewishness". In *The Collected Essays and Criticism.*

Vol. 3: *Affirmations and Refusals, 1950-1956.* Chicago: University of Chicago Press.

Grosskurth, P. (1986). *Melanie Klein: Her World and Her Work.* New York: Knopf.

Grunberger, R. Band of brothers. *AJR Journal*, March 2001.

Hayman, R. (1990). *Proust: A Biography.* New York: HarperCollins.

Heilman, S.C. (1998) *Portrait of American Jews: The last Half of the Twentieth Century.* Seattle: University of Washington Press.

Herzl, T. (1898). In *The American Hebrew*, New York.

Herzl, T. (1899). Antwort an Nordau. *Die Welt,* February 3.

Himmelfarb, M. (1967). Secular society? A Jewish perspective. *Daedalus*, 156, 220-238.

Ilnytzky, U. (1998). Literature's top 100. The Associated Press, July 22.
Jones, E. (1957). *The Life and Work of Sigmund Freud.* New York: Basic Books.

Joyce, J. (1975). *Selected Letters.* London: Faber and Faber.

Joyce, J. (1986), *Ulysses.* (edited by Hans Walter Gabler). New York: Random House.

Katz, J. (1989). *Private Enterprise in the Construction of Palestine at the time of Second Aliyah.* Ramat-Gan: Bar-Ilan University Press.[Hebrew]

Kazin, A. (1998). Laughter in the dark. *The New York Review of Books.* April 23.

Keogh, D. (1998). *Jews in Twentieth-Century Ireland: Refugees, Anti-Semitism and the Holocaust.* Cork: Cork University Press.

Krull, M. (1986). *Freud and His Father* . New York: Norton.

Marmorstein, E. (1969). *Heaven At Bay.* London: Oxford University Press.

Mosse, G. (1985). Nationalism and Sexuality: Respectability and Abnormal Sexuality in Modern Europe. New York: Howard Fertig.

Nabokov, V. (1980). *Lectures on Literature.* New York: Harcourt Brace Jovanovich.

Nadel, I.B. (1989). *Joyce and the Jews: Culture and Texts.* Iowa City: University of Iowa Press.

Nolan, E. (1995). *James Joyce and Nationalism.* London: Routledge.

Pawel, E. (1989). *The labyrinth of exile: A life of Theodor Herzl.* New York: Farrar, Straus, Giroux.

Proust, M. (1954) *A La Rechrche du Temps Perdu : Sodome et Gomorrhe.* Paris : Gallimard.

Proust, M. (1992). *In Search of Lost Time.* (tr. C.K. Scott-Moncrieff & T. Kilmartin, revised by D.J. Enright). London: Chatto & Windus.

Recanati, J. (1979). *Profils juifs de Marcel Proust.* Paris: Buchet, Chastel.

Reik, T. (1953). *The Haunting Melody: Psychoanalytic Experiences in Life and Music.* New York : Farrar, Straus, & Giroux.

Rizzuto, A.-M. (1998). *Why Did Freud Reject God?: A Psychodynamic Interpretation* New Haven, CT: Yale University Press.

Robert, M. (1977). *From Oedipus to Moses.* Garden City, New York: Doubleday.

Rolnik, E.J. (2002). Psychoanalysis moves to Palestine: Immigration, integration, and reception. In this volume.

Rothman, S. & Isenberg, P.(1974). Freud and Jewish marginality. *Encounter,* December, 46-54.

Sartre, J.-P. (1965). *Anti-Semite and Jew.* New York: Schocken.

Scholem, G. (1989). *Od Davar.* Tel-Aviv: Am Oved. [Hebrew]

Schorske, C.E. (1998). *Thinking With History: Explorations in the Passage to Modernism*. Princeton: Princeton University Press.

Shattuck, R. (1974). *Marcel Proust* . New York: Viking Press

Simon, E.M. (1996). Betrayal and redemption: The transcendent Jew in the works of Kazantzakis, Joyce and Bellow. In H.J. Schrader, E.M. Simon & C. Wardi (Eds.) *The Jewish Self-Portrait in European and American Literature*. Tubingen: Max Niemeyer Verlag.

Sprinker, M. (1994). *History and Ideology in Proust*. Cambridge: Cambridge University Press.

Steyn, J. (1999). *The Jew: Assumptions of Identity*. London and New York: Cassell.

Strozier, C.B. (2001). *Heinz Kohut: The Making of a Psychoanalyst*. New York: Farrar, Straus, & Giroux.

Tindall, W.Y. (1959). *A Reader's Guide to James Joyce*. New York: Octagon.

White, E. (1999). *Marcel Proust.* New York: Lipper/Viking..

Wilson, E. (1928). A short view of Proust. *The New Republic.* March 21.

Yassour, A. (1986). Philosophy-religion-politics: Borochov, Bogdanov and Lunacharsky. *Studies in Soviet Thought. 31*, 1-32.

Zimmerman, M. (1979). Leopold Paula Bloom: the New Womanly Man. *Literature and Psychology*, 29 , 176-84;

Acknowledgements

The author would like to acknowledge the help and encouragement generously offered by John Bunzl, Nilli Diengott, Avner Falk, Amihud Gilad, Daniel Guttwein, Zmira Heizner, Lia Koffler, Eran J. Rolnik, and Elliott M. Simon.

Chapter 2

The Temporal Emblematics of Belonging: Position and Validity in Israeli Political Discourse

Dan Diner
University of Leipzig

This chapter presents a general framework for understanding ideological and historical changes in Israel's history. Diner's analysis is quite abstract and offers a general typology of modern states and modern ideologies. The conceptual framework here is both psychological and historical, offering a lucid and powerful survey of the whole history of the Zionist movement in Palestine/Israel and its ideological needs and constrains. The chapter covers some events in detail, but draws broad conclusions about general trends over decades and centuries. The result is a highly original analysis of ideologies and historical turning points.

1. Introduction

In ethnically composed polities, the attributes of belonging take on the quality of political currency. From their symbolism and emblematic order, one can read the significant signs of belonging and participation valid at any given time. And that is especially true in national polities determined to forge a binding common ground for groups of differing origin in the population. Against the backdrop of such normative communality, the respective diverse pre-histories compete with each other for position and distinction. We may ask: just how much distinctiveness can prevail in the struggle of the various particularisms amongst one another and then be incorporated into the identificational corpus considered legitimate or even obligatory for the society as a whole? What amount of the respective group-specific past, memory and custom is embodied in the binding symbolism and emblematic arsenal of a present valid for all? The struggle over the particular distinctive components in the composition of the society's communality is a permanent battle over the symbolic resources both limited and necessary for the polity's functioning. In turn, the struggle over the relative validity of those components in the common identity is a process characteristic of states with as yet uncompleted internal and external legitimacy. Such states—in order to justify themselves both internally and to the outside—require both a continual symbolization of historical elements lying in the distant past and the permanent evocation of the aura of authenticity. Such polities are founded on the fiction of long memories, of ethnos.

In polities relying solely on constitution and the rules of law, other criteria are valid, even if their citizenry is composed of members of diverse ethnic groups. For such states, the ethnic composition of their respective population and the associated differing memories is irrelevant for their national self-identity. Their legitimation is ultimately anchored in the validity of institutions, and thus in the dominance of rules and procedures. Of course, such polities also derive their origin from historical acts of founding - mostly revolutions. Yet those acts took place in a time that consciousness grasps as part of the present. Ultimately, they invoke the arsenal of ideas and legacy of the Enlightenment. They are grounded in universal values committed to the freedom of the individual and the protection of human and civil rights. In any case, as polities bound to the present they are obliged to neutralize the differing pre-histories and origins of their composite populations, and in any event to disengage those pre-histories from the ambit of the political sphere. In the private domain, individuals can, alone or together with others, indulge in the memory of illustrious pasts, yet those pasts remain banned from the spaces of public validity and valorization. Democratic states founded solely on constitutional law derived from the values of the Enlightenment are thus polities with a short memory. They are based on the conceptual world of demos.

2. Choosing Past, Present, and Future

The United States is the principal prototype of a polity that strives to neutralize the differing origins of its constituent populations in the iconic shape of the abstract citizen. Those who wish to join the American communality are thus required to leave attributes of their previous affiliation outside the door. They take their place in a centuries-old stream of the acceptance of immigrants in a land with liberty and equality for all. A country disencumbered of all hindering pre-histories and pasts, prepared to stand in a here and now free of history.

In this regard, Israel is antipodal to the United States. It belongs to that category of polities that invoke a distant and, as it were, mythical past. In the case of the Jewish state, the pivot is "Biblical" justification. Such "Biblical" justification does not command recognition and validity only among religiously observant Jews. The recourse to ancient historical eras is equally a secular phenomenon. Of course, that secular discourse of self-validation and justification, in contrast to the dogmatic discourse of the religious, is oriented toward empirical proof, i.e. historically demonstrable evidence and its universal communicability.

The recourse to long past historical realities as the basis for historical claims to be realized in the present would appear quite problematic. After all, such a claim is not geared to some virtual historical hereafter; rather, it is intended to be actualized in the here and now. For the Jewish state, the consequences of such a claim are nothing short of dramatic. The guiding intention was to establish in Palestine, as the "Biblical" Land of Israel, a future presence for the Jews as a people and nation—and this in the presence of another, an Arab population in and on the land. Simply by virtue of that contravening presence of another people on the terrain, it was necessary to invoke an ancient past by summoning up those virtual times. Two time periods were counterposed to the present: the remote past and the claim of ancient historical patrimony associated with it, and a utopia whose establishment was projected into the distant future.

The resort to ancient past eras, the "Biblical" myth, is largely a part of the arsenal of the right. By contrast, the Zionist left sought composure in the notion that all contradictions would eventually be dissolved and reconciled in the ultimate utopia envisioned. Their universally attuned self-identity was torn as it tried to cope with the hardly compatible circumstances of the conflict in and for Palestine:

after all, that conflict necessitated justifying force against Palestine's Arabs, who by dint of their mere physical presence in the land laid claim to the only real time, the present. Yet force proceeds from virtual time. Ultimately, both past and future are arrayed against the existing status quo.

Virtual times mobilized to alter the status quo operate under a constraint for self-justification. After all, they intrude on a condition congruent with peace and the binding universal obligation to maintain it. Those intending to transform the status quo have always faced the necessity of having to legitimate their agenda. In turn, the rituals of justification are acted out in the form of historical discourses, a veritably obsessive occupation with long bygone pasts in order to invoke ancient patrimony so as to justify claims arrayed against the valid present. In such a discourse, various conflicting claims are posed against each other in temporal dislocation. And in such a counter-posing of time periods, arguments necessarily miss their target. Thus, the only means of communication that remains is the language of force. The collision of differing times is the fundamental constant in the conflict between Arabs and Jews in Palestine/Israel. To an even greater extent, conflicts over times and the conjunct tensions that periodically erupt also exist within the Jewish population in Israel between groups of different ethnic origins. These conflicts are far less dramatic than the core conflict between the two adversary peoples who, in their discourses of legitimation, lay claim to the contested land. In the temporal conflict between groups in the Jewish population that identify with differing origins, what is principally in contention is the relative position of respective diverse pre-histories within the frame of a shared political association, the State of Israel. Against the backdrop of such a common bond, they are constrained to exercise a high degree of reserve in that struggle over position and prestige. It is clear, however, that the iron anthropological rule of priority of temporal "seniority" demands its due. So it is that the newcomer in Israel is required to demonstrate where he or she belongs by the active amassing of time in the land. In this respect, Israel is no different from other immigration countries, if it weren't for the external discourse of legitimation bound up with and burdened by the persistent presence of the Arab population in the land.

Yet a contradiction emerges here: on the one hand, you have the validity of a virtual legitimating time anchored in ancient, quasi-mythical pasts, a bygone age that the once evolving, and now existent Jewish state has mobilized for fundamental justification, in its own eyes and those of others. And on the other, there is the validity of real time in its concrete unfolding. The justification that falls back on mythical elements and "Biblical" time is valid principally vis-à-vis the Arabs, the Palestinians. In the internal dynamics of the relations between the various Jewish populations within Israel, the temporal yardstick of their respective presence in the land is a subsurface criterion for position and prestige. Nonetheless, the pecking order grounded on the accumulation of time in the land can be shattered by the temporal order of the mythical past, which is valid principally as a discursive justifier to the outside. The legitimation accrued by presence in the land can be annulled by invoking the sacral conception of time so distinctive to religious discourse. Evoking the religious frame and the congruent image of eternity suspends the validity of secular time. Due in significant measure to the need to legitimate the Jewish state to the outside, the religious interpretation of mythical history internally is invested with something akin to a power of veto over the historically real time sequences in the land.

3. Internal Divisions and Identity

The different groups in the Jewish population in Israel competing over position and prestige are symbolized by different time layers and their respective emblematic order. As mentioned, the temporally successive groups of immigrants and their offspring conduct themselves in keeping with a behavioral pattern that is characteristic of immigrant societies: the established are always superior to the newcomers. This human constant and its everyday and social manifestations are overdetermined by another difference in belonging: namely that between Western, *Ashkenazi* Jews, and Eastern Jews, originating in the Islamic world, commonly termed S*ephardi*. Over and beyond any purported external differences in appearance between *Ashkenazi* and Eastern Jews, differing cultural forms of self-identity are salient. Despite all their internal differences, the Western Jews developed the consciousness of a bond between Jews as a people, a web of cohesion that approximates the Western conception of what constitutes a nation: namely the Jewish people qua *ha-am ha-yehudi* [Hebrew: The Jewish People]. During the nineteenth century, that notion of a Jewish people was infused with elements that increasingly tended to correspond to those of a European nationality. While religious ritual and religiously shaped customs and mores faded, the languages and secular cultures marking the collective bonds and unity came ever more to the fore.

The idea of the Jews as a nation, central in the conceptions of eastern and central European Zionism, was not limited solely to this most clear and patent form of Jewish national consciousness. It also was salient in other blueprints of collective Jewish self-identity in Europe's East. Increasingly, Jews there also came to view themselves as an ethnic group in the population (to use more contemporary discourse). It is true that these national conceptions of a Jewish people could not manage without some bond to Judaism and Jewish tradition, conceived in whatever secular terms. Yet despite all the still- binding religious components in such conceptions, they differ from the exclusively religious sense of identity common to Eastern Jewry. Although the general ongoing tendency for religion to modulate into nation was also evident in the Islamic world in the nineteenth century, the transformation of the millet into nation there differed from the largely secularizing and ethnicizing effects of modernity in the context of Western and Eastern Christianity. In any event, the self-identity of Eastern Jews remained imbued far more with religious elements, and much less nationalistic than that of the *Ashkenazi* Jews in Eastern Europe. The Jews of the Islamic world thus tend to feel a sense of belonging more to a religiously connoted *am yisrael*, the people of Israel, than to the Jewish people, *ha-am ha-yehudi*.

In Israel, the Eastern Jewish self-identity tends to infuse national Israeli identity with religious symbolism and emblemata as the binding attributes of membership in the collectivity. Secular components more in tune with a Western understanding of nation are devalued as external and alienating, indeed as not genuinely Jewish. One should recall, after all, that hybridity by secular marriage is possible in the West but not in the Islamic world. In addition, the religious components of collective self-identity merge with those of the overarching mythical narrative. They are invested with an importance extending far beyond the circle of the religious camp.

In competing for position and prestige in the community, the religious and national attributes of belonging are counter-posed. As I have explained, these components can certainly be additionally charged by inscription with the "ethnic" difference between *ha-am ha-yehudi* and *am yisrael*, the Western and Eastern constituents of Jewish belonging. If Jews from an Eastern background try to distance themselves from the religious components of their origin by moving toward Western i.e. national attributes, they assimilate themselves to a discourse, and thus to the concomitant criteria of position and prestige, more in keeping with the forms of self-identity prevalent among Western Jews. Such a discourse, in turn, is largely formulated in terms of history.

For its part, European historical thinking tends to link up with the secular roots and premises of the Enlightenment, thus following the cadence of the historical progression of Western civilization. Transposed to the internal Israeli conflict over "seniority", such a conception of history tends to maintain a progression and appropriate valorization in keeping with the sequencing of the successive waves of immigration. But in Israel, the absolutist character of the religious legitimation and its conjunct contra-historical understanding of time ruptures such a ranking grounded on historical sequencing and a pecking order based on who arrived before whom, as is commonplace in most countries of immigration. The religious interpretation of the mythical narrative, indebted to the concept of eternity, annuls the Western historical understanding of time. In the great scramble for position and prestige, it is able to provide all who espouse the religious emblematic order with a surplus gain. The invoking of religion, the public enactment of religious ritual and the political display of religious symbolism can shorten the otherwise long path the new immigrant or socially marginalized individual must travel to arrive at the sanctum of belonging. It can also invalidate claims to belonging otherwise bound up with particular spans of time. There is a principle oriented to the whole: namely that sacred time annuls secular time.

4. The Return

The blending of sacral with secular components of the claim to belonging to, and being a part of the Jewish state, is notorious. Thus, in contrast with practices in ordinary countries of immigration, the Jewish newcomer in Israel is not seen as a foreign who must acculturate and adopt to the new country, but as a "returnee." Such a return is not conceptualized in individual terms. Rather, it holds for individuals only to the extent that they participate in this "return" as part of a collective committed to a trans-historical, so to speak timeless and eternal temporal frame, the so-called Ingathering of the Exiles codified in the *hok ha-shvut*, the Israeli "Law of Return" of 1950. That fiction facilitates the following transformation: with their arrival in the

Promised Land, immigrants shed, qua "returnees," the historical time adhering to their biography, accommodating to a sacrally modulated sense of time. Such a fictive conversion, only to be realized in the projected future, does not require a concrete successful process of acculturation for its validation. Rather it occurs via the authority and transformative power of that juridical magic moment when Israeli citizenship is granted. The religiously anchored claim of the Jews to the land annuls all other attributes of a right to belonging moored in real time. If it were otherwise, that fictive claim to the land (itself asserting supra-historical authority) would be extinguished in favor of the claim of that population previously resident and still in the land, in accord with the reality of the present—namely of the Palestinian Arabs.

The sacral character of mythical time as the basis for the claim of "return," of being "restored" to the land, and thus of invoking the legitimating nexus of a bygone era—is obvious in the religious discourse employed. The Jew formerly present in the prestate *yishuv* or who later came to Israel is not simply a privileged immigrant eager, for whatever reasons, on exchanging his or her previous place of residence for another. Their "return" that annuls historical time is also an *aliyah*, an "ascent" to the Promised Land, a one-way pilgrimage without return. As an *oleh*, the immigrant accepts the obligation to expunge from collective memory the entire span running from the historical departure or expulsion of the Jews from ancient Israel to their contemporary return, erasing it as meaningful historical time. In this sense, *aliyah* does not merely signify a change in place but rather a no less sacrally charged change in time.

Along with its sacred meaning, the concept of *aliyah* also has a quasi-secular significance insofar as *aliyah* serves to qualify and enumerate the successive waves of immigration considered basic building blocks in creating the polity. That chronicling follows key historical events in European history. In the listing of *aliyah* waves, it is noteworthy that only four are singled out as such. By contrast, the so-called Fifth *aliyah* (1933-1939), i.e. the immigration of German and German-speaking Jews from Central Europe in the 1930s in the aftermath of the rise of National Socialism, was known in the parlance of that time as *aliyah hadasha* or "new immigration" to distinguish it from the preceding four. All the later waves to Palestine and Israel after 1945 are no longer given any special enumerative designation whatsoever. It would appear that only the first four *aliyot* are granted a formative significance for nation building.

The relative significance of succeeding immigration waves in the self-constitution of the Jewish *yishuv* and later in the State of Israel diminished successively in proportion to the increasing distance in time to the prime *aliyot*. Particularly after 1945, the *yishuv*, meanwhile imbued with the myth of authenticity as a Jewish polity in the making, was confronted with a wave of immigrants whose fundamental formative experience in Europe had been the war and the Holocaust. In those decisive years in world history, they experienced the time of Europe, while the *yishuv*, unhinged from mundane temporality and seemingly turned within, pursued its national and social paths in utopia beyond the present.

5. Narratives and Icons

As a constitutive temporal icon, the year 1948 represents something akin to a compromise between two narratives of originally unequal valence. On the one hand, the narrative of the *yishuv*, a purportedly indigenous and authentic body politic, that on top of it thought itself superior to all other Jewish narrative. On the other, the narrative history of the Holocaust survivors. The tales of the latter quite evidently put to shame the self-image of that authenticity of the *yishuv*, basking in the new radiance of its self-styled historical confirmation. In any event, that narrative was advised to keep its silence, since it demonstrated in all wretchedness the defeat of those life worlds that had sprung from the European there and then. Weighed down, the narratives of the European Diaspora crouched under the burden of their refutation, gratefully resorting to conversion in a grand gesture of forgetting accompanying the acceptance of the symbolism and emblematic order of the *yishuv*. It was not until 1961 that the Eichmann trial justified their plaint, even if the evidence they presented was in the name and language of collective memory.

The compromise between the narratives of the *Ashkenazi* Diaspora and that of the *yishuv*, is manifested in the iconic year 1948. It draws heavily on elements of legitimacy derived from those circumstances that placed a moral obligation on the international community to grant the Jews a place of their own. The emblematics of this moral self-obligation bear the markings of another locus, the insignia of "Auschwitz". It is the Holocaust survivors who represent Israel's universal legitimacy and who reconcile that legitimacy with the universally far less acceptable claim to unilateral self-justification via mythical time and fictive antiquity. After all, it was necessary to justify and account for the resort to force against the local population, which indeed represented the status quo and the attributes of the present, namely the Palestinian Arabs. Ultimately, the violence sprang from the despairing readiness on the part of both Jewish narratives, of the survivors and of the *yishuv*, to participate jointly in the baptism by fire of military self-recognition.

Thus, the icon 1948 symbolizes a compromise between the quasi-salvational providential chronology of the *yishuv* and the *aliyot* comprising it on the one hand, and the events in Europe that mark the epochal boundary of 1945 on the other. In the year of Israel's establishment, it was not only two contrary narratives that were interlinked; two totally different legitimacies also merged in this temporal monument. Given the diverse origins which later make up the Jewish population of the state of Israel, the year 1948 was in almost every way an *Ashkenazi* date. Flowing into this icon and its associated memories is a history of experience almost totally reflective of the European sequence of times and events. The immigrations immediately subsequent to 1948 also assimilated to this narrative by making it their own. They were assisted in this process by the fact of their European origin, their experiential histories bound to Europe and the events that had transpired there, as well as the memory so forged. To this extent, the year 1948 is principally an *Ashkenazi* icon of time. Despite all the indigenous endurance and vitality they reflected, the boundaries of the Israeli state established at that time derived their universal legitimacy from the cataclysm in Europe. Thus, the borders of Israel down to 1967 had ultimately been legitimated by the Holocaust. To this extent, these were, in a symbolic and legitimating sense, what could be termed the "borders of Auschwitz."

After the establishment of the state, none of the succeeding waves of immigration were added to the enumeration of the first four or five *aliyot*. The immigration waves following 1948 appeared obliged to subscribe to the foundation narrative and to canonize its symbolism and emblematics. This was especially true of the flood of immigrants in the 1950s and 1960s, stemming largely from Arab-Islamic countries. The context of that immigration wave differed significantly from that of European history. Although they were touched by the cataclysm of 1945, it had a completely different meaning for the Jews of the Islamic world: namely decolonization and the consequences of the Arab-Israeli conflict. As their ticket of entry into Israel, the Jews from these countries had to echo a different, i.e. *Ashkenzi* narrative. In any event, the act of belonging in Israel demanded an enormous renunciation on their part: ranging from the nullifying of their own pre-histories to the distortion of their primarily traditional and religious self-identity. They were subjected to a process of modernization that, over and beyond all social demands for adaptation and conformity, went hand in hand with homage to an ideal of national homogenization linked to an ethos of social equality—the transformation of sacral attributes of belonging into those of a secular ethnos. And such a process of acculturation, marked by institutional features, was in turn tied to the dominant emblemata of the year 1948 and its *Ashkenzi* pre-histories. Their locus was Israel in its 1948 boundaries and their legitimacy, interlinked with Auschwitz. In 1967, that frame of legitimacy would be burst asunder.

1967 heralded Israel's grand transformation. With the conquest of the "Biblical" heartland, the Jewish state, previously committed to an essentially secular emblematic order, charged on into the vaults of mythical time. That temporality had not simply been invented, it lurked covert in the very fabric of the justifying historical narrative. Encircled by the 1948 borders legitimated by Auschwitz, up to then that mythical historical narrative had existed on the margins until propelled to the surface by the unanticipated success of a sweeping victory. In any event, it seemed that nothing was done by the more rational and prudent to put a reasoned damper on the passions welling up from the deepest depths. From this watershed on, the "Biblical" myth of *eretz yisrael* took on something akin to supralegitimacy. Other justifications of the state were now out of fashion if not anathema. In any event, it seemed that a higher degree of legitimacy was attributed to the icon of 1967 than the iconic year 1948.

There has been much talk about the contrast between *eretz yisrael* and the State of Israel. This counter-posing does not just reflect and embody the antipodal character of national-religious mythologies and secular legitimations. Successive layerings in the Jewish populations and their origins are also aligned with that opposition. The events of 1967 heralded the supplanting of one narrative by another. In the eyes of the majority of Eastern-Jewish Israelis, the "Six-Day War" represented something tantamount to the bona fide founding event of the body politic. For them as Israelis, this war was after all the first truly relevant armed confrontation they had experienced. And for Jews who joined the *yishuv* and fledgling state through *aliyah*, participation in Israel's wars was analogous to a ritual of initiation, a demonstration of their conversion from then and there to here and now. In addition, the conquest of the "Biblical" heartland and the concomitant revaluation of the mythical legitimation of the state accorded the Eastern variant of Jewish belonging and its religious emblematic order and symbolism far more space and salience than the secular-*Ashkenazi* (and thus ethnic-national) insignia associated with the year 1948. The Jewish state also gained mounting acceptance in the eyes of those whose self-identity was more in tune with the religiosity of *am yisrael* and less with the national criteria of a Jewish people European in its origins.

The national-religious emblematic order permeated the political and public arenas of the body politic. And after ten years of incubation, it finally came to state power in 1977. Until that juncture, Eastern resistance to *Ashkenazi* hegemony and social institutions had been limited to the demand to make the nationally propagated ideal of equality a living reality. That ideal had in practice been shunted aside by dint of the argument of accumulated time common to countries of immigration and the associated claims to position and standing in the unfolding pecking order.

In the early 1980s, social protest among Eastern Israelis seized on another language: the discourse of religion, linked with a distinctive sacral emblematics of timelessness. By its nature, such an emblematic order neutralized the dominant insignia of claims to position and prestige based on social and historical time. And in view of the "Biblical" justifications binding on the body politic, all secular argumentation based on the salience of a set of temporal stages of presence in the land, stratified according to the phases of immigration, grew silent. After all, the secular discourse of national legitimation was also indebted to the myth of "Biblical" history, even though it clothed itself in worldly, quasi-historical trappings. Only after a substantial segment of Eastern Jewry in Israel had adopted the emblematic order of the Orthodox ticket, accommodating in text and external appearance to the East European guardians of the true faith—did they gain position and prestige. In defensive irritation, the champions of the secular-*Ashkenazi* narrative were forced to relinquish many of the ranks they had occupied and to make room for others.

6. Tentative Conclusion: A New Order?

In the aftermath of 1967, many changes were also taking shape in the circles of authentic East European religious orthodoxy. The ideology of the unity of the land and its quasi-holiness that spread everywhere after the conquest of the "Biblical" heartland also penetrated into the ranks of Jewish observant orthodoxy that had until then opposed the Zionist-secular myth of the "Biblically" grounded nation. They and an Eastern Jewry caught up in profound religious transformation from the end of the 1970s and the early 1980s, in alliance with secular nationalists, drove from the centers of power and influence the milieu which perceived itself to be originally and authentically Israeli. Nationalist myth and religious ardor, coupled with the emblems of the year 1967, had an increasingly salient impact on the previously dominant narrative bound up with 1948. In 1993, a surprising about-face was heralded with the Oslo accords and Yitzhak Rabin, legitimized by his status as a hero of both the 1948 and 1967 wars, proclaimed a withdrawal from the territories of exalted eschatological pathos back to the sobriety of a secular present. In 1995, as the living icon of an Israel in the boundaries of its historical establishment, he was gunned down, the victim of an assassination underpinned by mythical and sacral ideology. The assassin seemed the very incarnation of the symbolism and emblemata of the era that had sprouted from the soil of 1967. It appeared that Israel was not yet ready to change its ways. And such a tendency seemed but confirmed by the election results of 1996. The country bowed down once again before the yoke of mythical and sacral pasts.

The consequences of the right to "return" to *eretz yisrael*, that juridical magical moment in which the immigrant is transformed into a equal member of the collective, religiously grounded—an element that annuls the temporal claims to a place in the hierarchy that otherwise exist in immigrant societies—are delusive. They act to blur the experiential realities in the land, in particular the insights gained in conflict with the Arabs and Palestinians. As a result of constant immigration, the history of conflict beginning in 1948 at the latest appears to be repeatedly masked, covered over by the eschatological claim to the "Biblical" foundation myth. As though caught in a compulsive repetition of the past, Israeli society seems constrained to relive that fundamental experience of belonging. The "right of return" enshrined in Israeli law acts as a demographic damper on recognizing the realities in the land. That became evident over the past decade in the so-called Russian immigration. As if in cinematic slow-motion, that influx runs through the phases of secular Israeli memory.

Secular Israeli remembrance is a memory stamped by conflict. It links up with the pre-State of Israel chronologizing and then moves on to take the year 1948, the constitutive founding event of new legitimacy, as the point of departure. From that juncture on, this memory traverses the decisive existential points in the history of conflict with the Arabs, coming to insight and maturity in the process. If the year 1956 stood at odds with the self-image of the nation besieged, the year 1967 seemed to evoke the narrative both of the Holocaust and eschatological concepts of salvation. For a time they ran in parallel, but gradually moved further and further apart. The year 1973 marked the revoking of the exalted self-confidence of '67 and spurred differing and contrary developments. It heightened eschatological currents, giving impetus to little articulated tendencies toward doubt pulsing just below the surface. In turn, the 1982 Lebanon war helped spark a moral and political turn. This was kept alive by the blazing of the *Intifada* that erupted in 1987, and was finally realized with the Oslo accords.

The maturity of the Israeli polity and the associated "educational history" as genesis of the conflict tended toward recognition of the dominant realities on the ground, which was appropriately personified in the figure of Yitzhak Rabin. The indigenous Israeli memory, which evolved from 1948 on in the matrix of a bloody history of formation, may be overshadowed by two types of belonging: the religious orientation indulging in a mode of eschatological timelessness, and another sense of belonging, able to exercise a direct and immediate civil influence by dint of a privileged arrival in the land, by way of *aliyah*. And it was able to do so without having become a part of Israeli memory and its experiential history. The 1990s wave of *aliyah*, coming from the former Soviet Union, felt oppressed by the pervasive everyday burden of religious symbolism and emblemata of belonging. Today some pointers have shifted: the barometers indicate a victory of the symbolism and emblemata of those narratives whose terminus a quo was the year 1948. Yet it is likely that the far more profound and deepset conflict between the narratives is of a different duration, and will persist.

Translated by William Templer

Chapter 3

Towards a Critical Analysis of Israeli Political Culture

Moshe Zuckermann
Tel-Aviv University

The theoretical framework introduced in this chapter is the social criticism framework of the Frankfurt School, associated with such theoreticians as Adorno, Horkheimer, Marcuse, and Fromm. This framework embodied a bold attempt to combine psychoanalytic ideas with the Marxian tradition of uncovering and unmasking collective ideologies. Moshe Zuckerman approaches his subject matter, the major ideological themes in Israeli political culture, inspired and informed by the Frankfurt School. His goal is to analyze the production of a common identity, which is by necessity a "False Consciousness". To uncover the process responsible for the creation of this consciousness, what is habitually hidden must be uncovered, and what is hidden is the Other. It so happens that there are three groups of Others that haunt Israeli consciousness: Holocaust survivors, who are physical survivors but psychical victims, Palestinian natives, and the ultra-Orthodox Jews of Israel, who represent the historical presence of the Diaspora. Uncovering the production of ideology means stripping away layers of guilt and anxiety. At the end of this process Zuckerman makes it clear that getting rid of the false ideology means a radical de-Zionization of Israeli society.

1. Introduction

There can be no doubt that psychoanalysis has revolutionized academic and cultural thinking in the twentieth century. Its prominent position can be deduced from the influence it has exerted equally on the humanities, on the social sciences, and on the field of cultural studies, as well as from the vehemence with which its salient opponents have repeatedly denigrated it, delegitimized it, and declared its demise. Of course, the degree to which it offers tools for an accurate analysis of society or politics remains an open question, giving rise to frequent controversies. Freud's works already develop not only an ontogenetic strand of theory (i.e. in regard to the fate of the individual person) but also a phylogenetic strand (reconstructing the cultural evolution all of mankind). But despite Freud's impressive attempts to establish connections, these strands of theory have not eliminated the conceptual problems arising with the transition from the individual to the collective. Categories of repression, rationalization, sublimation, and the unconscious, for example, which are generally considered fundamental in the psychoanalytic theory of the individual psyche, are not accepted as self-evident in supra-individual theory at all. If they enter into the analysis of collective behavior, they generally exhibit an isomorphic character as analogy, and the language of their application is that of metaphoric comparison.

Yet, the theoretical and empirical work of the early Frankfurt School made an attempt (which in hindsight looks quite successful) to connect categories of macro-sociological analysis of society with central categories of psychoanalysis. Starting from the view of an essentially repressive structure of society, it investigated the structures of socialization within the bourgeois family, including the Oedipally-based psychological predispositions to the internalization of authority, and thus also to the authoritarian relationship with any and all forms of social domination. The political explosiveness of this original theoretical approach lay in the fact that the concept of ideology (in its Marxian meaning as "false consciousness") could no longer be grasped solely in the rational categories of a reason inspired by the Enlightenment. It had to be rethought as a state of consciousness (partially) determined by unconscious psychological needs, and which itself has far-reaching influences on the worldview and political behavior of individuals and groups. Here, the concept of the so-called "authoritarian personality" assumed a paradigmatic position. As a "social character" (as Erich Fromm called it; see Fromm, 1947), individually developed, but at the same time supra-individually formed by the social context of its emergence, the authoritarian personality manifests the psychological-emotional matrix of a fundamental dependence on authority, both in the marked desire to exercise authority over those weaker than oneself and in the urgent longing to submit to the authority of those stronger. The investigations of this carried out by Adorno and others were able to demonstrate the significant affinity between this particular form of "character structure" and fascism, or, more generally, anti-democratic social and political formations (Adorno et al., 1950). Generally, such an approach is less concerned with a linear causal connection between depth-psychological determinants and external behavior than with the derived results of such depth-psychological influences on politics, which are often very difficult to recognize, and their sedimentation in the realm of ideology. Precisely for this reason, the examination of the mutual effects of individual psychology and collective politics should be limited in the sense of Adorno's objection to Arthur Koestler: "There is no 'political neurosis', but psychological deformations influence political behavior, without explaining the latter's deformation entirely" (Adorno, 1971a, p. 91). Based on this, Adorno could go further and claim that the structure of fascism and the overall technique of fascist demagogues were authoritarian, while at the same time emphasizing that "as surely as the fascist agitator takes up certain inner tendencies of those to whom he appeals, he still does so as the agent of powerful economic and political interests" (Adorno, 1971b, p. 62).

2. Memory and Discourse

Are psychoanalytic categories useful in the analysis of Israeli political culture, and in particular in the analysis of the memory of the Holocaust and its impact, a force which influences it in its own specific way? To the degree that the question aims at the influence of psychological deformations on political behavior, in line with the above, the answer is yes only in the sense of the effect of this psychological deformation on the ideologized Holocaust discourse of the Israeli society. Seen in this way, the empirically demonstrable ideological manifestations in this discourse provide the necessary starting point for the analysis. The following paid advertisement by the Zionistic-revisionist Betar youth movement [Betar, inspired and led by Jabotinsky, was founded in 1923 in Riga, Latvia, and has been active since then all over the world] published in March 1999 in the Israeli daily newspaper *Ma'ariv* provides a paradigmatic example:

THERE IS NO OTHER GERMANY!
To the Prime Minister of the State of Israel, Benjamin Netanyahu
From the World Leadership of the Betar Movement.
The German Ambassador in Israel has informed the Foreign Minister
that, in their view, 'Jerusalem is not Israel's Capital'.
This is a declaration of war!
As Jews, as citizens of Israel, and in the name of the Betar Movement,
we demand that the German Ambassador be expelled from Israel and
that the Israeli Ambassador be recalled from Germany to Israel. There is
no new Germany! 1000 years before its founding, the roots of the Third
Reich were already firmly anchored in the hearts of the Germans, and
the Germany of today is a hothouse for hatred of Jews. From here to the
call for the destruction of the Jewish state is a short distance.
Mr. Prime Minister, today you are the highest representative of the
Jewish people. Keep our six million murdered brothers in mind and act
in accordance with your conscience.

Signed: The World Leadership of the Betar Movement.

The suppression of the fact that the event in question was not a specific announcement by the German Ambassador, but of the European Union's Ambassador, at the time of the announcement an office which happened to be held by the German *chargé d'affaires* in the framework of the European Union's common foreign policy, may be tolerated. One always requires a clearly profiled enemy when one is apparently so unsure of one's own profile that one must operate with all the greater aggression and whipped up all the more self-righteously. But of course we must ask what lies at the bottom of such lunacy. How can we explain this rhetoric of a "declaration of war", this historically arguing ahistorical idea of a thousand-year, exclusively anti-Semitically pervaded German prehistory of the Third Reich? The paranoid idea that a "call to destroy the Jewish state" issued by today's Germany is almost immediately imminent? Betar is a right-wing to an extreme right-wing movement, and thus should not be considered representative of all currents of Israeli political culture; nevertheless, this newspaper advertisement contains motifs that can be regarded as indicative of the general reception of the Holocaust in Israel. To examine this, it is first necessary to consider a number of structural elements of the connection between the Holocaust and Zionism.

Basically, we can say the following: Zionism, increasing in strength since 1945, not only viewed the Holocaust as the irrefutable argument justifying its own political solution to the "Jewish Question", that had finally turned into a catastrophe immediately before. It also objectified this understanding of history through a massive cooptation and instrumentalization of the memory of the victims, as well as through a political-ideological way of dealing with the survivors. This resulted in an objective (i.e. not intentional) discrepancy between the Holocaust survivors who had arrived in Israel and the state-sustaining Zionist ideology. For to the degree that state Zionism, based on the doctrine negating the Diaspora, understood the Holocaust as the ultimate manifestation of what must be negated, it could, in the end, encounter the surviving victims of the catastrophe only as examples of living warnings against what must be negated. The survivors personified everything that the so-called "national renewal" sought to overcome, and they paradigmatically embodied and represented the "Diaspora Jews", who were to be replaced by the "New Jews". This historical confrontation had several dimensions. There was the ignorant, arrogant question of many Israelis, "How could you let yourselves be led to the slaughter like lambs?" Then there was the coupling of "heroic courage" with the "*Shoah*" in the title of the official, state-established Holocaust Memorial Day. There was the Israeli silence about the Holocaust in the 1950s, at the same time as German expiation was materialized in the restitution payment treaty of 1952, and there was the ideology, proclaimed with immense Zionist pathos, of the "new beginning" now possible in the new country. This must be understood correctly: many of the Holocaust survivors needed precisely such an ideology to help them survive, and many became Zionists as the "conclusion" drawn from the horror of their own biographies. But this does not change the fact that the objectively existing discrepancy indeed had an objective effect. It led to a chasm, almost impossible to bridge, between the individual realities of personal life worlds (or psychological grappling) and the official, state sphere. The latter not only had to ignore these worlds of life for material and political reasons, but which also had to work directly against the aspects of victimization, helplessness, shock and horror, disease, and despair that dominated the psychological-mental world of the survivors. The opposition between the image of the healthy, self-defending, productive "New Jew" and the (stereotyped) idea of the sick, weak, and helpless Holocaust survivor could be overcome only ideologically, specifically through a unified ideology of "homecoming", of a "melting pot", and of a "new beginning". The Holocaust survivors' personal internalization of this state-mandated "overcoming" characterizes the (aforementioned) socially legitimated, private survival strategy on the one hand, and the collective ideological aspect of the "new consciousness" or the reformulated "new identity" demanded by the new state.

It is thus that the "Jew after Auschwitz", which Zionism very soon could use to its own purposes, was created. The "Jew after Auschwitz" became the irrefutable argument of the Jews' historical teleology as construed by the secular national movement: if anyone still needed proof of the urgent necessity of establishing, and a Jewish national homeland, world history had furnished such proof and such "final" proof. But since this representation was being formulated from an objective standpoint, the protagonists of what had been functionalized as a national argument had to be removed from their self-determined, subjective identities (whose contours, though, would be very difficult to reconstruct). The anonymization of the victims, as manifested in the industrial mass destruction, paradoxically continued *mutatis mutandis* in the Zionist ideologization of their fate, a concomitant of adducing their memory as a national historical argument.

Thus seen, the historical event of the Holocaust and its Zionist ideologization were from the beginning complementarily coupled with the double meaning of the Holocaust as turning point, first in the sense of a breakdown of civilization (*Zivilisationsbruch*), on the one hand, and then as the hub of modern Jewish national history, on the other hand. For to the degree that the Holocaust was not grasped as a catastrophe of humanity, but as the Shoah of the Jews, the structural foundations for a co-optation by particularistic, nationalistic, interpretation were in a sense already laid. The individual group identities of the murdered victims evaporated in the "Six Million" code, making the "Jews" an overarching, discrepancy-eliminating category. Moreover, those survivors who did not immigrate to Israel did not form any clearly identifiable, autonomous social group in their new countries, while those who did immigrate to Israel were, for years, not mentioned. Hence, Zionism could occupy the vacated historical space and fill it with meaning and senselessness as the culmination of civilizational development (namely the orgy of murder for its own sake, and thus the certainty of the constant potential to regress into barbarity) was given a somehow "positive" secular sense. This made the (historically quite understandable) co-optation of the monstrosity a heteronomous ideology, not only in regard to the particularistic political interest, but also in regard to the nature of what happened in Auschwitz, in its universalistic civilizational context.

This is hardly surprising, for the silence about the Holocaust (and the initial inability to even begin to understand what had happened) accompanied, from the beginning, a clear practical interest: the political solution of the "Jewish question", i.e. with making the unprevented past catastrophe an argument for preventing a future one. But because this meant a fundamental rejection of all Jewish efforts at assimilation or acculturation, the universal perspective was automatically blocked. One could be in favor of the instrumentalization of the Holocaust by the newly-founded Israel and the materialization of expiation by the so-called "other Germany" as the unspoken complementary relationship of particularistic interests, but Hannah Arendt's *Eichmann in Jerusalem* (1963), the idea of a universal banality of evil arising from modern civilization, had to remain opposed in Israel to the present day.

3. Guilt and its Repercussions

As we have said: without having recourse to individual psychological structures, but considering their collective sedimentation in political ideology, two kinds of ultimately unmastered feelings of guilt can be made out in the political culture of Zionism. First, there is a the feeling of guilt accompanying the foundation of the state at the expense of the Palestinians; and second, there is the primarily preconscious or unconscious feeling of guilt connected with the cultural or psychological negation of Diaspora Jewry in general and of the Shoah survivors in particular.

It took several decades of the most intense political and ideological work before the Palestinian experience and perception of the founding of the Zionist state as the catastrophe (*al-nakba*) of the Palestinian people could find its first modest entry in Israel's political discourse. For years, the central ideologemes of the Zionist narrative were constantly perpetuated, without even permitting the consideration that, even if these ideologemes could be interpreted as containing a kernel of truth, there was also in reality a historical catastrophe and painful exile of the other collective, an unspeakable destruction of entire life worlds and the ruin of individual human fates. Thus it could be claimed time and again that the Arabs had rejected the UN partition plan of 1947; that there was no Palestinian people; that the Palestinians were interested only in destroying the Zionist state, etc. Despite the wrongs committed in part systematically against the Palestinians in the

1948 war (as clearly revealed in recent historical research); despite the knowledge of the terrible suffering of the Palestinian exile, which has entered Israel's public sphere increasingly since the 1970s; and despite the in part extremely brutal occupation of the West Bank and Gaza Strip, the history of Palestinian suffering was (with some marginal exceptions) almost completely blocked out of common Israeli everyday experience and even more so from the sphere of official public discourse. Of course, one may be tempted to explain and argue this away with the two collectives' objectively existing and politically formally proclaimed status as enemies: in a state of continually perpetuated violence, also increasingly committed by Palestinians, there is little mental, much less political room to recognize the suffering of the other, especially of the "enemy". Consider the ease with which Palestinian partisans could be mutated to "two-legged animals" in Israel's everyday political rhetoric. How could it come about that the then-Prime Minister Menachem Begin could imagine that, by surrounding Yasser Arafat in the Beirut bunker, he had trapped Adolf Hitler in the Berlin bunker; how the Palestinians, turned into victims by Israel, could become the "successors to the Nazis" precisely in this country? It appears as if here something went far beyond the usual image of the enemy and normal rhetoric of conflict. The total demonization of those toward whom one had become fundamentally guilty, the deflection of one's own intolerable guilt, and its projection onto the source of the feeling of guilt, that is the victims.

Here an already existing and, so to speak, historically "legitimized" pattern is available. To the degree that the Palestinians figure as concrete evil and, in metaphorical comparison or in the sense of a "real" historical succession of evil in itself, to the degree that this evil is tied to the Nazis or the Holocaust, "Palestinians" and "Nazis" are accorded a virtually interchangeable status and the categories of perpetrator and victim are so thoroughly mixed that, even in one's own historical guilt, one may see oneself as victim. This explains why the status of Jerusalem, a topic of political dispute in the context of the Middle East conflict, can degenerate into a reason for a "declaration of war", not only in connection with the concrete enemies on site, the Palestinians, but also in the imagined reaction of "the Germans" or "Germany". For if the real declaration of war against the Palestinians is applicable to "Germany", then the paradigmatic characteristic of "the Germans" as the originators of the Shoah can be projected onto the Palestinians – after all, with both groups there is only a "short distance" to the "call for the destruction of the Jewish state". Thus, the assumption that there "is no other Germany" (and that there must not be one) accompanies the fixed idea that there can be no other Palestinians than those comparable to Nazis. The end of their demonization would necessary mean dealing with the guilt accrued toward them (just as the end of the demonization of Germany would sooner or later mean relinquishing the instrumentalizing approach to Germany's historical guilt).

Of course, we know that not all Israelis think in the terms of Betar's newspaper announcement and that Israeli political culture is in no way exclusively characterized by that extremist relation to the Palestinians. Yet, it remains to ask whether the common moderate position, a peaceful attitude toward the Palestinians that nonetheless insists on strict separation, that liberal, enlightened tendency to peacefully exclude those whom (for their own good) one does not want in front of one's eyes, whether this can't ultimately also be traced to an unconscious feeling of guilt. We are familiar with the conscious feeling of guilt motivating many of those Israelis oriented toward a real, historical reconciliation with the Palestinians. It remains to examine more closely the aspect of guilt among those who, out of obvious liberality, insist on purifying isolation, thus wishing (political) freedom for the victims, in order to be rid of them.

The other guilt feeling of Israeli Zionists relates to Zionism's ideological and practical cultural negation of Diaspora Jewry and the psychological non-perception of the Holocaust survivors that accompanied this ideological negation at a particular historical moment. Here we have the phenomenon of a constant "return of the repressed": in its beginnings, the historical awakening of political Zionism understood itself also as the uprising of the younger generation against the older. The rigor of the general "patricidal" liquidation of everything the Diaspora tradition stood for in the real life worlds and in the cultural self-understanding of "exiled" Jews meant that the objective continuation of the Diaspora became a constant threat to the self-image of the Zionist so-called "new Jews", and thus the object of increased ideological and psychological aggression. In no other country was Yiddish, the language of a*shkenazi* exile, so persecuted as in the pre-statehood Jewish community in Palestine and in Israel in the early years after its foundation. The image of the "unhealthy" body of the Diaspora Jews was contrasted with the athletic body of the new "muscle Jews" and treated as a model of what must be overcome in revolution. It is no coincidence that, in the usage of the official state ideology as well as in everyday Israeli communication, the Hebrew term *galut* (exile) and the attribute *galuti* (exile-like) became outright terms of abuse.

The problem was that not only that the Diaspora did continue outside of Israel, but also that, within Israeli society, despite a pathetically proclaimed melting-pot ideology and diverse real melting-pot projects, the Diaspora could not be "put down" or overcome, whether in the appearance of the Orthodox (not to mention the ultra-Orthodox) Jews or in the self-understanding and disposition of various ethnic communities, which consciously or unconsciously refused or at least objectively eluded the *ashkenazi*-secular idealized image of the *sabra*. Zionism required Israel's massive import of Diaspora Jews to start up its political project, and so, in its putative political solution of the Diaspora problem, it affirmed perforce the continuing presence of what it wanted to do away with and completely integrated what was to be negated.

In this connection, the religious component has played, and still plays, a central role. On the one hand, Zionism was positively molded by the pathos of self-determination of European national liberation movements. On the other hand, it was also inspired by a major negative factor. Since Zionism understood itself as the self-emancipatory national movement of the "Jewish people" and (in essential contrast to messianic-utopian religious faith) secular nationalism had always articulated itself in concrete territorial categories, Zionism had to work to gather the Diaspora communities scattered throughout the world in the predetermined territory of the incipient state of Israel. That this would be Palestine as the "Land of our Ancestors" was a necessary conclusion for Zionism's mostly secular founding fathers. A role in this was played not only by the traditional "longing", but also and especially by the necessity to find a common denominator for the extremely heterogeneous exile communities that were mostly alien to or alienated from each other; and (seen from the standpoint of an explicitly positive determination) this common denominator consisted of nothing other than the common religious affiliation. Seen thus, from the beginning, religion became an invisible but integral layer of secular Zionist ideology.

But this integral part was suppressed at the same time: to this day, nothing enrages Israel's secular Zionists more than the ultra-Orthodox Jew. This has much to do with the secular Jew's self-understanding as a citizen. He is indignant that the ultra-Orthodox Jew does not serve in the army, that (despite his anti-Zionism) he lives "parasitically" at the expense of the state, that he wants to institutionally interfere with others' personal lives and eating habits, etc. But it seems as if something else is involved. First, the Orthodox Jew is the embodiment of what was believed to have been overcome, equivalent to "evidence" of the possible failure of the collective historical "patricide"; second, and unadmittedly, he is also the incarnation of a supposed authentic origin: the personification of a "true" Judaism. The bad conscience that often comes over secular Israelis when one asks them about their "Jewish identity" has partly to do with the fact that the positive identity of the "New Jews" in Israel, once ideologically proclaimed, has proven amorphous since the traditional hegemony of Ashkenazi-secular culture has been increasingly challenged. As non-Zionist and even anti-Zionistic ideas have entered the Israeli discourse, the religious sub-culture has gained a completely new status in the debate about the "identity" of Israelis. The famous metaphor of the "full wagon" of the religious and the "empty wagon" of the secular has meanwhile mutated to a matrix of a comprehensive cultural struggle in which secular Jews in Israel, greatly enraged, want to defend "their" country, but are driven by a latent feeling of inferior identity and have nothing special to hold up against the storm of "true" Judaism. The premodern mixes here with the modern, but above all, the explosive debate is dominated by the "uncanny" feeling of having too hurriedly written "something" off, the feeling of the "return of the repressed".

Something similar, though on another level, can be said regarding Holocaust survivors in Israel. As we have seen, they provide Zionism with crucial and final evidence for the justification for its central ideological postulate: the negation of the Diaspora. In this instrumentalizing sense, the authors of the Betar announcement can to this day afford to call on the Israeli Prime Minister to "keep our six million murdered brothers in mind" when they want to expel the German Ambassador from the country for a parochial, current political interest. In actual fact, except for such heteronomous interests, "our six million murdered brothers" were of little use to the state-supporting ideology of Zionism. But since the postulate of negating the Diaspora has always contained a layer of guilt, but at the same time the Zionist argument was maintained for its own *raison d'être*, in the first decade after Israel's founding, the Holocaust and the survivors who immigrated to Israel had to be kept out of public discourse. But when the Israeli Holocaust discourse was stripped off its hegemonic Zionist dimension, various narratives of specific life worlds and communities increasingly differentiated, and other, non-Zionist patterns of reception entered the debates on the Jewish past. This belated confrontation with what had always been latently present proved to be the "return of the repressed": something that had nothing to do with the conventional Zionist teleologization of the Holocaust for the state of Israel, but all the more to do with the real suffering of the older Diaspora generation. The "new discovery" could also be rapidly Zionized, but at the same time it also permitted the consciousness of repressed guilt about its ideological dealings with the Diaspora and especially with the latter's prototypical protagonists.

Of course, it remains unclear how much these layers of psycho-collective knowledge can contribute to breaking up encrusted ideological dogmas and convictions in the Israeli political culture. As psychoanalysis in particular can teach us, they can be rationalized away and ideologically instrumentalized all too easily. Constant critique of ideology is necessary; but no less necessary is the willingness to deal with what has for so long been repressed. This is but one contribution of psychoanalysis to the understanding of the real political world.

References

Adorno, T.W. (1971a). Bemerkungen über politik und Neurose. In T.W. Adorno, *Kritik: Kleine Schriften zur Gesellschaft*. Suhrkamp: Frankfurt-am-Main.

Adorno, T.W. (1971b) Der Freudsche Theorie und Der Struktur der Faschistichen Propaganda. In T.W. Adorno, *Kritik: Kleine Schriften zur Gesellschaft*. Suhrkamp: Frankfurt-am-Main.

Adorno, T.W., Frenkel-Brunswik, E., Levinson, D.J., & Sanford, R.N. (1950). *The Authoritarian Personality*. New York: Harper & Row.

Arendt, H. (1963). *Eichmann in Jerusalem: A Report on the Banality of Evil*. London: Faber and Faber.

Fromm, E. (1947). *Man For Himself*. New York: Rinehart & Co.

Chapter 4

On Marginal People: The Case of the Palestinians in Israel

Ramzi Suleiman
University of Haifa

Coping with an imposed and painful marginality is the fate assigned to Palestinians living inside Israel's border, most of whom (but not all), are nominal Israeli citizens. The question addressed here is that of the meaning of this kind of citizenship, and the place of Palestinians within Israeli citizenry. What psychological consequences could this imposed marginality have, except anger and frustration? Identity is tied to collective memory, and this connection, having been examined in earlier chapters, is now looked at from a fresh perspective. The analysis presented here is both historical and psychological, and is far from detached. Ramzi Suleiman is both a sophisticated social psychologist, at home with prevailing theories and experiments, and a Palestinian who has experienced this imposed marginality all his life. This chapter offers a unique perspective both theoretically and personally.

1. Introduction

Freud's best-known work on social psychology (Freud, 1921) emphasizes the illusory nature (and real consequences) of group commitments and group behaviors, originating in a special kind of object-love, often having negative consequences. It also makes a simple distinction between in-groups and out-groups, and points out correctly that our love for comrades and brethren is limited by the boundaries of group belonging. Majority-minority relations are not among the concerns addressed. It is clearly there that whatever illusions we may share inside our group, and whatever strong emotional bonds we may have, our existence is always marked by the harsh realities of power differences. The situation in Israel is marked by a lopsided division between a dominant Jewish-Israeli majority, and a Palestinian minority. The complexity of identities, as they are tied to collective memory, is bound to affect any interaction between two national groups. Here the painful history of the past one hundred years has dictated a unique set of constraints.

The relations between these two groups have been studied, of course, and the question of minority group identity has been under the lens of academic research for at least forty years, but it seems fair to claim that all social-psychological research on the collective identity of Palestinians in Israel to date has adopted a static perspective. Reviewing this body of academic research reveals that its focus has been mainly on investigating various aspects related to the relative centrality of the national, civic, and religious sub-identities of this minority. As examples, Peres (1967) measured the degree of centrality, solidarity, and valence of different self-identifications. Hoffman and Rouhana (1976) and Lazarowitz et al. (1978) measured the relative importance, attractiveness and salience of self-identifications. Other studies in the fields of social psychology and sociology indicate a growing interest in comparing the perceived importance of the civic (Israeli) and ethnic (Palestinian) identities, and the construction of typologies based on their perceived importance (e.g., Tessler, 1977; Smooha, 1988, 1992; Rouhana, 1993, 1997; Suleiman & Beit-Hallahmi, 1996, 1997; Suleiman, in press). Notwithstanding the difference in focus and approach, all studies, including the ones cited above, consider the ethnic and civic sub-identities of the Palestinian minority as relatively stable constructs. This is not to say that the dynamic nature of these sub-identities was left unnoticed by all researchers. To assert that this is not the case, we mention in passing the extensive research by Smooha (cf. Smooha, 1988, 1992), which provided important data regarding the dynamic change in the preference of collective identification and suggested socio-political explanations to account for these changes. What is argued here is that no systematic attempt was made to provide a conceptual model for understanding the fundamentals of such dynamics.

This chapter constitutes an attempt to respond to this challenge by proposing a dynamic model for understanding the construction of ethnic identity among members of the Palestinian minority in Israel. This model assumes that the generating forces behind the dynamic construction of this identity are, to a large extent, determined by the minority's civic status and by its conflictual relationship with the dominant Jewish majority. In addition to describing the basic elements of the model, we will demonstrate its usefulness in understanding some important issues concerning the cohesiveness of this minority and its relatedness to certain elements of Arab and Palestinian culture.

To set the stage for the proposed model, we start by making two claims: First, we argue that the Palestinian minority constitutes a marginalized group in the Jewish State. Second, we argue that the State policy, and the practices of the State and Jewish public towards the Palestinian minority, are strategies and practices of power and domination.

2. Civic Marginality

A proper account of the state of affairs that lead to marginalizing the Palestinians in Israeli society requires that one undertake a political analysis of Zionist ideology, together with a historical analysis of the antecedents and precedents of *al-nakba*, the Palestinian catastrophe of 1948. Because such analyses are beyond the scope of this chapter and is being covered in others (Diner, 2002, Zuckerman, 2002, Brunner, 2002), we will confine ourselves to briefly mentioning that the marginilization of Palestinians in the Jewish State was an inevitable consequence of the Zionist ideology and praxis. The expulsion of hundreds of thousands of Palestinians in 1948, the destruction of hundreds of their villages and other related atrocities, were more than sufficient to convey to all Palestinians remaining in their homeland that the newly formed Jewish state excludes them from the realm of citizenship or partnership in the state and even considers them as potential enemies. Subsequent practices by the State, mainly the military rule imposed until 1966 on this torn minority, the ongoing expropriation of Palestinian land and the severe official and non-official discriminatory measures, have all enhanced the message of animosity and exclusion.

Of special importance in this context are governmental and nongovernmental discriminatory policies and actions which resulted in keeping in place the physical distribution of Palestinians in underdeveloped villages and in some ghetto-type neighborhoods in some cities like Haifa, Jaffa and Lydda. In addition to the obvious socio-economic disadvantages of excluding the Palestinian minority from urban spaces, this exclusion has deprived this minority of social and cultural experiences that are characteristic of modern civil communities.

Paralleling the marginalization and even total exclusion from the state economy, geography, and government, and in the service of such marginilization and exclusion, Palestinians in Israel were, and still are, kept out of Israel's civil and cultural spheres. Borrowing from David Grossman, the renowned Israeli novelist, they continue to live as the "present absentees" of the State of Israel, both as individually and collectively (Grossman, 1993).

The fact that the Jewish State has always maintained an exclusionary stand with regard to the Palestinian minority in its midst is well documented. In fact, most of the relevant literature is in perfect agreement in asserting the ethnic (Jewish) nature of Israel (cf., Smooha, 1990; Sa'di, 1992; Beit-Hallahmi, 1993; Yiftachel, 1993; Bourhis et al., 1997; Rouhana, 1997), and the exclusionary nature of its ideology and policy vis-à-vis the Palestinian minority (c.f., Bishara, 1995; Rouhana, 1997; Rouhana & Ghanem, 1998). Because Israel defines itself as the State of the Jewish people, it has always had a clear policy opposing assimilation, or integration, of the Palestinian minority. Moreover, Israeli policy has always been firm in rejecting any autonomous status for the minority, thus blocking the option for a dissociated mode of acculturation (Sa'di, 1992).

To summarize, we argue that the marginality of Palestinians as citizens is embedded in the definition of Israel as the State of the Jewish people. This implies not only that members of the minority are denied their right to equal and full citizenship, but also that this right is automatically ascribed to non-citizen Jews. The exclusion of the Palestinian minority from the boundaries of equal citizenship is doubled by the fact that Jewishness, as defined by the State of Israel, is tied to Judaism, and creates a religious, as well as an ethnic, membership category.

It is worth stressing that the marginality of members of the Palestinian minority as citizens is manifest in almost all aspects of the civic and public spheres and not only in the discriminatory allocation of public goods. This entails the marginalization of the minority, as a collective, from the state culture, myths, and symbols. In its least pernicious manifestation, cultural marginalization takes the form of alienation and absence. More often, it takes the form of devaluation, negative stereotyping, and dehumanization. Although negative perceptions and negative stereotyping of minorities are, regretfully, universal phenomena, it should be noted that the Palestinian minority case is more problematic than that of immigrant minorities like Indians in England or Algerians in France. This is because many values of the Zionist ideology, and State collective history, derive their positive valence from excluding the Arab or Palestinian Other. '*Geulat Haadama*' (redemption of the land) has been a core ideal of the Zionist ideology before and after 1948. This ideal prescribes that the land should be "redeemed" from the hands of the indigenous Palestinians who have been considered as aliens occupying the land, which historically and rightfully belongs to the Jewish people. Another important ideal was '*Kibush Haavoda*' (the conquest of work) according to which early Jewish settlers sought to exclude Palestinians from the job market. 'Redemption of the land' and 'conquest of work' are two major examples of positive Zionist ideals having ethnic exclusion at their core.

3. Power and Domination

Israeli social scientists have traditionally emphasized the traditionalism - modernity dimension in their research on the Palestinian minority. According to this perspective, research on this minority has entertained questions related to the ability and readiness of the minority to assimilate into (the more progressive) Western culture. Implicit in this tradition is the assumption that the Jewish majority serves the analysis only as a modernizing agent. Critical social scientists and historians, starting in the 1970s, have rightfully criticized this approach, while shifting the focus of their research to the analysis of geo-political and historic-political dimensions of the conflict between the Jewish majority (and State) and the endogenous Palestinian minority (Beit-Hallahmi, 1993; Sa'di, 1992; Rouhana & Ghanem, 1998; Yiftachel, 1993). Shifting the focus from the Palestinian minority (as the research object) to the study of intergroup relations implies a shift in focus from the traditionalism-modernity dimension to the study of majority-minority power relations within the specific geo-political and historic-political context of the conflict.

The analysis of the Jewish State policy vis a vis the Palestinian minority, as a relationship determined by power and control is most explicit in Ian Lustick's pioneering work. In his book *Arabs in the Jewish State: Israeli's Control of a National Minority* (Lustick, 1980), he analysed the foundations of the system of control imposed by the State to subdue the Palestinian minority, as well as its various transformations over time.

It seems fair to conclude that the main characteristic of the State and Jewish majority practices toward the Palestinian minority is that of power and domination. With respect to the dynamics of identity construction, it is argued here that the asymmetric power relation between the State (and Jewish majority) and the Palestinian minority is both unconsciously and consciously internalized by members of this minority, and constitute a major generating force for the dynamic construction of their collective identity. In the following sections of this chapter we shall go further to claim that the juxtaposition of this generating force with the minority's civic marginality has resulted in the marginalization of the Palestinian minority with respect to ethnic (Palestinian) identity. If we want to imagine the psychic consequences of such painful marginality, Freud's observations are directly relevant. Because identification is the original form of emotional ties with an object (Freud, 1921), it is clear that ethnic marginality and alienation from one's ethnic culture may have serious negative effects on one's self-esteem and his/her general psychological well being.

4. Controlled Selection and Ethnic Marginality

The main proposition of this chapter is that the construction of Palestinian ethnic identity in Israel is a dynamic process, and that the mechanics of this process are controlled by the power relations which exist between this minority and the dominant majority. More specifically, it is argued that at any historic instant, the selection, by members of the minority, of elements of their ethnic identity, as embedded in their collective memory, is predominantly subdued by the discourse of power which characterizes their relation with the Jewish state (and its Jewish majority) at that instant.

The dynamic nature of Palestinian ethnic identity in Israel could be inferred from several studies on minority self-categorization. The most striking data in this respect was obtained in a pioneering study conducted by Peres & Yuval-Davis (1969) on the eve of the 1967 war and immediately following it. In the summer of 1966 the researchers requested their respondents to rank order a number of relevant identification labels according to their appropriateness for describing their social identity. The result showed that labels, ranked from most preferred to least prefer, were (1) Israeli, (2) Israeli-Arab (3) Arab (4) Palestinian (5) Muslim/Christian. In the summer of 1967 a follow-up study was conducted using the same labels. This time the order was (1) Arab (2) Muslim/Christian (3) Israeli-Arab (4) Palestinian (5) Israeli. The civic-Israeli identity, which a year earlier had headed the list, was relegated to its bottom. While one may argue that the extreme changes reported by the above mentioned research were affected by the dramatic Arab defeat in the 1967 War, subsequent research lends support to the argument that the change in Palestinian minority self-identification is a continuous process. Most convincing in this respect is the extensive longitudinal research conducted by Smooha on representative samples of the Palestinian minority in Israel in 1976, 1980, 1985, 1988, and 1990 (Smooha, 1992).

As outlined above, the selection, by members of the minority, of elements of their ethnic identity, as embedded in their collective memory, is predominantly subdued by the discourse of power characterizing their relation with the Jewish State and Jewish majority. The extreme asymmetry in power relations between the two parties, the historical victimization, and the ongoing oppression and exclusion of the Palestinian minority have driven the dynamics of ethnic identity construction to a point of crisis. This crisis is characterized by ongoing erosion of the minority's identity to the point of ethnic marginality. The exclusion of Palestinians from the civic sphere, juxtaposed with the process of controlled selection (governing how they relate to their ethnic culture), has driven them, as a collective, to the threshold of ethnic marginality. The vacuum created by their alienation from their ethnic culture is partially occupied by their assimilation of a marginal, and distorted, version of an Israeli ghetto-type culture.

It is important to stress here that the State policy has been always instrumental in intentionally reinforcing ethnic and cultural marginality. This was accomplished through the activities of various institutions, especially the educational system and official media, which continues to play a key role in reinforcing the production and reproduction of an "Israeli Arab" marginal culture (Bishara, 1995).

The principle of controlled selection proposed here could be useful in making some interesting observations regarding the behavior of members of the minority in various contexts. For example, it can provide a partial explanation as to why for almost fifty years after the establishment of the State of Israel and the expulsion of the majority of the Palestinians from their homeland, little, if any, has been done to commemorate the Palestinian collective trauma (*al-nakba*). It may also explain why in recent years Palestinian high school students show strong reluctance to enroll in advanced courses on Arabic language and culture, a trend which have brought some schools to assign these courses as obligatory courses in their curriculum. A related issue concerns the manner in which educators, mainly in formal educational institutions, develop and promote ideological curricula and cultural activities. In an attempt to avoid cultural contents that are in conflict with the State and majority ideology, they often limit the organization of cultural activities to some "neutral" activities, such as traditional folkloristic events, exhibitions of peasant and Bedouin ornaments and the like.

5. Heterogeneity

It is reasonable to assume that the process of controlled selection and civic marginality may have differential impact on different Palestinian groups and individuals. Various factors may account for such differential impact such as differences in the individuals' socio-economic status and aspirations and in their capacity to draw on the group's collective memory. If the above assumption is valid, then one might expect a resulting heterogeneity in the relatedness of members of the minority to the civic and ethnic components of their collective identity. Research findings support this assumption by showing that members of the minority can be clustered into a number of categories defined by the manner by which they combine their ethnic and civic identities (cf. Tessler, 1977; Suleiman & Beit Hallahmi, 1996; Suleiman, in press). For example, Tessler (1977) found that 29% of his sample categorized themselves as Israelis, 41% categorized themselves as Palestinians and 23% categorized themselves as both Israeli and Palestinian. Suleiman & Beit-Hallahmi (1996) conducted a re-analysis of data reported in Suleiman & Beit-Hallahmi (1997). Using an Individual Differences Multi-Dimensional Scaling method (Takane et al., 1977; Young et al., 1978) they found that their participants could be clustered into three main sub-groups based on the different modes which they used for combining the national and the civic components of their collective identity. One sub-group (comprised of 18% of the participants) could be seen as a 'dissociative' group since its 'identity space' was one-dimensional, and this single dimension could be defined as 'national'. A second group (comprised of 11% of the participants) can be defined as an 'assimilative' group, since its 'identity space' included only a 'civic' dimension. Still, the majority of the participants (71% of the participants) could be defined as an 'acculturative' group since its 'identity space' was two-dimensional, defined by both a national and civic dimensions.

The discrepancy between the results obtained in different studies (like those cited above) may be partially attributed to methodological differences, but it may also reflect the dynamic process involved in the construction of ethnic identity. To demonstrate that this might be the case, consider the results reported by Smooha (1988) according to which in a representative survey conducted in 1975, 12% of the Palestinian minority used a 'combined identity' label (Palestinian-Israeli, or Palestinian in Israel) to describe their collective identity. In a follow-up survey conducted in 1987, the percentage of those using a 'combined identity' in 1987 increased up to 40%.

It may be of interest to note that the heterogeneity resulting from the various modalities in solving the tension between a minority's ethnic identity and civic status may be inferred from various social psychological theories. One such theory is Social Identity Theory (SIT) proposed by Henri Tajfel and his colleagues (cf., Tajfel, 1978, 1981, 1982). According to SIT, members of the minority will use various strategies in order to avoid feelings of low self-esteem. They may leave or dissociate themselves from their low-status group and try to join the high-status majority group (an assimilative orientation). Another strategy is 'social creativity', according to which individuals may seek 'positive distinctiveness' for their group by redefining the dimensions of comparison between their group and the majority out-group. Altering the evaluation criteria, or the referent out-group are common 'creative' strategies. Finally, low-status group members may choose to directly compete with the majority out-group through mobilizing the group, as a collective, and challenging the status quo. Collective mobility, by challenging the status quo, becomes an option if individual mobility is difficult, and if members of the minority perceive the status difference as unstable.

Another theory that is highly relevant to the discussed issue is the

Acculturation Typological Perspective (Berry et al., 1986; Berry et al., 1989). It argues that the tension experienced by members of the minority between identification with their ethnic group, and identification with the superordinate group (dominated by the majority) does not necessitate a categorical preference between the two identities. The theory posits that members of the minority may use one of four acculturation strategies: Assimilation, integration, dissociation, and marginalization. Members of the minority who adopt an assimilation strategy will eventually categorize themselves in a manner that emphasizes their identification and assimilation into mainstream culture (dominated by the majority). An integration strategy will result in self-categorization that emphasizes the belonging both to the ethnic minority and to mainstream society. A dissociation strategy will result in self-categorization that emphasizes only membership in the ethnic minority, and a marginality strategy will result in excluding both minority and majority identities from one's self-categorization. In this case the self may be categorized primarily in terms of other relevant social categories.

Social Identity theory and the Acculturation Typological Perspective do not relate explicitly to the possible heterogeneity of minorities with respect to the ways minority group members relate to their civic and ethnic identities. Nonetheless, based on SIT such heterogeneity can be inferred if one assumes that not all members use the same strategy to avoid low self-esteem. Similarly, it can be inferred from the Acculturation Typological Perspective if one assumes that different members of the minority may use different acculturation strategies. The theoretical analysis advanced in this chapter reaches a similar conclusion with regard to the minority's heterogeneity. Nonetheless, it bears a number of fundamental differences from the above two approaches, especially from the SIT approach.

First, our analysis stresses the dynamic nature of the process of construction of collective identities, as opposed to the static nature of the models mentioned above, including Freud's (1921). Secondly, unlike SIT, it does not presume that the main objective of minorities is to assimilate into a majority-dominated society, nor does it assume that such tendency is driven by the psychological need for achieving a positive self-esteem. Finally, the proposed model views the process of minority self-identification as more reactive and less pro-active than suggested by SIT. The reader of the SIT literature is left with the impression that the minority is proactive in making its category choice.

In contrast, the analysis brought here emphasizes that although members of the minority strive to maintain their ethnic identity and culture, they are forced to select from their collective memory only those elements which they perceive as less conflictual with the hegemonic dominant group. Their marginal ethnic identification and the synthesis they achieve between their ethnic and civic identities should be viewed as results of forced choices within the framework of minority-majority relations that are governed by power and domination.

To conclude this point, the proposed model argues that the socio-economic heterogeneity of this minority, the differential capacity of its members to gain access to their collective memory, subjective interpretations of political realities, and political outlooks, all imply a parallel heterogeneity in the shaping of minority ethnic identity. As demonstrated above, the predicted heterogeneity in ethnic identification is validated by results from several studies indicating that the Palestinian minority is significantly heterogeneous with respect to ethnic identification. Despite some positive aspects, such heterogeneity also has some clear disadvantages. This is because a highly heterogeneous minority may lack the critical mass of group members who share congruent interests and goals. Not only does the lack of group solidarity and cohesiveness hamper the instrumentality of the group in achieving its common goals. It also reflects negatively on the psychological well being of the group's members.

6. Conclusion

In this chapter we argued that since the establishment of the State of Israel, the Palestinian minority in Israel has been experiencing a continuing process of civic and ethnic marginalization. While civic marginality is implied by the mere definition of the State not only as a Jewish state, but as the state of the Jewish People, ethnic marginality is the product of a controlled process of self-defeating selection from the minority's collective memory. This process has been mainly driven by the power relationships existing between this minority and the hegemonic Jewish majority.

We conclude by suggesting that the analysis of the construction of a given collective identity should be undertaken within its specific past history, partly embedded in its collective memory, and its aspired and hoped-for future. The latter's chances of becoming a reality depends on the existence of a critical mass of group members with congruent interests and goals. This can be achieved only if enough group members see their interests and goals as satisfactorily congruent with collective ones. The significant heterogeneity in the way members of the Palestinian minority relate to their collective memory implies a corresponding fragmentation with regard to how they relate to their aspired collective future. The ongoing oppression and exclusion of this minority by the majority in the Jewish State has resulted in a conflictual relationship between the collective past of the minority, its aspired-for future, and its here-and now reality as a marginalized minority. We argue that the complications of this conflict have created the manifestations of a collectivity in a real and permanent crisis. Marginality, and the constant awareness of being marginal, used to be considered the fate of Jews in the Diaspora (Lewin, 1948). What Lewin so insightfully pointed out was that marginality is not caused by belonging to numerous groups, but by an uncertain belonging. In its successful attempt to transcend the Diaspora and create sovereignty for Jews, Zionism has created a new kind of marginality for the indigenous Palestinian minority.

References

Beit-Hallahmi, B. (1993). *Original Sins: Reflections on the History of Zionism and Israel.* Brooklyn, N. Y.: Interlink.

Berry, J., Trimble, J., & Olmedo, E. (1986). Assessment of acculturation. In W. Lonner & J. Berry (Eds.). *Field Methods in Cross-Cultural Research.* Newbury Park, CA: Sage.

Berry, J., Kim, U., Power, S., Young, M., & Bujaki, M. (1989). Acculturation attitudes in plural societies. *Applied Psychology, 38,* 185-206.

Bishara, A. (1995). The Israeli Arab: Readings in the truncated political discourse. Journal *of Palestinian Studies, 24,* 26-54.[Arabic].

Bourhis, R. Y., Moïse, L. C., Perreault, S., & Senécal, S. (1997). Towards an interactive acculturation model: A social psychological approach. *International Journal of Psychology, 32,* 369-386

Brunner, J. (2002). Contentious Origins: Psychoanalytic Comments on the Debate over Israel's Creation. In this volume.

Diner, D. (2002). On the temporal emblematics of belonging: Position and validity in Israeli political discourse. In this volume.

Frued, S. (1921). Group Psychology and the Analysis of the Ego. In *The Standard Edition of the Complete Psychological Writings of Sigmund Freud.* Vol. 18, 65-144. London: The Hogarth Press.

Grossman, D. (1993). *Sleeping on a Wire: Conversations with Palestinians in Israel.* New York: Farrar, Straus and Giroux.

Lewin, K. (1948). *Resolving Social Conflicts.* New York: Harper & Row.

Lustick, I. (1980). *Arabs in the Jewish State: Israel's Control of a National Minority.* Austin: University of Texas Press.

Peres, Y., & Yuval-Davis, N. (1969). Some observations of the national identity of the Israeli Arabs. *Human Relations, 22 ,*219-223.

Rouhana, N. (1993). Accentuated identities in protracted conflicts: The collective identity of the Palestinian citizens in Israel. *Asian and African Studies, 27,* 97-127.

Rouhana, N. (1997). *Palestinian Citizens in an Ethnic Jewish State: Identities and Conflict.* Yale University Press: New Haven.

Rouhana, N. & Ghanem, A. (1998). The crisis of minorities in an ethnic state: The case of Palestinian citizens in Israel. *International Journal of Middle East Studies, 30,* 321-346.

Sa'di, A. (1992). Between state ideology and minority national identity: Palestinians in Israel and in Israeli social science research. *Review of Middle East Studies, 5,* 110-130.

Smooha, S. (1988). *Arabs and Jews in Israel.* Vol. 1, Boulder: Westview Press.

Smooha, S. (1990). Minority status in an ethnic democracy: The status of the Arabs in Israel. *Ethnic and Racial Studies, 13,* 389-413.

Smooha, S. (1992). *Arabs and Jews in Israel.* Vol. 2, Boulder: Westview Press.

Suleiman, R. (in press). Perception of the minority's collective identity and voting behavior: The case of the Palestinians in Israel. *The Journal of Social Psychology*.

Suleiman, R., & Beit-Hallahmi, B. (1996). Individual Differences in Perception of the Collective Identity of Arabs in Israel. Unpublished manuscript.

Suleiman, R. & Beit-Hallahmi, B. (1997). National and civil identities for Palestinians in Israel. *The Journal of Social Psychology, 132* , 219-228

Tajfel, H. (1978). *Differentiation Between Social Groups: Studies in the Social Psychology of Intergroup Relations*. London: Academic Press.

Tajfel, H. (1981). *Human Groups and Social Categories: Studies in Social Psychology*. Cambridge: Cambridge University Press.

Tajfel, H. (1982). Social psychology of inter-group relations. *Annual Review of Psychology, 33*, 1-39.

Takane, Y., Young, F. W., & De Leeuw, J. (1977). Nonmetric individual differences multidimensional scaling: An Alternating least square method with optimal scaling features. *Psychometrika, 42*, 7-67.

Tessler, M. (1977). Israel's Arabs and the Palestinian Problem. *Middle East Journal, 31*, 313-329.

Yiftachel, O. (1993). Debate: The concept of 'ethnic democracy' and its application to the case of Israel. *Ethnic and Racial Studies, 15*, 125-136.

Young, F. W., Takane, Y., & Lewyckyj, R. (1978). ALSCAL: A nonmetric multidimensional scaling program with several individual differences options. *Behavioral Research Methods and Instrumentation, 10*, 451-453.

Zuckerman, M. (2002). Towards a critical analysis of Israeli political culture. In this volume.

Chapter 5

Unconscious Defense Mechanisms and Social Mechanisms Used in National and Political Conflicts

Rafael Moses
The Hebrew University

We must confess that for all of us Rafael Moses had served as the main inspiration for the idea of the Vienna conference. He has been among the early pioneers of the application of psychoanalytic ideas to long-term political conflicts, and has been widely recognized as a world leader in this field, even though most psychoanalysts have kept their distance from such efforts. Moses took a clear stand in opposition to separating the public and the private spheres in psychoanalytic interpretation. Some of his psychoanalytic colleagues had found this nothing less than stunning, but he kept on working. Since the 1960s he has been actively involved in thinking and writing about the Israeli-Palestinian conflict and about the unconscious aspects of all social conflicts. Eventually, his work became internationally recognized and appreciated.

As this chapter demonstrates, Rafael Moses combined an immense curiosity about political leadership and political processes with a sensitivity to the plight of common citizens, who are often the victims of leaders and processes beyond their control. This curiosity is expressed through the references to many concrete personalities and events in modern history and politics.

In addition to being a curious psychoanalyst of broad interests, Rafael Moses was a solid and erudite scholar. The theoretical armamentarium that made psychoanalytic interpretation possible for Moses ranged from Freud's own ideas in what we regard today as the classical era to later (once dissident) theoretical developments proposed by Melanie Klein, W.R. Bion, and Heinz Kohut. These more recent ideas offer several ways of approaching the basic issue, which is the theoretical leap from the individual psyche to group ideologies. While focusing on unconscious mechanisms, Moses did not deny the importance of conscious and intentional behavior. He gave it its due share of importance in analyzing history. This was the other side of his departure from keeping psychoanalytic interpretations confined to the consulting room and to individual personalities.

As Moses himself pointed out, the readiness to analyze group ideologies and collective prejudices, and to demonstrate their unconscious sources, and the mechanisms at work behind them, leads to harsh criticism when applied to the analyst's own collectivity. It may naturally lead to assent and applause only when directed at the Other. Moses had been consistent over the years in applying psychoanalytic insights to his own clan, so to speak, thus incurring the wrath of those in power.

1. Introduction

One of my preoccupations over the past 20 years or more has been to understand as much as I could about psychological motivations, processes and mechanisms in the Arab-Israeli and Palestinian-Israeli conflict. Since I lived this conflict during these years, and before, one of my own motivations understandably was, trying to deal actively with a very painful problem that created a great deal of helplessness for me and all of us here. Also, because I lived this conflict on the Israeli side, I was able, so I believe, to understand better the psychological processes that were taking place on the Israeli side. There is, however, good reason to believe that many, if not all, of these mechanisms, are at the same time similarly taking place on the other side of the conflict, and on every side of every political conflict.

Unconscious defense mechanisms are known to us from studying the individual. There is, therefore, a methodological problem in my assumption that these same mechanisms can be found in groups and in parties to a conflict. I am not the only one making these assumptions (cf. Benedict, 1946; Volkan, Julius, & Montville, 1990-1991; Volkan, 1988; Ettin, Fidler, & Cohen; 1995; Rangell & Moses-Hrushovski, 1996; GAP Report No 103, 1978, and others) and yet I feel that I should state my case for them.

We are here faced with the problem of when and under what circumstances a mechanism used by one individual can be accepted to have become a group mechanism. I once (Moses, 1982) used a number of similes to relate to this quandary and asked: Is it like the voices of many singers which coalesce to form the singing of a choir? Or like the music made by an orchestra, composed of many individuals and groups of instruments? Or is it more like the economic production of the individual members of a society, as it comes together to comprise the Gross National Product of a nation? At what point does the idealization of a teacher by most of the class become a group phenomenon? I believe that with unconscious defense mechanisms, we can say, similarly, that when a large number of the members of a group use an unconscious defense mechanism at the same time, we can speak of a group phenomenon.

2. Projection and Narcissism

Perhaps the most obvious of such mechanisms is that of projection. The individual, when he does not wish to face a hostile thought within himself, ascribes it to 'the other'. It is the other who wants to attack him, to do him in, and many more forms of aggression, lesser or greater, not the person himself who has such 'bad' wishes. In a conflict between nations or societies we today speak of 'the demonization, or the dehumanization, of the enemy'. This is a special form of projection, which allows the members of that group to view those of the other group as less than human, as demonic. Therefore, they are not as good as we are, not as human or humane; hence, we, the members of our group, are allowed to 'defend' ourselves and to do things to the other which, were he more human and less demonic, our conscience would not allow us to do. Our whole view of the enemy, of the other, is then distorted in a way which makes it possible for the leaders of that society to mobilize its people against this wicked enemy.

Illustrations in this conflict of ours abound: the Israeli view of the Syrians, the Palestinians, the Egyptians - all especially forceful at certain times of tension with 'the enemy'. And vice versa.

This demonization and dehumanization, then, are examples of stable, consistent, ongoing, rather than transient, forms and manifestations of the projection mechanism. They also bring us close to another mechanism, which we will discuss in more detail when we talk about narcissistic proclivities, namely pre-emptive action based upon the certainty that the enemy is bad and is plotting to do us in. We then have the right, nay, perhaps the duty, to attack him first. As regards projection, we should also remind ourselves of the widespread phenomenon of projection of the superego, when we rely on our leaders to make judgments for us and thereby abdicate our own responsibility; and the projection of the ego ideal, most blatant in an example like that of Jim Jones in Jonestown, all of whose followers committed mass suicide because he wanted them to (Mills, 1979).

Perhaps this is an appropriate place to make another statement relevant to our moving from the individual to the group: namely, that such mechanisms can be and often are used by leaders of a country or a society to manipulate its members. Sometimes this is done in good faith, sometimes not; sometimes consciously and sometimes unconsciously. How we judge it, will of course depend on where we stand: are we members of that group or are they our enemies ?

This brings me to another phenomenon: that the use of such mechanisms by the individual is supported and bolstered through its being shared by his/her friends, by his/her family and finally it receives a widening echo through formulations in the media, newspapers or television, which make it almost self-evident that this is indeed how the world around us looks.

Let us move on to narcissistic tendencies and phenomena. Can a parallel be drawn between the narcissistic traits, affects and proclivities of an individual and those of a nation? Is there an analogy between the genesis, the development of narcissistic needs and sensitivities, the psychology and psychopathology of the self of the individual and those of the group and the nation? My view is that all of the attributes of normal group narcissism can be observed in the State of Israel. Kohut (1976) describes the process of idealization of the leader. In the history of the State of Israel we find idealized leaders in the case of the first

President, Chaim Weizmann, and the first Prime Minister, David Ben Gurion.

The idealizing cathexes of these leaders, in Kohut's words, hold the group together and ensure its cohesion. They also exert a force against the formation of splinter groups, a danger that recurred in our society from the early times in the 1940s when an internecine struggle between right-wing and left-wing Zionism was raging, to recent days, finally leading up to our latest elections. I will mention later how much depends on the leader of the society, and whether he functions in analogy to a good or a bad mother. This is part of the mechanism of projective identification and the way it is handled by the mother in relations to the child, and by the leader in relation to his group or nation.

Group cohesion is also supported by a shared grandiose self (again borrowing from Kohut): the shared belief in the grandiose past and future of the group. Such a shared grandiose self, incidentally, is discernible in the beliefs and actions of Yugoslav Prime Minister Milosevic. This complex of beliefs became public some 10 years ago, when his rhetoric focused on the battle of Kosovo in 1389, where the Moslem Turks defeated the Serbs. In his view, this was a national event which must not be forgotten, in our terms, or those of Volkan (1994) a "chosen trauma". Please keep in mind once more that the use of a grandiose self in a nation and by a leader can be either benign, or malignant. We will have a chance to return to this theme.

We are now pondering the question: to what extent is there a grandiose self in the individual, in the family, in different groups and finally in the society or the nation. This is perhaps most easily demonstrable in the families of schizophrenic patients. Here it has been shown (Lidz et al., 1965) that the symptom of megalomania in the patient has its roots in the deep conviction of his mothers that her son is indeed the center of the universe, her universe. In working with these families as a whole, it soon becomes evident that the other family members expressed the grandiose ideas about the patient as representing an aspect of themselves.

Let us move on to neurotic families, families just like our own. Here, though it may be harder to accept, I am sure that we can similarly find grandiose ideas, only more secretly. We encounter the 'specialness' of most of those who willingly submit themselves and share our psychotherapeutic or psychoanalytic work. Such thoughts relate to both one's origins and to one's potential. If we dared look more closely, I believe that we would find such grandiose ideas and contents in each one of us. Some of our scientist or politician friends, or patients, sometimes confide in us that they dream about winning a Nobel Prize. How secret, and how realistic, these ideas are varies from one person to the next. Some may realize such dreams, most don't.

There is to be found in ordinary people, individuals and families, a similar but opposed negative narcissistic affect: a feeling of shame, of inferiority, of worthlessness. This parallels the grandiose feeling and serves as its opposite. Often we move from one extreme to the other within us, frequently not aware of what exactly transpires in us at a given moment. So much for the individual and the family as the smallest social unit or group. We will now want to look at larger, but still small, groups to look for grandiose ideas and affects. Indeed, here we can see a group pride or group patriotism in a variety of groups. The German term *Lokalpatriotism*, interestingly, has become an integral part of colloquial Israeli Hebrew. I think there is such a pride in the small child's class or nursery School. It focuses first around the nursery school teacher rather than around the group. We also all know the child's pride, strong and omnipotent, towards the father's strength and the mother's beauty as well as other attributes of both.

Similar group narcissistic phenomena can be seen in a wide variety of groups throughout the development of the individual: my school as compared with other schools; my class as compared with other classes. The pride in groups of adolescents is well-known and has been described by poets and eternalized in popular literature and drama. The world-famous musical play *My Fair Lady* demonstrates this where, again, shame and inferiority are also strongly visible. But we, as adults, have no less special pride and grandiose feelings about our kind of work, about our work group, be it the university, our department within the university, our hospital and many more. It is also true for political groupings, for geographical areas, cities, to mention only one. We all can give many examples.

How about the phenomenon of group narcissism in Israel, the country and the people? Jewish religious traditions tell us we were the Chosen People from the beginning, chosen by God over all other nations and peoples. As the sufferings of Job were seen as a special trial inflicted on someone especially elected, so historical events are seen by many in relation to the Jews: Ongoing persecutions are often seen as signs of a special relationship to God. The settling of Palestine in the first half of the twentieth century was tied to a stringent ideology (see, among others, Eisenstadt 1985; Moses & Kligler, 1966) and to a sense of mission. If not the fulfillment of a messianic prophecy, it was at least the realization of a dream dreamt for 2000 years. In his pioneering, in making the desert bloom, with the hoe in one hand and the gun in the other, the Israeli immigrant could combine the grandiose group (and individual) self with the stringent ideology.

Indeed, Israelis have over the years by and large tended to stress the assets of their country, the advantages of Israeli cities, landscape, food, and character, all compared to those of others. We might ask: Do such boasts seem like the phallic narcissism of the adolescent, not yet sure of his worth and therefore needing constant confirmation from the outside? Is it a defensive grandiosity, analogous to the arrogance and haughtiness of a person with a narcissistic personality disorder?

Two historical examples can help us examine the border between normal and pathological narcissism in Israel. The first is the period between the Six-Day War in 1967 and the Yom Kippur or October War in 1973. There is agreement among a number of researchers that this was a time of grandiosity and omnipotence for Israel. In 1967, there was a three-week long threat to Israel and to its people, fears of being overrun with terrible consequences imagined. Some wondered how to flee, some actually fled. After expecting the worst, the unexpected happened. In six short days, the armies of three neighboring Arab nations were defeated with a negligible number of casualties. The territory under Israel's rule grew to 3 times its previous size. It seemed that a country threatened with extinction had become a regional power. Thus it was not only the land but also the national ego that was inflated (cf., inter alia, Gonen, 1978). This became a period of narcissistic inflation, which lasted, with much pride, arrogance and splendid isolation, until the Yom Kippur War. I am writing of this concisely because I want to move on to other things, but much documentation can be quoted to bear this theory out. This general mood influenced the processing of information preceding the October 1973 War. Objective information was misinterpreted and the threat of war, for which there were obvious signs, was ignored, as indeed it had been thirty two years earlier by the United States at Pearl Harbor. The 1973 War punctured the narcissistic inflation and led to a lowering of the value of the national self, and led to a degree of depression.

Israel's narcissism can be also be examined in relation to the Israel Defense Forces (IDF). It is probably the most central, the most sensitive vessel of Israel's narcissism and its grandiose national self. Every Israeli has major emotional ties to the IDF. All of us, our children and some of our fathers served in it. The Defense Forces, with an emphasis on Defense (as in the precursor of the army before 1948, the 'Defense' underground army known as Haganah, Hebrew for defense), play a large role in the lives of Israeli citizens. They are identified with it. In terms of narcissism, the army, and to a lesser degree the flag, the anthem, the government, or the Prime Minister, is an extension of the individual self of the citizen; as such it becomes part of the group self, for better or for worse. In Israel, the successful exploits of the Israel Defense Forces since 1948 raised the self-esteem of the nation; even more so because Jews had no such institution prior to the Zionist settlement in Palestine. Amongst its dramatic successes were the Suez Operation in 1956. Later on, there were a number of daring raids carried out outside Israel, some of a James Bond type, particularly one carried out in Beirut without the shedding of innocent blood. Then came the 1967 Six-Day War with its dramatic victory over Egyptians, Syrians and Jordanians with which the Israel Defense Army reached its peak of narcissistic pride, and of being the vehicle of the national grandiose self. Only the Entebbe rescue operations of hostages hijacked to Idi Amin's Uganda in 1976 presented a feat to be added to this list.

However, we must ask: Is Israel different in this respect from other nations? Or do others share this characteristic of grandiosity? This ties in also with the question of the borderline between normal and pathological narcissism of the nation. I have proposed to call the normal group narcissism of a nation patriotism and its pathological version chauvinism. Pathological narcissism seems to have been clearly demonstrated in Nazi Germany and in the regime of Idi Amin; and in the regime of Slobodan Milosevic. But it is also evident in extreme terrorist organizations, be they Arab, German, Italian, Japanese, South American or Jewish. Yet it is sometimes difficult for us to decide whether a nation's narcissism is still within the range of normalcy. Thus de Gaulle and the France he represented: "La France c'est moi!"

showed a particularly grandiose style, a chauvinism which at times was extremely effective, yet at others seemed to harm France more than help her. But France's national pride and high self esteem certainly existed before de Gaulle and continued after him. Napoleon showed grandiosity. The Germans too have shown unusual national pride quite a while before Hitler. Thus their national anthem, just like other anthems, but only more so, emphasizes that Germany is to be set over all others, "über Alles". Johan Gottlieb Fichte had claimed philosophically, in 1808, that the regeneration of the world depends on the German spirit (see Fichte, 1968). I would think that this idea is analogous to the messianic vision of the Jews. I thus believe that this is a characteristic of all nations: to feel superior, special, better than others, than all others, especially its neighbors and rivals. In part it is probably defensive, to ward off feelings of worthlessness, of shame, and of inferiority. But it also clearly serves the purpose of group cohesion. Some grandiosity seems the right glue for such cohesion.

3. Identification

Earlier in this essay, I presented the concept of projection. There is also the mechanism of identification, and obviously in nations the identification with one's leader and leaders and with their acts and statements. Churchill, in Britain's most difficult hours in World War II, was a leader who, like Nasser in the early 50s, invited his followers to share in the greatness of the moment. Freud already spoke of the more stable and long-term identifications of followers with their leaders and the goals and causes they represent, and told us of the narcissistic supplies they provide. He also spoke about identification, and rivalry, with the other members of the group. To add one more example of identification, it is clearly discernible when negotiators from two sides come together to try and work out a mutually acceptable plan. Often, the negotiators are then way ahead of their constituents in that they have been able to move forward on an agreement, in part by identifying with their counterparts. They now need to work hard at it to bring the constituents, to where they, the negotiators, already are. All these phenomena, then, can be seen on both sides of our conflict and of any political conflict.

The mechanism of projective identification has been widely

postulated, particularly by Kleinian psychoanalysts, as taking place between two persons (see also Ogden, 1982; Zinner & Shapiro, 1972; Zinner, 1976). I believe that we can discern it equally well in political process. I want to focus here on one particular aspect of it, first as it happens between the child and his mother. When the child projects a strongly unpleasant affect or conflict into his mother, this serves as an opportunity for the mother to help the development of the child (Meissner, 1980, 1987; Ogden, 1982; Grotstein, 1982). As the child recurrently projects and identifies with psychic content that it feels to be bad (e.g. aggressive and destructive), the opportunity is for the mother to "hand it back" to the child in more moderated, muted, detoxified and therefore acceptable form. This coincides with Bion's view of the mother as container (Bion, 1963). Projective identification thus is a mechanism which can further the adaptive and integrative growth of the infant/child, as the good mother is able to contain her child's unacceptable wishes and feelings. If the mother is not able to do so, the projected psychic content will be returned in unmodified, i.e. "bad" form and will thus cause obvious difficulties. There is an analogy here not only to the analyst and the analysand, but also to the leader and his function for the large group, his followers. The citizens project their often conflicted and more archaic content onto or into the leader. It may then be accepted in its raw and primitive form by the leader and 'returned' or reflected back to the constituents in moderated and detoxified form, less raw and archaic, less threatening. Parallel to a good mother, this would be a moderate leader, whom we would call "good", who would not be tempted to exacerbate the conflict and its archaic content. The extreme, rigid leader, on the other hand, would not only be unable to moderate such projections, he would, in fact, thrive on them. He would use them to escalate a conflicted situation through a demagogic dramatization and a polarization of attitudes. A warmer, more flexible, more moderate leader would also make his constituents feel better about themselves because he is a more tolerant and containing leader, thus encouraging a a more mature, moderate, flexible and permissive social system. A tough, extreme and rigid leader would lead his followers to more aggressive positions and behavior, to more extreme positions, because of his emotional inability (and lack of desire?) to tolerate or hold unacceptable psychic content within himself. The existence of such a mechanism in political process opens up a vista of interesting possibilities of understanding.

We encounter here a sometimes quite confusing mixture of unconscious processes and external reality. But this confusion is not new for us. Freud (1922) spoke of the fact that a person who feels persecuted, by his "enemy", often also his love object, frequently faces the reality that this "enemy" does, in fact, harbor unconscious aggressive wishes against him. Henry Kissinger reportedly said that a person who is paranoid may still be persecuted in reality. Indeed, we will always expect to see a consistent interaction between inner and outer reality in all psychic mechanisms. The important 'other' and the environment are always directly or indirectly involved. For example, projection does not mean projecting psychic content into a vacuum; rather, it stimulates, facilitates or strengthens psychic content already there in the receiver; and the content already there invites the projective identification.

It is one further step from here to another phenomenon in political process. Let me use an example from 20 years ago so as not to make it too controversial. You may remember that the mechanism of projective identification also includes a wish to control what is projected or him in whom one projects. The ultranationalist settlers on the other side of the green line (the 1967 borders of Israel) projectively identified with the one-time Prime Minister Menachem Begin. They thereby pushed him to adopt some of their extreme positions. Viewed from the other side, Mr. Begin projectively identified with the position of the settlers, who could express loudly some of the views that he could or would not allow himself to declare. By egging them on, probably mainly unconsciously, to maintain a consistently more militant position, he served his own ends in several ways: He covered his right flank politically and so he was able publicly to maintain a less extreme position. He used their extreme political position as leverage for allowing himself to be a little responsive, yet not too much so, to the constituency on his right. This enabled him to neither lose that constituency nor to follow their extreme position. I believe that President Clinton has at times acted similarly with groups both on his extreme right and left. Mr. Netanyahu in Israel on the other hand did not seem to take a middle stance, and thus apparently did not use this mechanism.

Here again, part of this mechanism is unconscious and another part is deliberate and therefore conscious. We have seen an example of this in projection. What is particularly impressive is the deliberate use for political aims of mechanisms that are in part unconscious (see, e.g. Moses 1986, 1990; Moses-Hrushovski, 1994; Moses & Moses-Hrushovski 1997). To return to the example of the settlers and Mr. Begin, it is beyond doubt that these intentionally and with much conscious effort attempted to influence the national leader to act in accordance with their activist views. They would do so by arguing their case and by various political maneuvers. But such real and intentional behavior by no means excludes the concurrent operation of unconscious mechanisms. Both parties, the settlers and the Prime Minister, also interact through unconscious egging on and thus gain vicarious gratification. We know this particular mechanism both from observing family dynamics (Ackerman, 1958; Wynne, 1965; Haley and Hoffman, 1967) and from Ruth Eissler's 'scapegoats of society' (1953). Both are closely related to projective identification.

Other mechanisms will be mentioned only briefly here: denial in political process (Moses, 1989a), entitlement and shame in political process (Moses & Moses-Hrushovski, 1990; Moses, 1989b) and the interesting question of whether there is a perpetuation, or perhaps even a reversal, of the victim role. Two topics which must be further addressed are unconscious guilt and then, more at length, mourning.

4. Unconscious Guilt

I gave an Annual Freud Lecture in 1983 in Vienna about unconscious guilt in political process. To give you some idea of the reactions of some of my fellow countrymen at the time, let me tell you about two events. The first one occurred when I gave one of my papers to a psychoanalyst friend for his critical reactions, and he said: but this is anti-Semitic !! The other took place in Vienna. The Annual Sigmund Freud Lecture was usually attended by the President of Austria. Thus diplomatic personnel, at least from the countries from which the speakers came, usually attended. The Israeli *chargé d'affaires* was present during my lecture, but walked out without a word to me, in protest. I presume that both reacted to the fact that I concentrated on Israel and did not talk about other countries and that I had ignored the reasons and circumstances which led to the events that brought about the use of Israel's mechanisms of defense. It is evident that unconscious guilt is clearly discernible on the Israeli side of the conflict in three main areas.

First: The impact of the Zionist movement and the setting up of a Jewish Homeland in what was then Palestine on the Arab population of these areas. Did we take away their country from the occupants of Palestine and expel them? I am sure you know that there are opposing versions of the history of those days.

Second, most of us in Israel are aware of the two blatant massacres committed by our side: that by the forerunners of the Likud Party in Deir Yassin, the Arab village near Jerusalem in 1948; and that committed by Israeli border police in 1956 at the time of the Suez Operation, when almost fifty Arab villagers were killed in Kafr Kassem, an Arab village in central Israel when they came home from work after a curfew had been declared. True, both of these events took place at a time of war, but that does not, to my mind, excuse them.

Third, the treatment of the Arab citizens of Israel, and later those of the administered territories, through discrimination, lack of respect and at times in humiliating ways. It is unavoidable for a Jewish Israeli to live in Israel without reacting to the roadblocks which we pass many times, where we were waved on while our Palestinian neighbors were submitted to checking of documents, examinations of cars and often humiliating examinations of the persons themselves. We cannot but have guilt feelings about that because all of these were acts carried out by Israelis in the name of Israel, in our name.

However, expressions of guilt feelings have been and are noticed in public life only very marginally indeed, if at all. I believe that this is a general human reaction. Of all the terrible inhumanities committed in the twentieth century, very few have led to a clear and obvious evidence of guilt feelings by the perpetrators. The next question is whether these guilt feelings do become translated into actions, and if so in what ways. There are several reports in the literature which can help us look at this question (Redl, 1954; Hartmann and Loewenstein, 1962; Sandler, 1962; Malmquist, 1968).

We always seek approval from our superiors. Children search for approval from their parents, and states in politics from the international great powers. Then one rationalizes one's behavior. Others try to hide such acts or lie about them. A third way is to expect or even to provoke what are seen as unjust accusations. One can then feel righteous at being treated unfairly and stay with the anger that this brings up. Here we already see a beginning of guilt changing into aggression to rid oneself of it, at least consciously. Children clearly show a need to provoke punishment to alleviate guilt feelings. In nations this is much harder to discern and even more so to demonstrate. Freud (1924) said in this context about the individual:

> ...an unconscious sense of guilt, is often recognized by a 'negative therapeutic reaction' .. It constitutes one of the most serious resistances and the greatest danger to our ... aims. ...On the other hand, often a neurosis which has defied every therapeutic effort may vanish if the subject becomes involved in the misery of an unhappy marriage, or loses all his money, or develops a dangerous organic disease...one form of suffering has then been replaced by another; ... all that mattered was the constant amount of suffering." (p. 166).

In international relations, guilt could lead to the behavior of provoking a war; but would then be hidden by the blatant aggression.

We also see displacement of guilt to others; reaction formation against the guilt, again with a feeling of having been unjustly treated. We know there is both in families and in societies a split between the more gentle and the more harsh sides. In families there are permissive and strict ways of educating children. In societies, we find extreme groups, such as settlers in Israel, or terrorists who serve a function for the large group and thus are tolerated and perhaps indirectly encouraged by the latter. The majority of the population can then gain some vicarious gratification of its aggressive wishes (through the actions carried out), while at the same time righteously condemning them. But unconscious guilt feelings will be mobilized.

Guilt can also be moderated through the phenomenon of group conscience. In its extreme form we have the war superego compared to the peace superego described by Freud (1932). One's narcissistic needs may be met through obtaining the approval for guilt-producing acts from one's subgroup, thus convincing oneself that one is praiseworthy in spite of, or perhaps because of, the deed committed. This again will come from family, friends, and some mass media as well as the leader of the subgroup and the cause. It turns out that even professional killers in the USA need to convince themselves repeatedly that their victim is indeed bad and unworthy of continuing to live (Arlow, 1973).

We have seen how guilt can be alleviated through the mechanisms of displacement and projection. Finally, the most interesting way of dealing with guilt feelings is when one is able to shove aside the guilt through aggressive behavior. Sometimes a person, or a state, will even accuse the other before he himself is being implicated. In the extreme case this can lead to the pre-emptive strike, based on a correct or incorrect evaluation of the danger that exists. What is clear is that it is easier to fight one's pangs of conscience outside than within oneself.

We often see mothers who when a child has been almost run down by a car will discharge their anger, and their guilt, through hitting it. We also know well family members, who deal with their guilt about a loved one's death through illness by taking the doctors to the courts. Children as well as adults may react with recalcitrant obstinacy (*Trotzreaktion*), at times accompanied by a projection of the superego onto the parent or an authority figure. These, then, are a large variety of mechanisms for dealing with guilt which are more familiar to us in the individual than in the group. Some we can recognize in the group already and others we need to study in more detail.

5. Mourning

I am now coming to the last of the mechanisms I would like to deal with in this chapter, namely the process of mourning. It is of special interest to us because it seems to be essential for groups and nations to enter a peace process or to complete it. To put it differently: The absence of mourning processes often obstructs or delays a peace process. The need for a mourning process is related to another psychological phenomenon: the fear of change, which all of us know from its clinical presence, in ourselves and in others. The recognition that we are in the midst of a process of change, such as in psychotherapy or psychoanalysis and in the long drawn-out peace process of the Middle East, bodes ill for us. We will not be able to continue with the same well-known patterns from the past but will have to adapt to new, strange, so far unknown conditions and ways of living. In our human experience, this is frightening. The step to be taken seems irreversible and irrevocable. And yet peace, just as health and successes of various kinds, seem such an eminently desirable goal that we feel badly to have queasy feelings about facing it or them.

The danger is that people who have an unconscious fear of peace will act out their negative feelings. In our conflict, the ways in which this can be done are legion: to use bulldozers to ready land for more settlements, to open up a tunnel under the Temple Mount in Jerusalem without consulting others on both sides; to escalate tensions on some cold or warm front, through individual or collective action; by carrying out or condoning violent acts against innocent Palestinians; or by finding ways to increase the humiliation of Palestinians that is already part of the daily scene. However, these acts can also be carried out intentionally for political reasons. This is another example of the mixture between unconscious and conscious, i.e. intentional and planned behavior.

In addition to the ubiquitous fear of change and the holding on to familiar patterns of safety (cf. also Sandler, 1965), work of mourning (as Freud called it in 1917) is required of us at many different levels of development in order to be able to move forward. We must mourn the past in order to leave it behind us, just as we must mourn the loss of a loved one in order to proceed with our life. In the process of mourning we will concern ourselves with the loved person, our memories of him/her, the person we love that is suddenly no longer there. By doing so, by remembering times spent together, we will gradually, slowly detach ourselves emotionally from that person. It is a painful process and it is often tempting to try to avoid it and hold on to the loved one who is gone. But the process of mourning is essential if we want to proceed with the business of living, to be free for new events and new relationships.

The same is true for participating in a peace process. Here, as with individuals, there are also incomplete and pathological mourning processes which do not allow the mourner to continue the ongoing peace process. We saw one aspect of this when the Sinai peninsula was returned to Egypt in 1982, as part of the Egyptian-Israeli peace settlement. For example, we interviewed Jewish settlers in Ofira/Sharm-e-Sheikh in the Southern Sinai before they had to leave their chosen Paradise. Many of them refused to set a date for their own move back to Israel, even though the date for the evacuation of the area was unequivocal. They postponed it from week to week. But, with our help, this became only a transitory postponement of mourning processes, which did not cause serious problems (Moses, Rosenfeld, & Moses-Hrushovski , 1987).

It is crucial importance whether a state or a government encourages mourning processes in its people at a time when it faces or is definitely engaged in a peace process which will involve the giving up of territories. It is then analogous to an individual who has undergone an amputation of a limb, but has not been able or willing to mourn the loss of that limb. The phenomenon of having pains in a leg or an arm that is no longer there is called 'phantom limb'. It stops only when the emotional mourning process of the limb has been completed. The same is true for other parts of the body, but also for functions one is able to carry out and needs to be ready to give up, such as in passing from one developmental stage to another and in old age. Similarly, the territories to be returned by Israel, both in Sinai in 1982 and in Gaza, the West Bank and the Golan Heights today, need to be mourned.

We have all come to take them into us as parts of ourselves even though they were not part of the State of Israel as it was constituted in 1948. The land gradually became part of the national body-self. We have visited there, have enjoyed the special treats of each region, especially after 1967, when all of a sudden the territory we could visit became 3 times as great as before. In the same way, then, we have to give up what we have made into a part of ourselves. This requires a process of mourning.

The role of the leadership in such a process is vital. It is striking that, when a switchover took place in 1999 from a government that hardly encouraged the Israeli people to prepare to take leave from parts of the land, to a government known to be committed to handing back territories, many more people, including settlers, indicated that they are ready to give up lands, even their own. This demonstrated the essential role which a government plays in helping the people prepare for giving up land and for the mourning process that goes along with it. Thus mourning is a prerequisite for the adaptation to a new phase, in the individual and in the group. A special, interesting, and related function of mourning has been described by Pollock (1963). It may induce creativity, especially of the artistic kind (among others, he used the German painter Kaethe Kollwitz as a convincing example). But mourning is also a prerequisite for any organization which wants to adapt itself to newly changing circumstances (cf. Kernberg, 1984).

Thus, the process of mourning is essential for any country entering or engaged in a peace process; particularly so when land needs to be given up, but not only then.

In this chapter I have taken you a long way, from one defense mechanism to another, from projection through identification and projective identification to a variety of narcissistic phenomena and finally to unconscious guilt feelings and how we deal with them and to processes of mourning. I have tried to provide you with an amount of depth sufficient to convince you, yet also of width and perspective so as to give you an overview. I don't know if I have succeeded in demonstrating the ubiquity of unconscious defense mechanisms in political process.

Before summing up, a brief foray into the social area. I feel strongly that in large groups, societies, nations, not only do unconscious defense mechanisms take place, but there are also social, societal reactions that help a society to deal with the events that affect it. These have been less well described. It is only in recent years that we are beginning to focus on them more. Regression in a society at times of crisis when it needs a strong, charismatic leader (Chruchill in World War II, but also Nasser in Egypt in the 1950s) is one example. Mourning processes in a society, healthy, incomplete or pathological, are another. Sometimes a society espouses a trauma it has undergone, even many, many years ago, what Volkan has called a chosen trauma. Thus, as mentioned above, the Serbs have chosen to see their defeat by Turks in Kosovo in 1389 as a national trauma which must not be forgotten. Israel has chosen the destruction of the Second Temple in 70 A.D. and the episode the zealots in Massada , where the zealots, according to the myth (not supported by historical evidence), killed themselves rather than be taken captive, as a national trauma to be held on to. Whether the Holocaust, a very real trauma indeed, will, when there is enough distance from it, becomes such a chosen trauma is an important and interesting question. Which similar traumas on the Palestinian and Arab side have been or will be chosen is a topic which I can only ask about, but not tell you.

To sum up and reiterate, here is my hypothesis: that individual defense mechanisms in the group, society, and national and societal reactions serve as ways of society to deal with its history and its traumas as well as with its present-day development; particularly in relation to political conflicts.

References

Ackerman, N.W. (1958). *The Psychodyamics of Family Life*. New York: Basic Books

Arlow, J. (1973). Motives for Peace. In H.Z. Winnik, R. Moses, & M. Ostow (Eds.), *Psychological Bases of War*. New York: Quadrangle, The New York Times.

Bion W.R. (1963). *Elements of Psycho-Analysis*. London: Heinemann.

Eisenstadt, S.N. (1985). *The Transformation of Israeli Society*. London & Jerusalem: Weidenfeld & Nicholson.

Eissler, R. (1953). Scapegoats of society. In K. Eissler (Ed.), *Searchlights on Delinquency*. New York: International Universities Press.

Ettin, M.F, . Fidler, J.W. & Cohen B.D. (1995). *Group Process and Political Dynamics*. Madison, CT: International Universities Press.

Fichte, J. G. (1808/1968). *Addresses to the German Nation*. New York: Harper.

Freud S. (1917). Mourning and Melancholia. In *The Standard Edition of the Complete Psychological Writings of Sigmund Freud*. Vol. 14, 239-258. London: The Hogarth Press.

Freud S.(1922). Some neurotic mechanisms in in jealousy, paranoia and homosexuality. In *The Standard Edition of the Complete Psychological Writings of Sigmund Freud*.
Vol. 18, 223-232. London: The Hogarth Press.

Freud S. (1924). The economic problem of masochism. In *The Standard Edition of the Complete Psychological Writings of Sigmund Freud*. Vol. 19, 157-185. London: The Hogarth Press.

Freud S. (1932). Why War? In *The Standard Edition of the Complete Psychological Writings of Sigmund Freud*. Vol. 22, 197-215. London: The

Hogarth Press.

GAP (Group for the Advancement of Psychiatry) (1978). Report No. 103. Self-involvement in the Middle East Conflict. New York: Mental Health Materials Center.

Gonen, J.V. (1978). The Israeli illusion of omnipotence following the Six-Day War. *Journal of Psychohistory*. 6, 241-271.

Grotstein , J. (1982). *Splitting and Projective Identification*. New York: Jason Aronson.

Hartman, H. & Loewenstein, R.. (1962). Notes on the Superego. *Psychoanalytic Study of the Child*, 17, 42-81.

Jacobson, E. (1957). Denial and repression. *Journal of the American Psychoanalytic Association*, 5, 61-92

Kernberg, O. (1984). The couch at sea: The psychoanalysis of organizations. *International Journal of Group Psychotherapy, 34,* 5-23.

Kohut, H. (1976). Creativeness, Charisma, Group Psychology: Freud's self-analysis. *Psychological Issues, 34*, 379-425.

Lidz, T., Fleck, S. & Cornelison, A. (1963). *Schizophrenia and the Family.* New York: International Universities Press.

Meissner, W.W. (1980). A note on projective identification. *Journal of the American Psychoanalytic Association, 28,* 43-67.

Meissner, W.W. (1987). Projection and Projective Identification. In: J. Sandler (Ed.), *Projection, Identification, and Projective Identification.* Madison, CT, International Universities Press.

Mills, J. (1979). *Six Years with God.* New York: A & W Publishers, Inc.

Moses R. & Kligler, D. (1966). The institutionalization of mental health values.
Israel Annals of Psychiatry, 4, 148-161.

Moses, R. (1982). The group self and the Israeli-Arab conflict. *International*

Review of Psycho-Analysis, *9*, 55-65.

Moses, R & Hrushovski-Moses, R. (1986). A form of denial at the Hamburg Congress. *International Review of Psycho-Analysis*, *13*, 175-180.

Moses, R. (1983). Guilt feelings in the political process. *Sigmund Freud Bulletin* (Vienna), 7, 2-14.

Moses, R . (1984). Dehumanization of the victim and of the aggressor. In V. D. Volkan, D.A. Julius & J.V. Montville (Eds.) *The Psychodynamics of International Relationships*. Lexington, MA: .Lexington Books

Moses, R . (1986). Watergate as a Universal Phenomenon. In: H. Lobner (Ed.) *Psychoanalyse Heute*. Vienna: Verlag Orac

Moses, R. (1987). Projection, identification, projective identification - their relation to political process In J. Sandler (Ed.) *Projection, Identification, and Projective Identification*. Madison, CT: , International Universities Press.

Moses, R. (1989a). Denial in Political Process. In: E.L. Edelstein, D.L. Nathanson & A.M. Stone (Eds.), *Denial: A Clarification of Concepts and Research*. New York: Plenum Press.

Moses, R. (1989b). Entitlement and Shame: Their relation to Political Process. In H.P. Blum, E.M. Weinshel, & F.R. Rodman, (Eds.) *The Psychoanalytic Core: Essays in Honor of Leo Rangell*. Madison, CT: International Universities Press.

Moses R. & Moses-Hrushovski R. (1990). Reflections about Entitlement. *Psychoanalytic Study of the Child , 45*, 61-78.

Moses, R., Rosenfeld, J., & Moses-Hrushovski R. (1987). Facing the threat of removal: Lessons from the forced evacuation of Ofira. *Applied Behavioral Science, 23*, 53-72

Moses-Hrushovski R (1994). *Deployment: Hiding Behind Power Struggles as a Character Defense*. Northvale, NJ: Jason Aronson.

Malmquist, C.P. (1968). Conscience Development. *Psychoanalytic Study of the Child, 22*, 308-333.

Ogden, T. (1979). On Projective Identification. *International Journal of Psycho-*Analysis, *60*, 357-373.

Pollock, G.H. (1989). *The Mourning-Liberation Process*. Madison, CT: International Universities Press.

Rangell, L. and Moses-Hrushovski, R. (Eds). (1996). *Psychoanalysis at the Political Border- Essays in Honor of Rafael Moses.* Madison, CT: International Universities Press.

Sandler, J., et al. (1962). The classification of superego material in The Hampstead Index. *Psychoanalytic Study of the Child, 17*, 107-127.

Scheidlinger, S. (1952). *Psychoanalysis and Group Behavior*. New York: W.W. Norton.

Volkan, V.D., Julius, D.A. & Montville, J.V. (1990-1991). *The Psychodynamics of International Relationships*. Lexington, Mass: Lexington Books.

Wynne, L. (1965). Some indications and contraindications for exploratory family therapy. In. I. Boszormenyi-Nagy & J.L. Framo (Eds.), *Intensive Family Therapy*. New York: Harper & Row.

Zinner, J. (1976). The implication of projective identification for marital interaction. In H. Grunebaum & J. Christ (Eds.), *Contemporary Marriage: Structure, Dynamics & Therapy*. Boston: Little, Brown.

Zinner, J & Shapiro, R. (1972). Projective Identification as a mode of perception and behavior in adolescents. *International Journal of Psycho-Analysis, 53*, 523-530.

Chapter 6

Contentious Origins: Psychoanalytic Comments on the Debate over Israel's Creation

José Brunner
Tel-Aviv University

The concepts of patriotism, identity, identification, narcissism, and chauvinism are the center of numerous discussions about the nature of nationalism and national ideologies. Is each and any kind of nationalism potentially pernicious and destructive? Can there be cases of "healthy", positive, and productive national self-regard? This chapter is part of the discussion which has been going on the in West for generations. Earlier chapters in this book, especially those by Moses and Suleiman, set the stage for this case study by Brunner. The phenomenon under investigation is the appearance of public stock-taking and soul-searching within the Israeli elite vis-à-vis the obvious injustice done to the Palestinians by the Zionist project. Actually, this phenomenon goes back a hundred years, but the critical voices have become stronger in recent years, as Palestinian resistance and doubts about Zionism have grown. Brunner uses this case study to apply Kohut's idea of "good" narcissism, which shook up the world of psychoanalysis when it was first introduced. His conclusion is that a "mature", well-balanced kind of national identity is not only desirable, but possible, and may even be within reach.

1. Introduction

As we all know, the State of Israel was officially founded on May 14, 1948. This essay examines the debate on the historical origins of the

State that has been in progress in the Israeli media over the last decade and still has not come to an end. In this debate the traditional Zionist narrative on Israel's creation has been subjected to revisions by a number of critical historians and social scientists who have been called "New Historians" or "post-Zionists".

This public debate can be taken as a polemic offshoot of the weighty tomes of research on the early history of Israel authored by the academic protagonists involved. However, the debate in the Israeli press has to be considered an event that, although related to some of the protagonists' scholarly endeavors, constitutes a distinct phenomenon, deserving analysis in its own right. It is noteworthy, for instance, that some of the claims that generated strident exchanges in Israeli newspapers in the middle of the nineteen-nineties had already been published in scholarly books in the course of the nineteen- eighties, but failed to cause a scandal at the time. Moreover, the controversial term "New Historian" as the epithet for a more critical stance among Israeli academics was coined already in 1988, without attracting much fire (Morris, 1988). As we shall see, in contrast to the scholarly publications, the public debate on Israel's creation emerged only after the 1993 Oslo agreements between Israel and the Palestine Liberation Organization, which led to the establishment of enclaves of Palestinian self-rule in the Israeli-occupied West Bank and the Gaza Strip, and were designed as a framework for an ongoing peace process between Israel and the Palestinians.

Numerous accounts, from a variety of angles, of the debate that has become visible in the Israeli press since 1994, have already been published, both in Hebrew and English (e.g. *History and Memory* 1995; *Kol Ha'ir*, 1995; *Theory and Criticism* 1996; Livneh, 2001; Mahler, 1997; Weitz, 1997; Peled, 1999; Shapira 1999; Silberstein, 1999). In fact, this essay draws in part on the author's earlier account, which examined the first three years of the debate from a psychoanalytic angle (Brunner, 1997/98).

Anita Shapira, one of the main protagonists of the debate, has expressed puzzlement at what she has described as the "astonishingly passionate" nature of the debate on the founding of Israel (Shapira, 1995, p. 9). The aim of this essay is to expose the debate's underlying emotional dynamics and explain its logic. But this cannot be done without a presentation of some of the exchanges. In order to highlight the emotions involved, each of the first four sections outlines some of the main points of contention and the rhetorical strategies deployed by the protagonists involved.

But why stay on the surface level of newspaper polemics rather than delving into the depths of the underlying scholarly contributions? Because, as Benedict Anderson (1991) has shown in his widely-read *Imagined Communities*, reading the daily newspaper constitutes the major "mass ceremony" of modern times, by means of which members of literate collectives come to imagine themselves as related to one another and thus as members of one nation. As this essay shows, the press constitutes not only a locus where collective identity is constructed or imagined, but also an arena where prevalent notions of national identity can be publicly contested, that is, where collective imaginations can be subverted.

Moreover, in its fifth section this essay introduces a psychoanalytic interpretation in order to come to terms with the emotional impact of this controversy. Taking its cue from Heinz Kohut, the founder of the psychoanalytic school of thought commonly known as self-psychology, the essay argues that the dynamics in question have to do with collective narcissism; hence it seeks to reveal some of the narcissistic anxieties and satisfactions involved in the debate.

The debate on the creation of Israel provides a fruitful case study for psychoanalytic inquiry, since creational moments are particularly important in the life of a nation. Like all moments of birth, they are emotionally charged and heavy with significance. Hence they are the subject of myth as much as history. Myths of origins are stories that express the understanding or imagination a collective has of itself and its place vis-à-vis other collectives. Moreover, stories about origins form a special kind of discourse that grounds and organizes social experience. They are never restricted to the past to which they ostensibly refer; they always also say something about this past's meaning for the present, for in telling stories about origins, the past is made to press on the present and the future tends to become destiny.

2. Going West

In 1994 Ilan Pappé, a historian and political scientist at the University of Haifa, published in the daily *Davar* a scathing review of a book by Anita Shapira, a historian at Tel Aviv University. He claimed that rather than providing a scholarly discussion of the history of Zionism, Shapira's work was propagandist in that it reproduced the Zionist terminology it pretended to analyze. He concluded his review with the statement that

> scholars of all disciplines who deal with the past and present of Israeli society cannot remain loyal to their academic and intellectual duties without getting rid, at least to some degree, of the straightjacket which the Zionist ideology has forced on them (Pappé, 1994a, p. 20).

Rather than regarding the Zionist settlement of Palestine as a unique and moral project, as presented by Shapira, Pappé suggested regarding it as a colonialist venture, whose only unique feature was its timing.

Beyond Shapira, Pappé's attack was directed at the work of affirmative scholars in general, those scholars whose narratives extend or amend myths that have become part of the Israeli-Jewish collective consciousness. Affirmative intellectuals present the creation of Israel in a heroic terminology, not unlike the one which the political elite of the Zionist movement has used to mobilize legitimacy and support. Explicitly or implicitly, the Zionist project and its realization in the creation of the Jewish state are depicted as an Ingathering of the Exiles, the return of the dispersed Jewish collective to its historical homeland, where it has managed to rebuild itself from the abyss of complete destruction in the Holocaust into a self-determining collective subject of modern statehood (cf. Zuckerman, 2002). Its achievements are portrayed as the result of efforts of moral self-sacrificing pioneers, achieved in the face of Arab intransigence by superhuman efforts of the few who fought the many, a small nation which sought peace against overwhelming and hostile Arab others, who plotted its destruction. In this narrative the Jewish people appears as an ancient nation, a nation before the age of nationalism, as it were, with a singular historical destiny, surviving through the millennia despite universal persecution by others. Zionists are portrayed as a special kind of Jews, who can be justly proud of their auto-emancipation from persecuted victims into pioneers and warriors, thus turning Diaspora Jews into the obsolete Jewish Other of the collectively reborn, the farming and fighting Jews of Palestine (cf. Beit-Hallahmi, 1993, 2002).

On the other side of the divide are critical scholars like Pappé, who deny the uniqueness of the Zionist project. Instead of foregrounding aspects that present it as seeking a haven for the persecuted, i.e. as a moral enterprise, they stress violent aspects that led to the uprooting of others. Such critical narratives of the creation of the Jewish state turn the founding of Israel into an entirely modern deed, rather than a redemptive one that brings about the renaissance of an ancient people. Even in the rare instances in which critical scholars relate the Jewish settlers in Palestine to their European origins, they place them in the context of colonialism. As Ilan Pappé puts it in a "lesson in new history," published in the daily *Ha'aretz*:

> The State of Israel was created with the aid of Western colonialism. It intentionally uprooted the Palestinian population and justified this retroactively on the basis of Jewish 'uniqueness' resulting from the Holocaust (Pappé, 1994b. English translation cited from Shapira, 1995, pp. 19-20).

Since such critical narratives sever the history of the Zionist Jewish settlers in Palestine from the Jewish Diaspora, they present the Jewish-Arab confrontation, and above all the conflict with the Palestinians, as the cardinal issue in the origins and development of Israeli statehood. As Anita Shapira, one of the most articulate and outspoken opponents of the critical scholars has commented disapprovingly:

> They are not concerned with the processes that occurred in Europe in the nineteenth and early twentieth centuries which led to the emergence of Zionism and the desire to create a Jewish state. In their eyes, the problem of Palestine is isolated from the wider European-Jewish context and stands on a different plane, that of the Middle East (Shapira, 1995, p. 16).

This essay refers to academic iconoclasts who undermine Israel's myths of creation as *critical* intellectuals or scholars, rather than as "new historians" or "post-Zionists", as they tend to refer to themselves or are usually referred to by their *affirmative* opponents. The main reason for this is that rather than about epistemology or methodology in the writing of history, which characterizes the American divide between Old and New History since the beginning of the century (Himmelfarb, 1987), the Israeli debate is about the *affirmation* or *critique* of the myth of the creation of the Jewish state. As both sides agree, their dispute is "about the role of historians in the shaping of Israel's collective memory" (Shapira, 1995, p. 12; Pappé, 1995, p. 69). Other than for their opposition to the dominant Zionist mythology, the critical scholars do not necessarily belong to the same methodological or ideological camp. Benny Morris, now a historian at Ben-Gurion University in Beer Sheba, who introduced the term New Historians into the debate on Israel's origins, is a rather traditional positivist (Morris, 1988). University of Haifa historian and political scientist Ilan Pappé, on the other hand, is a self-declared relativist. Moreover, not all critical scholars are post-Zionists or oppose Zionism. While Ilan Pappé proclaims himself post-Zionist, Benny Morris (1997) stresses his Zionist conviction. Finally, although the subject-matter of the debate is history, many of the protagonists on both sides are not historians at all, but novelists, columnists, philosophers and social scientists, who look critically at Israel's past.

To some extent at least, the Israeli controversy surrounding the creation of the state can be examined from a generational perspective. Mostly, the critical intellectuals were born after 1948 or were still small children at that time; thus they speak in the voice of those who have to live with the results rather than the intentions of the acts of their parents. The crucial life experiences that marked this generation were the 1973 Yom Kippur War and the 1982 Lebanon War. Although she put it somewhat harshly, Shapira is right in stating that looking back on the 1948 war, "the new generation was less impressed by the 6,000 Jews who had fallen in that war than by the uprooting of approximately 700,000 Arabs from Israeli territory". In general terms, one may agree therefore with Shapira's claim that the

> shift in emphasis from the suffering of Jews to that of Arabs, from the heroics of *Palmah* literature to descriptions of acts of cruelty and atrocity, was an inseparable by-product of the transition from one generation to the next (Shapira, 1995, p. 14).

Although a generational perspective may offer some insights into the debate, it clearly is insufficient to explain it. First, not all affirmative intellectuals belong to the founder generation. There is, of course, a substantial number of affirmative scholars who belong to the same, younger generation as the critical academics. In fact, affirmative scholars form the majority of this generation of academics. Second, a generational perspective cannot account for the fact that the public debate on Israel's origins gained its momentum only in the course of the nineteen-nineties and did not emerge before then, although some of the relevant researches were published earlier.

Rather than turn the debate on the founding of Israel into a generational (Oedipal perhaps) conflict, it seems more appropriate, therefore, to relate it to historical and political events and processes. Above all the 1993 Oslo agreements between Israel and the Palestine Liberation Organization seem to have provided the necessary background for the public dispute between affirmative and critical intellectuals. These agreements raised the question of how a prosperous Israel with a democratic self-image could live with the violence immanent in its creation, which had turned the Palestinians into a nation of stateless refugees and second-rank citizens. The repercussions of this violence did not trouble Israeli society through much of its short history, but came to haunt it since the Lebanon war in the beginning of the 1980s, and the first Palestinian *intifada* (popular uprising) in the occupied territories starting at the end of 1987, which led to the 1993 Oslo agreements.

The debate may also have been made possible by a general trend typical of much of the left-wing section of the *ashkenazi*, i.e. Western, elite of Israel, which has moved away from an ethos stressing obligations and duties to the collective, towards an emphasis on the protection of individual rights. In the 1990s Israel was no longer dominated by the political discourse which was characteristic of the generation of founders, where, in the words of Yoram Peri, a political scientist and, at the time, editor of the now defunct daily *Davar*, "[t]he "we" preceded the "me", "together" was incomparably more important than "private". Israeli socialism was based on collectivism rather than equality' (Peri, 1994, p. 17). This change was part of the evolution of Israel from an étatist society towards a civil society in the United States style, which has been generated by Israel's continuous economic prosperity. Of course, all these factors contributed also to the conclusion of the Oslo agreement that was supposed to set an end to the occupation and the violence between Palestinians and Israelis, thus facilitating Israel's full membership in the globalized hi-tech Western world.

As a whole, therefore, the cultural space in which scholars critical of Israel's myths of creation came to play a public role emerged in the wake of concerns about the ethics of "the Occupation" (i.e. the Israeli occupation of the West Bank and Gaza since 1967) and warfare, dwindling state control, diminished fears concerning survival, the drift further towards the West, and the dialogue with the Palestinian leadership which started in Oslo. Thus, the debate on the founding of Israel is an aspect of a more comprehensive process of transformation that affected the self-consciousness of its Jewish community during the last decade and continues to manifest itself in the press, above all in the high-brow daily *Ha'aretz* (cf. Samet 1996; Karpel 1995; Karpel, 1996).

3. Magnificent Myths and Dangerous Doubts

The disdainful tenor of Pappé's attack on Shapira, which to a large extent constituted the opening salvo in the public debate on Israel's founding, is not unique. In fact, the term New Historians, suggested by Benny Morris as a self-definition of those who provide critical narratives of Israeli and Zionist history, derives from contempt for the work of affirmative scholars. Morris argued that these critical scholars were New Historians rather than revisionists, since previous treatments of the 1948 Arab-Israeli war were lacking in serious scholarship and constituted but tendentious and apologetic works of official history, written by "committed adult participants" who themselves had lived through 1948 and belonged themselves to the "generation of nation-builders". Since no body of true scholarship existed, he claimed, there was nothing to revise. Instead, new ground had to be broken by Israeli historians; hence the name New Historians (Morris, 1988).

Countering Pappé's review of Shapira, writer Aharon Megged fired a broadside in *Ha'aretz* against what he called "a suicidal impulse" or "a suicidal urge" of recent Israeli historiography. He argued that a new generation of historians endangered Israel's very existence by creating self-doubt in the hearts of the Israeli population concerning the legitimacy of the Zionist project and the origins of the Jewish state (Megged, 1994). This angry attack on Pappé and other critical scholars was cast in even more savage a tone than Pappé had used in his piece. Megged declared that anyone who called the Zionist movement and policies colonialist, identified with the Palestinians, i.e. with Israel's threatening and destructive other. Confronted with arguments such as Pappé's, he wondered whether Israel was driven "into self-destruction by a hidden biological force" (Megged, 1994, p. 27).

Megged left no doubt that as a combatant in the 1948 War he had a strong personal identification with Israel's collective self-image. He explained that the Zionist pioneers and soldiers, including himself, were never motivated by colonial aims and that their consciousness never was that of colonial masters. Megged seemed to fuse with the Zionist collective and to derive much of his pride from having been part of a national struggle against evil others, who set out to destroy Israel.

Megged viewed the growing pluralism of historical narratives on the creation of Israel as leading to what he called a "Spenglerian decline" of the nation as a whole. He regarded the refusal of the New Historians to fully merge with the Zionist "we" and to let their historical narrative be dominated by the collective self-image of the founders of Israel as tantamount to identifying with the Palestinians. Megged could disregard or dismiss the Palestinian historiography of the Jewish-Arab conflict as the narrative of the enemy, but he clearly was overcome with feelings of anxiety, rage and impotence, when faced with an internal, Jewish, voice whose presence in the public discourse of Israel could not be ignored. Thus, Danny Rabinowitz, a critical anthropologist, was right in claiming in *Ha'aretz* that the work of the New Historians did not allow people like Aharon Megged to age in peace. The hitherto hegemonic interpretation of his life and nation was forced to encounter an alternative, and thus "the black-and-white picture turns into a confusing texture composed of shades of gray" (Rabinowitz, 1994b).

Megged's attack on the critical intellectuals was followed by a long interview with Benny Morris in the largest circulation daily *Yediot Ahronot*, on December 16, 1994, under the title "They lied to us, they concealed the truth, they swept the facts under the carpet". In this interview Morris argued that the common beliefs of the Israeli public about the 1948 war were the result of a deliberate deceit, in which the facts of mass deportations and massacres were suppressed.

The course of the debate on the creation of Israel lends some credence to Morris's severe accusation. It seems that affirmative scholars often neglected to publish unpleasant facts they uncovered in official archives, and acknowledged them only when their critical opponents made further denials impossible. Even Shapira, a staunch defender of the affirmative narratives covering Israel's creation, admitted that many establishment historians, who took part in the 1948 War (often referred to as the War of Independence) and served later in the Israeli army's history unit, imposed self-censorship on themselves when confronted with compromising material in the archives. Shapira explained this by their feeling that the publication of sensitive documents, such as orders concerning the expulsion of Palestinians from their native villages, might be harmful to the public image of the Zionist project (Shapira, 1995).

As a second line of defense, when forced to acknowledge unpalatable facts, affirmative historians tended to argue that the critical scholars who published them distorted their meaning. Shapira contended for instance, that critical scholars, as she called them, New Historians, ignored the Palestinian rejection of the partition of Palestine in 1948 and the aggressive designs of the Arabs in the outbreak of the 1948 War of Independence. Instead, she pointed out, critical scholars portrayed Israel with a power and strength that were gained only much later (Shapira, 1995).

4. Tough Words and Powerful Passions

Even though the tone of this debate is fierce and the battle lines are drawn rather clearly, one also has to recognize that neither of the camps speaks in only one voice. For instance, while Megged opposed pluralism in historical scholarship on Israel, Shapira explicitly welcomed it as legitimate and enriching (Shapira, 1995, 1999). Largely, however, one can say that Israel's affirmative intellectuals are intentionalists. They focus on the soul-searching which accompanied the settlement practices of the Zionist founders of the state, emphasize the pure intentions of those fighting in defense of the nation and seek to justify the deeds of the latter by their self-conception as vulnerable and exposed to a threat looming over the nation from a hostile other. In contrast, critical intellectuals tend to be consequentialists; they are interested in long-term effects and outcomes. As the critical sociologist Gershon Shafir has pointed out:

Zionist historiography focused its research on the ideology. Thus it generated debate only on the good intentions of the immigrants, but neglected the actual consequences of the Zionist settlement policy. The results of this neglect, which may have been inevitable, haunted the [Zionist] movement throughout its history (Shafir, 1995).

Evidently, the aim of critical intellectuals is to undermine affirmative visions of the national past, which, so they claim, have been upheld by academics in conjunction with the political elite of the Jewish state in order to infuse the Israeli-Jewish collective with a narrow-minded national pride and relieve it from responsibility for the suffering imposed on the Palestinians.

One indication of the fact that the debate on Israel's creation encompasses deep-reaching currents of self-reflection is its extraordinary longevity. In August and September 2001, after seven years of debate in the press, passionate exchanges still fill entire pages in the newspapers, especially in the *Ha'aretz Magazine* (Karpel, 2001; Livneh, 2001). In fact, one of the most recent stages in this public debate again provides testimony to the highly charged nature of the debate. In a lengthy interview in *Ha'aretz,* Amnon Rubinstein, a professor of constitutional law, who in the past served as Minister of Education and who, by all accounts, is a liberal and levelheaded intellectual, attacks a whole series of critical scholars for being anti-Israeli (Karpel, 2001). In particular, he takes issue with an article published by Adi Ophir and Ariella Azoulai at the occasion of the centennial of the first Zionist Congress, which depicts Israel as conducting a form of military colonialism that no longer exists in Europe. Rubinstein calls Ophir and Azoulai's stance "Neo-Stürmerian", thus comparing their views to those of neo-Nazis. Though Rubinstein later apologized in print for using this expression, it is of course precisely slips of this kind that reveal the fierce emotions with which this debate is charged (Rubinstein, 2001).

On another occasion a few years earlier, Rubinstein (1997) had pointed to the threat to the "soul of Zionism" that he discerned in the work of the critical intellectuals. He compared their attack on the Zionist movement to that launched by ultra-Orthodox groups and accused critics of Zionism of neglecting the ubiquitous presence of anti-Semitism and underestimating the force of the "Jewish national will to life."

In fact, from the middle of the nineteen-nineties to today, critical intellectuals have attacked all established truths and violated every possible taboo concerning the creation of Israel, thereby provoking their affirmative opponents to use strong-worded replies and accusations. As mentioned above, critical sociologists and historians argued that the Zionist settlement in Palestine constituted a colonialist enterprise rather than an ingathering of exiles (Karpel, 1996, Kimmerling, 1999; Pappé, 2001). Repeatedly they have made the argument that during the 1948 War Israel drove out the Palestinians by following a more or less systematic policy of ethnic cleansing (Pappé, 1999a; Kimmerling 2000; Levy 2000). In this fashion they have drawn attention to the fact that 1948 was not only a constructive moment of state-creation or creation, but simultaneously also a date that signifies loss and destruction, and that entered the Palestinian national consciousness as *al nakba*, that is, as "the catastrophe". Thus, critical scholars claim, one can no longer refer to the 1948 war innocently as the War of Liberation or the War of Independence, as is usually done in Israeli parlance. In fact, the critical anthropologist Danny Rabinowitz supported the establishment of an official day of commemoration to mark the suffering inflicted on the Palestinians in the course of the creation of the State of Israel, a proposal that particularly incensed writer Aharon Megged in the early days of the debate (Rabinowitz, 1994a, cf. Megged, 1994).

For the critical scholars Zionism is not the highly moral, redemptive and peace-seeking movement that it pretends to be. They deny Zionism the pure motive of providing a safe haven for persecuted Jews from all over the world. Yosef Grodzinsky (1995) has argued, for instance, that rather than coming to Palestine out of their own free will after surviving the Holocaust, some of those who emigrated from displaced persons camps in Europe were recruited by brutal means by Zionist emissaries. Moreover, critical scholars claim that the Israeli political system cannot be regarded as the only democracy in the Middle East, embroiled in continuous warfare only because it is misunderstood, threatened and attacked by vicious neighbors. Instead, they depict Zionism as a cynical, violent, colonial and belligerent force and Israel as a militaristic, undemocratic and oppressive society. Indeed, there seems to be nothing that can be said in Israel's favor from this critical vantage point.

It is not surprising that this comprehensive moral devaluation of

Zionism and Israel that is the combined product of the work of those critical scholars has hit a raw nerve and led to strongly worded responses from affirmative academics, journalists and politicians. In a widely reviewed book devoted to the refutation of the claims of critical scholars, Ephraim Karsh, an expatriate Israeli working at King's College London, has accused critical scholars of trimming and twisting their facts, and of pretending to have discovered scandalous new data when in fact they were but recycling old ones. Karsh, an academic who belongs to the younger generation of affirmative academics, joins others who have accused critical scholars of scheming, lying and fabricating history in the service of an anti-Zionist or even anti-Israeli agenda (Sadeh, 1997; Siwan, 1997; Tevet, 1999; cf. Karsh 1997; Pappé 1999b).

5. Back to School

Recently the focus of the debate has shifted and its scope as well as its audience have widened. From a local debate it has turned into an international one. Arab intellectuals have begun to take note of the work of the critical scholars, (Said, 1998; Sid-Ahmed, 1999; cf. Segev 2000), while widely-read columnists, such as Jonathan Mahler (1997) Walter Laqueur (1998), Hillel Halkin (1999) and Bernard Avishai (2000), have commented on various aspects of the controversy in American periodicals ranging from *Lingua Franca* to *Commentary*.

Moreover, the debate no longer turns only on the myths, facts or stories of creation *per se*, but to a large extent addresses their influence on the minds of the young, that is, the way in which narratives of Israel's creation are transmitted to the next generation in Israeli schoolbooks. Since 1999 the representation of crucial moments of Israeli history in textbooks has been widely discussed in the press. Obviously, schoolbooks increasingly moved into the center of the debate on the origins of Israel, because their pages are the medium for both popularizing historical scholarship and disseminating national myths (Kim, 2001; Rotem 2001). There also is no doubt that some of the increasing ferociousness of the debate on Israel's creation has to be explained by the affirmative intellectuals' fears that critical views may gain the upper hand in the education of the young.

One typical *cause célèbre* is Tel Aviv University historian's Eyal

Naveh's ninth-grade ministry-approved history textbook *The Twentieth Century*. It states that the Jewish forces prevailed in 1948 because they were superior to the Arab forces in terms of planning, organization and equipment, as well as in numbers of trained soldiers. This explanation of a military victory may seem non-controversial, were it not for the fact that it contradicts the popular view, affirmed by more traditional intellectuals, that Israel's 1948 victory over the invading Arab armies was a kind of miracle or a result of superhuman heroism in which the few defeated the many. In fact, earlier schoolbooks did not give figures for trained soldiers. Instead they explained, as did a book of 1984, that in 1948 the Jewish community numbered 650,000 while the Arab states numbered 40 million (Bronner, 1999). Thus, rather surprisingly, Naveh found himself in the middle of a major media scandal, with many of the "usual suspects," such as Amnon Rubinstein and Aharon Megged, joining in a chorus of condemnations (Aloni, 1999; Bartal, 1999; Baumel, 1999, Briman, 1999; Megged, 1999; Rubinstein, 1999; Sa'ar, 1999a; Sa'ar 1999b; Segev, 1999; Yogev, 1999; Zand 1999).

In November 2000, the Knesset Education and Culture Committee decided to withdraw approval from another recently written history textbook, *A World In Change*, claiming that it misrepresents or ignores significant events in Zionist history. As Avirama Golan reported for *Ha'aretz*, "some committee members... suspected that the textbook had been influenced... by the thinking of the "New Historians" (Golan, 2000). As Golan explains, the move to deny official approval to this book was initiated by Yoram Hazony, head of the Shalem Center, a right-wing Jerusalem think-tank. Hazony, who holds a doctorate in political philosophy from Rutgers University, is a former aide to Benjamin Netanyahu. Together with other authors, he published a booklet that criticized *A World In Change*, among other things, for lacking photographs of major icons of Zionist historiography, such as David Ben Gurion, one of the state's founders and the first Prime Minister of Israel (Golan, 1999). Moreover, Hazony pointed the finger at planners of a new curriculum, which integrated the study Jewish history and the study of world history rather than keeping them separate, blaming them for "de-Judaizing" Israeli schools. Hazony directed his attack not only at intellectuals and educators who are outspoken critics of Israel's political myths, but also at a large number of mainstream scholars, who by no means can be seen as associated with post-Zionism or the New Historians (Eldar 2000a; Neuberger, 2000). In turn, Hazony has been accused by his opponents of McCarthyism and of being a Kahanist, i.e. having racist and extremely right wing, anti-democratic sympathies (Eldar, 2000b; Karpin, 2000).

As we can see, the scope and topics of the debate on Israel's creation may change, but its emotional and verbal ferocity stays the same. Since the debate's beginning in the middle of the nineties, affirmative intellectuals see themselves continually on the defensive, and perhaps rightly so. Despite the recent interference in history textbooks, it seems unlikely that the old heroic narratives on Israel's early history can be salvaged. They have crumbled under the onslaught of critical scholarship. For more sophisticated affirmative scholars like Anita Shapira this may not be much of a loss. From the very beginning of the debate she claimed that critical historians and social scientists erroneously targeted affirmative scholarship, while in fact many of the myths and distortions they criticized were to be found in textbooks only, but not in the scholarship of the affirmative historians. For others, however, the unmaking of myths seems to raise the specter of national disintegration, fragmentation, and despair. In August 2000, Zalman Shoval, former Israeli ambassador to the US, even warned delegates to a B'nai B'rith International Convention in Washington that the New Historians were "poisoning the minds of the younger generation" (B'nai B'rith, 2000). This, of course, was the accusation for which Socrates was sentenced to death in ancient Athens, more than two millennia ago.

6. All You Need is Love

It is interesting to note that in one way or another, affirmative academics, journalists and politicians tend to regard the critique of the myths of Israel's creation as undermining Israel's ability or will to exist as a collective. As the critical historian Gabriel Peterberg (1994) has perceptively remarked, those who interpret this conflict from an angle which differs from that of the Zionist actors are accused of completely negating the existence of the State. Indeed, affirmative intellectuals often respond to the devaluing critique voiced by critical scholars with the claim that an attack on the innocent, ideal and heroic self-image of Israel's creation forebodes a death of some kind and can bring about an end of the communal will to survive, instigating a national collapse.

The collective self-image of Israel has to be kept untainted, it appears, or otherwise the Jewish state will be annihilated.

This dual link between purity and strength on the one hand and impurity (or sin?) and death on the other is puzzling. It raises a host of questions concerning the emotional sensitivities, vulnerabilities and injuries at stake in the debate, for which a psychoanalytic perspective may be appropriate. Admittedly, extra-clinical applications of psychoanalytic categories of any kind are beset by a host of methodological problems. It is, of course, highly problematic to analyze public utterances of journalists, historians and social scientists by means of therapeutic concepts that were developed in and for the distinctly private realm of clinical practice, and which even within the four walls of the consulting room are highly precarious. But as has also been demonstrated repeatedly, all methodologies in the human sciences can be shown to be fundamentally problematic or flawed in one sense or another. In fact, when conducted in an abstract, general manner, methodological arguments resemble futile and somewhat obsessive attempts to pack and unpack one's suitcase in order to fill it in an ideal way while folding one's clothes without crumpling them.

The psychoanalytic inquiry into the public debate on Israel's creation undertaken here can thus be taken as a short journey, embarked upon in full awareness of the fact that some of the clothes one brings along for such a ride are bound to be inadequate for the weather conditions one encounters, while others will look rather wrinkled by the time one reaches one's destination. One can still claim that one has packed in a manner that is appropriate for the voyage, however, if one finds oneself dressed reasonably well on most occasions and is able to see most attractions without having to freeze or sweat too much. According to this criterion one can say, then, that the methodological equipment is good enough for this journey, if the psychoanalytic discussion provided here enriches our understanding of the emotional dynamics underlying the public debate on Israel's creation by pointing to dimensions of meaning and causally relevant factors that otherwise may have gone unnoticed.

First, let us cover the basics: a psychoanalytic perspective may be said to be relevant here since national identity is an emotional matter; it evokes strong und unexpected feelings of familiarity among strangers. People who have never met may share a feeling of closeness and affinity with each other simply because they are members of the same nation. This primary hold of national consciousness over the minds of people and its main power as a social force comes from the domain of the passions; it has to do with love. Of course, the function and dynamics of national consciousness should not be reduced to psychology and explained by unconscious factors. They are not wholly explicable by reference to feelings of belonging and the search for identity. Members of a nation use their collective identity also strategically, as an economic, cultural or political criterion of inclusion and exclusion, to gain advantages of one kind or the other, and to establish social hierarchies. Nevertheless, theories that do not take note of the deep emotional roots and affective quality of nationalism fail to attribute the appropriate significance to the quest for relatedness, collective identity and self-esteem. But even those historians and social theorists who acknowledge that nationalism involves an intense and passionate longing for attachment and association with others who are conceived as similar to oneself, often do not know what to say about this yearning. Instead, there is a general tendency in history and the social sciences to elaborate on nationalism and ethnic conflict from cognitive, economic, political, and cultural perspectives which have little to offer on the passions involved. As Thomas Scheff (1994) rightly notes: "Descriptions of nationalist movements note the passion, indeed the very pages crackle with it. But these descriptions do little to conceptualize, analyze, or interpret it" (p. 18).

How, then, can one interpret nationalism from a psychoanalytic point of view? Undoubtedly, nationalism or national identity forge emotional bonds with others because they are imagined to be akin to oneself. Thus, from a psychoanalytic perspective, the form of love and dynamic of passion at issue here can be defined as being of a *narcissistic* type. As Freud pointed out, the narcissistic choice of a love object leads a person to love "(a) what he himself is (i.e. himself), (b) what he himself was, (c) what he himself would like to be, (d) someone who was once part of himself" (Freud, 1914, p. 90). Ultimately, narcissists are only capable of loving others whom they can experience as being in some fundamental way the same as themselves or as ideal and idealizing mirrors of themselves.

Heinz Kohut, perhaps more than any other psychoanalyst, has developed a framework that addresses issues of narcissism. According to him, all individuals partake in some kind of collective narcissism, for without it they cannot define their identity and gain self-respect in a social and cultural vacuum. They always constitute themselves in an inter-subjective space in which narcissism comes into play when people identify with real and imagined others and are accepted and recognized by them. Applying this psycho-political perspective to the collective narcissism involved in national identity and nationalism, some of its forms may be said to give rise to a feeling of love that is akin to *infatuation*, a term that has not been used by Kohut and is introduced here into his frame of analysis.

Nationalist infatuation with the Fatherland or with one's own nation can serve to cover up feelings of individual or collective impurity and vulnerability by means of shared fantasies of past or present grandeur and illusions of belonging to an omnipotent, superior, morally special and historically unique state or nation. It reduces or eliminates boundaries between individuals of the same nation and seeks to establish a morally perfect union among them, while legitimizing the exclusion, debasement or persecution of others, who may be depicted as base and corrupt, but also as threatening and hostile.

As Kohut (1972) explains, for those who are excessively in love with their individual or collective self, infatuated as it were, mere otherness can be an offense that deserves to be punished. Otherness cannot really be tolerated by such narcissism, since it signifies a boundary and a limit to the power and purity of the national collective. However, as E. P. Thompson (1982) has rightly pointed out: "We cannot define who 'we' are without also defining 'them' — those who are not 'us.' Throughout history, as bonding has gone on and as identities have changed, the Other has been necessary in this process. Rome required barbarians, Christendom required pagans, Protestant and Catholic Europe required each other" (pp. 18-19). While serving as a creation of love among "us," collective self-infatuation inevitably leads to rage against "them," that is, against those who fail to be part of "us" because they differ in some significant way, such as race, language or religion, from "us," and against all those who refuse to mirror "our" moral and historical distinction and greatness. According to Kohut it is the narcissistic need to cover up an inner vulnerability, which explains the eruption of boundless rage against those who refuse to be conquered by the pathologically disturbed narcissist, and fail to serve as mirrors of success or objects of fusion. Kohut (1972) argues that there is "a specific psychological flavor" to narcissistic rage, which differentiates it from other forms of aggression:

> The narcissistically injured... cannot rest until he has blotted out a vaguely experienced offender who dared to oppose him, to disagree with him, or to outshine him.... The enemy... who calls forth the... rage of the narcissistic vulnerable is seen by him not as an autonomous source of impulses, but as *a flaw in a narcissistically perceived reality*. He is a recalcitrant part of an expanded self over which he expects to exercise full control and whose mere independence or otherness is an offense (pp. 385-6, emphasis in the original).

Collective self-infatuation, as defined here, leads to rage against all dissent and difference. This is but the other side of exaggerated self-love, self-reference, self-absorption, self-idealization and self-aggrandizement, a facade which serves to hide from oneself as well as from others unconscious but strong anxieties and fears that have to do with deep-seated feelings of vulnerability, fragmentation, emptiness and worthlessness. As Kohut (1971) elaborates in his analysis of individual narcissism, it is in order to escape from the latter, unbearable affects that they are repressed into the unconscious, for they would cause insufferable psychic pain. But in order to keep them stowed away safely, self-infatuated narcissists have to subordinate, appropriate or annihilate all others, since otherness might be threatening. The aim of such narcissists is to make all others part of their own self in order to use them as "mirrors" who provide them with the feeling of worth that they seek, or to eliminate them if they refuse to do so.

7. Mirror, mirror on the wall...

Applying this Kohutian approach to the Israeli debate, one may say, perhaps, that the critical scholars' main sin is their refusal to mirror the imagined grandiosity of their nation. Alternatively, one could argue that they hold up a looking glass that, instead of mirroring Israel's imagined beauty, shows its ugly features. Evidently, such devaluation inflicts substantial narcissistic wounds and is experienced as severely threatening by those who regard the collective self as highly vulnerable.

Obviously, Israel's creation involved experiences of being isolated, fragmented, weak and vulnerable in the face of overwhelming

Arab enemies, whatever the historical reality was in numbers of trained soldiers during the 1948 war. Only three years after the end of the Second World War and the Holocaust, the Jewish community in Palestine was certainly marked by strong fears of death. Then came the continuous narcissistic injury inflicted upon the Israeli collective by the refusal of its Arab neighbors to publicly and officially recognize Israel as a sovereign nation state during the first three decades of existence (Moses, 1982).

As long as Israel's enemies refused recognition, there was no internal debate on the creation of the Jewish state. But almost immediately after recognition from the Palestinians was gained within the terms of the Oslo agreements in 1993, as part of a process of territorial compromise and historical reconciliation, Israel's myths of creation became a subject of contention in the Israeli press. In many ways, it seems that only international and regional recognition, i.e. an external mirroring that allayed deep-seated existential anxieties and fears of extinction, allowed the debate on Israel's founding to emerge from within.

The narcissistic rage with which affirmative intellectuals like Megged countered critical voices becomes more understandable when one notes the way in which he fused his personal identity and pride with that of the Zionist collective. Perhaps, this fusion is the reason that he experienced the refusal of the critical scholars to mirror in their work the collective self-infatuation of the founders, as the infliction of a severe narcissistic wound, almost as annihilating. Such responses show that Israel's collective self is held together at least in part by grandiose fantasies that affirmative academics and thinkers have much difficulty in abandoning.

This also comes to the fore in the heated reactions to Naveh's textbook, which no longer presents the Israeli victory of 1948 as one of a David against a Goliath. Such anger is difficult to understand, unless it is seen as a reaction to anxieties triggered by what is experienced as a threat of fragmentation or disintegration. Of course, such anxieties are reinforced in a period of increasing individualization, privatization and globalization, which are all factors that constitute further attacks on group cohesion. Finally, the Second *Intifada* further reinforced fears of death and anxieties of a breakup of the Jewish state. Thus, in the face of the violence of the Second *Intifada* many critical voices have become silent again. Even Chief Justice Aharon Barak, undoubtedly a leading member of the Israeli elite, finds himself forced to deny in public pronouncements that a judicial decision, in which equal legal protection was accorded to Arabs, could be considered post-Zionist (Livneh, 2001; Lahav, 2001).

As we see, at present the founders and affirmative historians, intellectuals, and politicians experience any critique of established Zionist myths and practices as threatening decline and decay. This reaction may be a result of the diminishing external, regional and international, mirroring, which had allowed the surfacing of internal ambivalences concerning Israel's creation in the first place. It seems that the possibility of conducting an internal public debate on the state's origins is at least to some extent contingent upon feelings of safety and acceptance that have to be fueled from without, such as happened in the wake of the Oslo agreements.

At the same time, the anxieties evoked by the work of the critical scholars highlights one of the major weaknesses of their stance, in terms of the internal emotional dynamics of the Israeli debate. While the critical discourse on Israel's founding has done much to shatter myths that served to promote collective self-infatuation, the comprehensively devaluing tendency and disdainful tone of the critical scholars is not conducive to a collective self-appreciation that could serve as an alternative to self-infatuation.

The contours of such an alternative can be discerned in Kohut's work. He has stressed in an individual context that ideals, principles, and fantasies of grandiosity can become integrated into a self in ways that lead to enjoyment without devaluating others. This form of self-valuation does not hinge on the denigration of those who differ in one way or another from the self and, in contrast to infatuation, involves a calm and levelheaded form of love that is put here under the heading of *self-appreciation*, again a term that is not part of Kohut's vocabulary. Kohut calls this type of self-love "a higher form of narcissism," arguing that it leads to an "outlook on life to which the Romans referred as living *sub specie aeternitatis,*" involving "a quiet pride," deriving from one's special ability to accept one's own finitude, mortality and transience. According to Kohut, by valuing one's self in this fashion one may develop artistic creativity, a sense of humor, wisdom and an empathy with others, based on the recognition that the feelings of others are similar to one's own. Conspicuous in such instances of narcissism, Kohut claims, "is a non-isolated, creative superiority which judges and admonishes with quiet assurance." Kohut (1966) holds this type of narcissism in high esteem; as he comments: "I have little doubt that those who are able to achieve this ultimate attitude toward life do so on the strength of a new, expanded, transformed narcissism" (p. 81).

Transposing Kohut's approach from the individual to the nation, it is thus possible to speak of a narcissistic satisfaction provided by the feeling of belonging to a particular country or national collective, which does not necessarily have to be built on unconscious anxieties of disintegration, fragmentation, and death. Hence this form of narcissism does not have to lead to an exaggerated idealization of one's collective self and the concomitant exclusion, discrimination or subordination of others, as well as the acceptance of oppression within the collective. There are thus two sides to self-appreciation. While it is not to be exclusionist and oppressive towards others, it also must allow for an appreciation of the achievements, cultural creativity, sophistication, and enlightenment of one's own collective.

Though the critical scholars have managed to undermine some of the self-idealizations that are necessary for self-infatuation, in itself a devaluation of the Israeli or Zionist collective self-image does not and cannot contribute to the "quiet pride" which Kohut associates with appreciative forms of narcissism. While the public discourse of the affirmative scholars tends to demonize Israel's enemies of 1948, critical scholars usually depict them as passive victims of Zionist aggression and manipulation; demonizing the Israeli or Zionist leadership instead of the Arabs. Thus, the current critical positions on the founding of Israel often constitute only a negative to which affirmative narratives provided the positive, rather than transgressing beyond the division of the world into evil monsters and hapless victims.

Of course, it is highly doubtful that a self-appreciative collective narcissism can at all evolve when a nation feels under a severe threat, such as is the case during the Second *Intifada*. These conditions again raise the specter of disintegration and annihilation, whatever their historical origins and military reality may be. But even at some future stage, in which calmer reflection may again become possible, it is unlikely that collective self-appreciation can replace self-infatuation if intellectuals on both sides, Zionist Jews as well as Palestinian Arabs, will not encourage their nations to see themselves as active protagonists who exercise at least partial control over the historical processes and events in which they take part. If one regards the dynamics of the public debate on Israel's creation as one that is charged with narcissistic passions, it is obvious that it will not do to counter grandiose mythological moments of founding, heroic self-images, and pure victimhood, by declaring that Israel has been born in sin. Instead, it may be more helpful to develop narratives that acknowledge the errors and evil that both sides have committed, and of which they ought to be ashamed, but also to recognize the achievements of which they can be proud.

To conclude, this essay does not seek to draw on psychoanalysis in order to issue a call for reconciliation instead of critique. Evidently, all critiques contains an aggressive element, but, relying once more on Kohut, one can distinguish two basic forms of aggression: the types of aggression that Kohut has called "elemental" and "mature" belong to one category, while "narcissistic rage" belongs to the other. Kohut (1977) identifies elemental aggression with the beginning of life, holding it to be necessary for the establishment, development, and maintenance of a rudimentary self vis-à-vis others. In contrast, he speaks of mature aggression as one of the results of a successful analysis, in which narcissistic rage has been superseded (Kohut, 1972). Characteristic of both is that they are nondestructive, i.e. that while they may serve as means of delineation and assertion of one self against another and provide the emotional charge for the criticism of others, they do not seek to eliminate their object. Narcissistic rage, in contrast, seeks to wipe out all difference; it is not only aggressive but destructive. Based on this Kohutian distinction, the message of this essay is not that critique and controversy should be abandoned. Rather, its moral is that aggression may be constructive, but that it can be so only if it entails the recognition and at least some appreciation of one's Others, that is, one's victims, opponents and enemies, rather than seeking their destruction. For only thus can one hope that they will respond with nondestructive, productive aggression, both on an intellectual or political level, rather than with the blind, annihilationist force of narcissistic rage.

References

Aloni, N. (1999). Gentlemen, history is stormy. *Ha'aretz*, 10 December [Hebrew].

Anderson, B. (1991). *Imagined Communities: Reflections on the Origin and Spread of Nationalism*. London: Verso.

Avishai, B. (2000). Post-Zionist Israel. *The American Prospect*, 11 (12), May 8.

Bartal, I. (1999). "Old-new history." *Ha'aretz*, 21 October [Hebrew].

Baumel, A. (1999). A pluralist view, not a myth-destroyer. 15 December, *Ha'aretz Book Review Supplement* [Hebrew].

Beit-Hallahmi, B. (1993). *Original Sins: Reflections on the History of Zionism and Israel*. New York: Interlink.

Beit-Hallahmi, B. (2002). Political and literary answers to some "Jewish Question": Proust, Joyce, Freud, and Herzl. In this volume.

B'nai B'rith News (2000). http://bnaibrith.org/pr/zalman082900.html, downloaded 21/06/01.

Briman, R. (1999). Cut post-Zionist education. *Ha'aretz*, 31 August [Hebrew].

Bronner, E. (1999). In Israel, new grade school texts for history replace myths with facts. *New York Times,* August 14.

Brunner, J. (1997/98). Pride and memory: Nationalism, narcissism and the historians' debates in Germany and Israel. *History and Memory, 9,* 256-300.

Eldar, A. (2000a). Education and lies: Who took over the history books? *Ha'aretz,* 24 August [Hebrew].

Eldar, A. (2000b). Dr. Hasony's spiritual leader. *Ha'aretz,* 14 September [Hebrew].

Freud, S. (1914). On narcissism: An introduction. In the *Standard Edition of the Complete Psychological Works of Sigmund Freud.* Vol. 14, 73-102. London: Hogarth Press

Gans, C. (2001). Historical rights: The evaluation of nationalist claims to sovereignty. *Political Theory,* 29, 58-79.

Golan, A. (2000). A lesson in how to turn people off Zionism. *Ha'aretz,* 30 November. Downloaded from the English Internet Edition 26/06/01.

Grodzinsky, Y. (1995). Something nevertheless is missing in this story. *Ha'aretz,* 3 May [Hebrew].

Halkin, H. (1999). Was Zionism unjust? *Commentary,* November.

Himmelfarb, G. (1987). *The New History and the Old: Critical Essays and Reappraisals.* Cambridge, MA.: Harvard University Press.

History and Memory, 1995. Vol. 7, no. 1. Special Issue: Israeli historiography revisited.

Karpel, D. (1995). The national camp. *Ha'aretz Magazine,* 9 June [Hebrew].

Karpel, D. (1996). Ready to pay the price. *Ha'aretz Magazine,* 9 February [Hebrew].

Karpel, D. (2001). Independent in the field. *Ha'aretz Magazine,* 20 July [Hebrew].

Karpin, M. (2000). On his record. *Ha'aretz Book Review Supplement,* 22 September. Downloaded from English Internet Edition, 26/06/01.

Karsh, E. (1996). *Fabricating Israeli History: The "New Historians".* London: Frank Cass.

Kim, H. (2001). The post-Zionist ghosts and Sharon and Livnat. *Ha'aretz,* 13 March [Hebrew].

Kimmerling, B. (2000). From the Haganah chronology. *Ha'aretz,* 16 May [Hebrew].

Kohut, H. (1966). Forms and transformations of narcissism. *Journal of the American Psychoanalytic Association, 14,* 243-272.

Kohut, H. (1971). *The Analysis of the Self.* New York: International Universities Press.

Kohut, H. (1972). Thoughts on narcissism and narcissistic rage. *The Psychoanalytic Study of the Child, 27,* 360-398.

Kohut, H. (1977). *The Restoration of the Self.* New York: International Universities Press.

Kohut, H. (1984). *How Does Analysis Cure?* Chicago: University of Chicago Press.

Kohut, H. (1985). *Self Psychology and the Humanities: Reflections on a New Psychoanalytic Approach.* New York: Norton.

Kohut, H. and. Wolf, E.S. (1986). The disorders of the self and their treatment: An outline. In A.P. Morrison. (Ed.). *Essential Papers on Narcissism.* New York: New York University Press.

Kol Ha'ir, (1995). Zionism: The battle for rating. 6 October [Hebrew].

Lahav, P. (2001). A "Jewish state... to be known as the State of Israel": Notes on Israeli legal historiography. *Law and History Review, 19,* 387-433.

Laqueur, W. (1998). Acute culture war in Israel. http://www.nzz.ch/english/background1998/background9806/bg980620/israel. downloaded 21/06/01.

Levy, G. (2000). Perhaps there was no other possibility; but why lie all these years? *Ha'aretz,* 1 November [Hebrew].

Livneh, N. (2001). The rise and fall of post-Zionism. *Ha'aretz Magazinet,* 14 September [Hebrew].

Mahler, J. (1997). Uprooting the past: Israel's new historians take a hard look at their nation's past. *Lingua Franca,* August.

Megged, A. (1994). The Israeli suicide impulse. *Ha'aretz Magazine,* 10 June [Hebrew].

Megged, A. (1999). Enlightened like the brightness of the sky. *Ha'aretz,* 14 September [Hebrew].

Morris, B. (1988). The new historiography: Israel confronts its past. *Tikkun,* Nov.-Dec.

Morris, B. (1997). I did a Zionist deed. *Ha'aretz,* 16 June [Hebrew].

Moses, R. (1982) The group self and the Arab-Israeli conflict. *International Journal of Psycho-Analysis,* 9, 55-64.

Neuberger, B. (2000). McCarthyism, Israel-style. *Ha'aretz Book Review Supplement,* 22 September. Downloaded from English Internet Edition, 26/06/01.

Pappé, I. (1994a). The influence of the Zionist ideology on Israeli historiography. *Davar Supplement,* 15 May [Hebrew].

Pappé, I. (1994b). A lesson in New History. *Ha'aretz Magazine,* 24 June [Hebrew].

Pappé, I. (1995). Critique and agenda: The post-Zionist scholars in Israel. *History and Memory,* 7, 66-90.

Pappé, I. (1999a). Touching a raw nerve. *Ha'aretz,* 15 September [Hebrew].

Pappé, I. (1999b). The tribunal of academe. *Ha'aretz,* 12 November [Hebrew].

Pappé, I. (2001). Zionism as a colonial movement. *Ha'aretz,* 20 May [Hebrew].

Peled, Y. (1999). The worried Zionists. *Theory and Criticism,* 15, 135-143 [Hebrew].

Penslar, J.D. (1995). Innovation and revisionism in Israeli historiography. *History and Memory,* 7, 125-146.

Peterberg, G. (1994). The Stalinist. *Ha'aretz Magazine,* 17 June [Hebrew].

Peri, Y. (1994). The withdrawal into the private gardens. *Davar Magazine,* 22 July [Hebrew].

Rabinowitz, D. (1994a). Israel's original sin. *Ha'aretz,* 10 April [Hebrew].

Rabinowitz, D. (1994b). A confusing texture composed of shades of gray. *Ha'aretz,* 15 June, [Hebrew].

Ram, U. (1994a). Post-Zionist ideology. *Ha'aretz,* 8 April [Hebrew].

Ram, U. (1994b). The post-Zionist debate: Five notes of clarification. *Davar Magazine.* 8 July [Hebrew].

Rotem, T. (2001). Always a political minister. *Ha'aretz,* 4 May [Hebrew].

Rubinstein, A. (1997). The revolution failed, Zionism succeeded. *Ha'aretz,* 10 June [Hebrew].

Rubinstein, A. (1999). Old history, but accurate. *Ha'aretz,* 30 September [Hebrew].

Rubinstein, A. (2001). I transgressed the prohibition. *Ha'aretz Magazine,* 3 August [Hebrew].

Sa'ar, R. (1999a). Who threatens the official in charge of the history curriculum? *Ha'aretz,* 13 September [Hebrew].

Sa'ar, R. (1999b). Threatening letters to the author the new grade nine history textbook. *Ha'aretz,* 14 September [Hebrew].

Sadeh, S. (1997). The indictment: Fabricating history. *Ha'aretz Magazine.* 2 May [Hebrew].

Said, E. (1998). New history, old ideas. *Al Ahram* 378, 21-27 May. http://www.ahram.org.eg/weekly/1998/378/pal2.htm, downloaded 21/06/01.

Samet, G. (1996). Culture and history. *Ha'aretz,* 9 February [Hebrew].

Scheff, T. (1994). Emotions and identity: A theory of ethnic nationalism. In C. Calhoun (Ed.), *Social Theory and the Politics of Identity.* Oxford: Blackwell.

Segev, T. (1999). Look what you did to my myth. *Ha'aretz,* 17 September [Hebrew].

Segev, T. (2000). Damascus against the New Historians. *Ha'aretz,* 7 January [Hebrew].

Shafir, G. (1995). The colonial question. *Ha'aretz,* 10 January [Hebrew].

Shapira, A. (1995). Politics and collective memory: The debate over the "New Historians" in Israel. *History and Memory,* 7, 9-40.

Shapira, A. (1999). The past is not a foreign country. *The New Republic*, 29 November.

Theory and Criticism: An Israeli Forum (1996). Issue no. 8 [Hebrew].

Sid-Ahmed, M. (1999) Israel's new historians. *Al-Ahram* 450, 7-13 October http://www.ahram.org.eg/weekly/1999/450/op3.htm, downloaded 21/06/01

Siwan, E. (1997). The New Historians and the promise that wasn't kept. *Ha'aretz Book Review Supplement*, 25 June [Hebrew].

Tevet, S. (1999). New Historians or political activists. *Ha'aretz Book Review Supplement*, 15 December. [Hebrew]

Thompson, E.P. (1982). *Beyond the Cold War*. London: Merlin.

Weitz, Y. (Ed.) (1997). *From Vision to Revision: A Hundred Years of the Historiography of Zionism*. Jerusalem: Zalman Shazar Center [Hebrew].

Yogev, E. (1999). Who is afraid of critical history? *Ha'aretz,* 6 September [Hebrew].

Zand, S. (1999). The cries of the hyenas and the silence of the lambs. *Ha'aretz,* 16 September [Hebrew].

Zuckerman, M. (2002) Towards a critical analysis of Israeli political culture. In this volume.

Acknowledgement

I wish to thank Pnina Lahav, Yoav Peled and Arnona Zahavi for their comments on earlier drafts.

Part II

Psychoanalytic Treatment in Historical and

Political Context

If in the first part of our volume, six of our contributors have used psychoanalysis as an inspiration and as a source of hypotheses for explaining history and culture in general, in Part II the object under investigation is the practice of psychoanalysis as a form of psychotherapy. This is what most often the term 'psychoanalysis' refers to in public discourse, especially in the mass media. In the following three chapters constituting Part II of this book, the practice of psychoanalysis as the "talking cure", developed by Sigmund Freud, is being examined in its social and cultural contexts.

What is very much in evidence here is the connection between modern, secular, psychotherapy and modern Western culture. If we are looking at Israeli society, there is a clear connection to European-oriented, more secular Israelis, those individuals who have experienced a weaker kind of patriarchy during childhood.

Psychoanalysis as a clinical practice traveled to Palestine in the 1920s and was established in the Jewish community there in the 1930s, when a psychoanalytic institute was founded in Jerusalem. Eran J. Rolnik describes the early reception of psychoanalysis into the Jewish community in Palestine and offers a fresh look into events in the first half of the twentieth century. Among the contributors to this book we find three leading members of the Israel Psychoanalytic Institute of today, the same Institute whose early history is portrayed in Chapter 7: Emanuel Berman, Yolanda Gampel, and the late Rafael Moses. What we find here in the two contributions by practicing psychoanalysts (and in the chapter by Moses in Part I) is the ability to listen to the unsaid and unheard; a sensitivity to emotions and anxieties below the surface, the hidden world of dreams and silent nightmares. Beyond the uncanny ability to listen, what is revealed in these chapters is a sober and courageous kind of psychoanalysis, which is ready to commit itself not only to the interpretation of politics, but to both social action and a public political stance.

Chapter 7

Psychoanalysis Moves to Palestine: Immigration, Integration and Reception

Eran J. Rolnik
Tel-Aviv University

Psychoanalysis as a clinical practice traveled to Palestine in the 1920s and became marginally established in the Jewish community there in the 1930s, when a psychoanalytic institute was founded in Jerusalem. Eran J. Rolnik offers a thorough historical examination of the encounter between psychoanalysis and Jewish Palestine, as the early stages of the reception of psychoanalysis into Jewish society in Palestine are portrayed and analyzed. We are offered a fresh look into events in the first half of the twentieth century and into the forces working for and against the reception of psychoanalytic ideas and practices. Tensions between Zionism and the Zionist movement, and the individualistic bias of psychoanalysis *qua* psychotherapy naturally came to the fore. This chapter is marked by both originality and erudition. What emerges is a rich and lively picture of life in the Jewish community of Palestine in the days before World War II, with a special emphasis on cultural developments. The difficult experiences of immigrants, who were actually refugees forced to leave their homelands are described touchingly, and all involved come to life with their hopes, fears, and dreams.

> "Last night I had a vivid dream of Jerusalem. But it was a mixture of Vienna Forest and Berchtesgaden. It seems that my imagination cannot reach any further then that."
> Anna Freud to Max Eitingon (Letter of May 11, 1934)

1. Introduction

Most of the material in this chapter was first presented in Vienna, and as some of the participants in the Vienna conference had come to Vienna from the shores of the Mediterranean I wish to take this opportunity and approach the history of psychoanalysis as a particular encounter between East and West, between Eastern and Western intellectual traditions. Such an admittedly Eurocentric perspective may find its justification in the emblematic location chosen by our Viennese hosts to facilitate introspection into the identity making of Israeli society and its conflicts.

The following text hardly qualifies as a definitive diachronic narration of the early history of psychoanalysis in Palestine. My aim is to offer a 'panopticum', a panoramic view of the building blocks, imageries and aphorisms, which contributed to shaping the transmission of the Freudian paradigm in Jewish Palestine, a place that, albeit remote from Europe, cannot be said to have been indifferent to Central, and Eastern, European intellectual traditions. In the final part of this paper I will try to integrate my account of the early history of psychoanalysis in Israel within the broader context of contemporary psychoanalytic, and historiographic discourse. This will also allow me to partially succumb to one of the greatest seductions of psychoanalysis, namely its applicability in historical research and the study of political conflicts (Toews, 1999; Esman 1998).

While working on this chapter I gradually became aware of the effect that the location of our conference might have on the text presented before you. Regardless of how much one knows about the life of the founder of psychoanalysis, his name still keeps claiming the place of a metaphor in one's mind. To talk about the history of psychoanalysis in a private house that was turned into a museum is to come as near as possible to that imaginary point where a person's life, Freud's private life, transcends the limits of his biography, thereby becoming a discipline, dissolving into metaphor, and turning into a language that is both public and private. Yet I need not tell the 'Freudian reader' that this 'imaginary' point constitutes the heart of the psychoanalytic endeavor (which dates back to Freud's self-analysis): to understand and communicate that which is most personal and private.

Some of the most recent contributions to the historicization of psychoanalysis concentrated on the trans-cultural impact of the psychoanalytic movement. It seems that ever since the teachings of Freud became, in the words of W.H. Auden, a "whole climate of opinion", it has become rewarding to juxtapose the history of psychoanalysis in various contexts with the intellectual history of groups and societies whose main endeavor was not identical to that of the psychoanalytic movement itself. For this reason, the historiography of psychoanalysis is not only concerned with the conceptual or institutional history of psychoanalysis in countries far remote from the German cultural sphere. While studying the history of psychoanalysis we uncover the anatomy and unfolding of social and political developments not necessarily at the center of any particular psychoanalytic discourse (Forrester, 1997). This natural tendency of psychoanalysis, to serve as both the object and the subject of contemporary historiography, has attracted much attention in post-modern scholarship. Jacques Derrida has termed it: 'The Freudian impression'; the mark left by the event that carries Freud's name, on every aspect of human activity and self-understanding (Derrida, 1998; Rolnik, 2001a).

The historiographic tension that arose out the attempts to study the rapid diffusion and acceptance of the psychoanalytic movement both within and outside its immediate Viennese context gains a particular significance in the case of our study. Vienna was after all home not only to the universalist Freud but also to Theodore Herzl, founder of modern political Zionism (Beit-Hallahmi, 2002). This is not to say that the two had much in common in terms of their intellectual and personal pursuits. On the contrary; this fact may serve to illustrate the varied directions and the manifold identities, which fin-de- siècle Vienna could give rise to, at least with regard to its Jews.

An observation made by William Osler in 1914 strikes a suitable opening chord if we wish to survey the history of the reception of psychoanalysis in Palestine. "In estimating the position of Israel in the human values", wrote Osler, "we must remember that the quest for righteousness is oriental, the quest for knowledge occidental" (cf. Gilman, 1993). Righteousness and its traditional counterpart, knowledge, figure as two recurring subtexts in the evolution of psychoanalysis. Historians still tend to perceive Freud's theory as caught midway between knowledge and belief, between technique and ethics (Rieff, 1979; Rolnik 2001b). However, if we divest Osler's righteousness-knowledge parable of its ethno-religious connotation it will not be too hard to extend it into a parallel equation, one in which knowledge signifies the individual and the private, whereas righteousness stands for imageries that are more collective and public. In the course of my paper I will have to return to this parable as it can accommodate some of the tensions and paradoxical developments that arise when we follow psychoanalysis in its journey to Jewish Palestine. Aphorisms such as this one point to direction in which we should look for the historical mechanisms that molded psychoanalysis and cast it into a mental environment whose pretext was, and perhaps still is, rather antagonistic to the secular, critical and individualistic essence of Freud's teachings. If pressed to state the main thesis of my contribution I would consider this last sentence to be the thrust of my argument.

2. The Authority of the Past

Traditionally Europe has always thought of itself as an intellectual construct more then a real geographical entity (Hobsbawm, 1997). This phenomenon is all the more relevant to Freud's Vienna which at the turn of the century still echoed the notion that Eastern Europe, perhaps even the Orient itself, began at the eastern exit from Vienna. From Vienna one could look any which way one chose. Being of Jewish descent in late nineteenth century Vienna, with its rising anti-Semitism, had made it all the more necessary to look both directions, east and West, in search of identity.

But before we try to examine the conditions under which two such opposing historical phenomena such as psychoanalysis and Zionism could coexist, at least in the minds of some, let us take into account the broader social context in which psychoanalysis came into this world. One should not fail to notice the role it played in safeguarding the principle of intellectual honesty from institutional dishonesty, for which the Viennese political environment at the turn of the nineteenth century stood. The wish to be true to oneself, which became one of the dominant issues of the day, found its expression in the political discourse but also in the scientific and literary discourse of Vienna. And we note in passing that the ideal of complete honesty, this moral imperative which shaped the Viennese intellectual discourse of the day, has found its expression in the fundamental rule of psychoanalytic technique, thereby becoming a source of analytic self knowledge: 'Say anything that comes to your mind'.

From its first years onward, psychoanalytic theory has often been interpreted as an expression of the human need to lay bare the soul's unconscious experiential foundations. And it was, in fact, in light of such foundations that Freud ascribed such weight to both the collective human past and the past of every individual. It was all the more popular among the champions of Jewish-national particularism, who considered the new discipline as a fusion of radicalism and tradition and tried to enlist it for their own political ends. The relation of Jewish particularism to the universalism of European Enlightenment here also gained expression when Freud's early positivist ideas were welcomed as a form of quasi scientific support for Zionism's romantic endeavor of reconstructing a unified (and unifying) national past.

A look at the reception of psychoanalysis in pre-revolutionary Russia is here useful, keeping in mind that the basis for such a shift in focus away from Palestine lies in the sociocultural composition of the *Yishuv*, the Jewish community in pre-1948 Palestine. More specifically, that reception offers a wider context for understanding the ideological-cultural discourse framing the debate over psychoanalytic ideas in Palestine during the period.

Dubbed the "Second *Aliya*" and "Third *Aliya*" by Zionist historiographers, the double wave of Jewish immigration to Palestine following the century's turn, first between 1905 and 1914, then between 1918 and 1923, contributed in a decisive way to the ideological foundations of the Jewish immigrant community of Palestine under the British mandate (1918-1948). One of the chief accomplishments of those who immigrated, whose views in many respects represented those of the Russian intelligentsia, was the transformation of utopian-egalitarian ideas and socialist myths from Eastern Europe into concrete schemas for action for the Zionist movement. To be sure, the first encounter between psychoanalysis and the *Yishuv* cannot be considered a precise mirroring of the encounter between psychoanalytic theory and Russian Marxism. It did, however, bear the most prominent markers of that theory's Russian reception. The revolutionary impulses released by the advent of psychoanalytic theory, along with the possibilities at work in psychoanalysis as both Kulturwissenschaft and "healer of sick souls," rendered the psychoanalytic movement a welcome element in the discourse of many young communists, whose conceptual world offered space for a notion of "soul" not bound to class or nationality (Miller, 1998; Etkind, 1997; Rice, 1993).

In this manner, psychoanalytic therapy was granted a place of honor, as a way to liberate victims of bourgeois society's repressive mechanisms from their past-centered angst. Even after the October Revolution, as long as it was possible to uphold the analogy between individual mechanisms of repression and those of bourgeois society, revolutionaries such as Trotsky and Joffe fashioned psychoanalysis into a scientific-ideological party instrument, hoping to reconcile psychoanalysis with Pavlovian physiology (Knei-Paz, 1978; Etkind, 1994).

Despite the dominant political climate, Russian psychoanalysts tried to maintain their scientific weltanschauung with all means at their disposal. As late as 1927 and preceding his emigration to Berlin, Mosche Wulff, head of the Russian Psychoanalytic Association, managed to complete his study of the sexual life of Moscow's bus and streetcar conductors (Wulff, 1928; Etkind, 1997), perhaps a final token of the strenuous effort by Russian psychoanalysts to keep a place in post-revolutionary, proletarian discourse, hence to legitimate their existence. It is doubtful, however, that Wulff's dynamic psychoanalytic explanations for the potency problems in the group under study were at all adequate to the task of bridging the gap that now yawned between Marxist dialectics and Freud's theory of drives (Kloocke, 1995; Jaffe, 1966).

In the following years, the concept of the "unconscious" was treated with contempt, soon qualifying as hostile to the regime. The Marxist consciousness was no longer ready to tolerate a theory representing human beings as subject to the laws of an unconscious, past-mediated inner world (Miller, 1990). In any case, as "Freudian man" came to reveal his authentic features, the impossibility of aligning them with socialist ameliorative ideals became more apparent. Ever more clearly, principles of societal openness, sharpened awareness, and ideological flexibility were making way for a stress on the dominance of unconscious human drives, the human character thus being nigh-inalterable, in an essential manner. In 1932, Alexander Luria, the well-known neuropsychologist still serving as secretary of the Russian

Psychoanalytic Association, turned against Freud's "bourgeois psychology". In doing so, he categorically rejected both Freud's pessimism about social change and the central role psychoanalysis attributed to the irrational aspects of human nature (Solms, 2000; Luria, 1978). Still, the core of this conflict lay in diverging approaches to the past: psychoanalysts stressed the past's role in structuring the present and its interpretation; a basic premise of the Marxist dialectic was construction of a post-revolutionary, socialist society whose past either did not exist or was insignificant.

In the historiography of the Palestinian Jewish émigré society, we find frequent discussions of the tension between, on the one hand, the cultural heritage and past of individual immigrants and, on the other hand, the tendency of Zionist ideology to construct a collective past. From the onset of political Zionism onward, the need to build a society with a fixed, distinct identity meant establishing a Zionist meta-narrative: a narrative capable of embracing and overshadowing manifold historical experiences, cultural identities, and ethnic sensibilities, which would still tend to emerge from underneath the surface. As is possible to observe in national movements in general, the Zionist movement developed an instrumental relation to the past, attempting to give its followers the impression of a collective present and future through the construction of a unitary collective-mythological past (Hobsbawm, 1990; Wistrich & Ohana, 1995; Even Zohar, 1990; Sternhell, 1986). The image of the Jewish immigrant to Palestine itself served this purpose: the image was of a newcomer who had freed himself from the chains of an oppressive past, one presented in terms that were part historical part abstract and mythic, and who could thus henceforth determine his own fate.

3. Zionism as Cure

In its early days, the theory of psychoanalysis was in many respects especially attractive for those movements convinced of the human propensity to repeat the past. The subjection of the mental life of the individual to specific rules, the grounding of action and experience in an unconscious determinism, and the working to the surface of suppressed material, all constituted a paradigm that had become a focal point for sociocultural utopianism in Europe. At the time of the outbreak of the Great War, the psychoanalytic movement was often linked with experimental art, socialism, progressive education, and modernist literature. Growth, independence and honesty were also central motives in the rhetoric of the youth-culture that emerged in Europe following the Great War (Eksteins, 1989).

One of the dominant figures in the formation of the Jewish youth-movement was Siegfried Bernfeld, who was one of Freud's first students. Bernfeld's work pointed to the possibilities offered to Jewish youth through a fusion of the ideas of Marx and Freud (Eksteins, 1979; Hoffer, 1981; Bunzl, 1992). Robert Weltsch, Hugo Bergmann (Kafka's classmate in Prague, and later philosopher and first director of the Hebrew University's Jewish National Library), as well as Martin Buber, and Zvi Zohar (One of the key figures in the socialist Zionist youth movement) all formed part of Bernfeld's circle of disciples and later continued to debate Freud's ideas in Palestine. Granting young people a pioneering role within the Jewish national movement; Bernfeld's doctrine had a particularly strong influence on the ideology of the Zionist-socialist youth organization Hashomer Hazair (Margalit, 1971; Mintz, 1995). Likewise, an evocation of Freud by the young educator Meir Yaari (soon after his arrival in Palestine in 1921), at the onset of his pedagogic program, reveals a clear presence of Bernfeld's ideas:

> I consider it important that you carefully study Freud and his school. I do not know if many of us are fully capable of grasping his doctrine; but I hope that it will at least lessen tensions to some degree. Based on this practical experience [with Freud], what seems particularly important to me is the unfolding of the instincts. Be aware of the strength at work within you when you are carried away by manly eroticism (Mintz, 1995, p. 302).

This is taken From a talk that Meir Yaari sent from Palestine to Vienna, most likely at the end of February or start of March 1921.

The youth movements of the early twentieth century, *Hashomer Hazair* among them, saw one of their major roles as the transformation of a hypocritical and sanctimonious approach to sexuality, and the liberation of young people from a dulling of their instincts, from a sexual inhibition then typically associated with Jewish youth (Gluzman, 1997; Bunzl, 1997). In this vein, Yaari spoke of a "pure and proud generation of new immigrants" that had freed itself from "historical restlessness and the deadening of natural instincts." "We wish," he proclaimed, "to extol the unfettered young person who as an adult remains a child, who prizes and acts out the instincts, rather than treating them with contempt" (Mintz, 1995, pp. 374)

But while this optimistic, revolutionary image of psychoanalytic theory drew both socialists and Zionists into its vortex, Freud had begun to revise his theory of the human psyche, step by step. The significance of the appearance of essays such as 'Introduction to Narcissism' (Freud, 1914) and 'Remembering, repeating and working-through' (Freud, 1914) did not lie solely in their new definition of psychosis as a narcissistic neurosis incurable through analysis, or in the thesis that cure is only possible through analysis of the transference neurosis. With all their technical implications the essays also marked the onset of a new phase in psychoanalytic discourse, one concentrating on, among other things, the limits inherent in the new therapy and the scope of the psychic changes that were its goal (Bergmann, 1993). By the end of 1920 Freud has taken his theory beyond the pleasure principle and introduced the controversial concept of the death instinct which then threatened to alienate his theory from many of its early proponents.

Whoever desired to continue thinking of psychoanalysis as a rational scientific vehicle for utopian social principles, in order to use it for specific ideological-socialist goals, had to choose between establishing distance with the theory's new pessimistic aspects and ignoring the development that turned it into a critical theory devoid of any constructive aspirations. The approach to the Oedipus complex can here serve as a good example: The variety of efforts to make use of the concept in the context of pedagogic praxis did not keep step with theoretical developments within psychoanalysis itself. Years after continental psychoanalysis had altered its view of the Oedipus complex, coming to consider it an unavoidable and essential element in the individual's development, "avoidance" of the complex remained a major theme for advocates of collective child rearing. Well after psychoanalytic theory had abandoned the notion of the Oedipus complex as a basic flaw in the nuclear family, the same advocates continued to stress the role of environment in the emergence of the complex within the individual (Rapaport, 1958). We know that in 1930, Zvi Zohar, one of the prominent figures in *Hashomer Hazair* education planning, appealed to Ernst Federn, secretary of Vienna's Psychoanalytic Association, for support in the translation of Hebrew psychoanalytic literature needed for that socialist organization's educational purposes (Zohar, 1930; Liban & Goldman, 2000). We can not delve here into the various twists and turns that befell psychoanalytic theory in the *kibbutz* movement, but given the significant role this movement played in laying the foundations for the state of Israel, we can conclude by endorsing Eli Sagan's assertion that the child rearing practices of a society not only form the basic matrix upon which the society functions, but may prove to be the royal road to its collective unconscious (Sagan, 1999).

The assumption of the central role of the individual and his or her past history, the interpretation of human beings as ruled by unconscious conflicts grounded in the personal past, and the belief in a cure effectuated by a hermeneutic approach to psychic contents and unconscious experiences, these are some of the basic building blocks of Freud's dynamic-theoretical model of the human soul. These fundamentals seem to have experienced a transformation following their encounter with the Jewish community of Palestine. This raises the question of whether the dissective, interpretive, and individually-oriented psychoanalytic perspective was not opposed in a basic and radical manner to the collectivist view of the individual and the constructive-oriented premises of Zionist ideology and self-understanding. If this is in fact the case, how are we to explain the great interest in Freud's ideas manifest in Jewish Palestine from the early twenties onward?

4. The Hebrew Freud

The fact that the first essay by Freud to become available in 1928 to Hebrew readers was *Group Psychology and the Analysis of the Ego* (Freud, 1921) may point again to that knowledge-righteousness discourse which formed the basic matrix of psychoanalysis in its formative years. It seems that the local Jewish intelligentsia was inclined to perceive Freud's theory as an ethical, rather then critical, theory. One could indeed think of no better text in the Freudian corpus embodying the distance between drives and morals, between the individual and society. In this essay Freud discusses the mental mechanisms by which drives are turned into morals. Envy, according to Freud is the precursor of social Justice. Justice is how we deny ourselves all those things we would like to deny the other.

The translation that was commissioned by the 'Hebrew Teachers Association' was the first among a series of essays written by Freud whose common denominator was the applicability of psychoanalysis to the understanding, or rather the making, of society. Hebrew readers encountering Freud for the first time were taken by what they perceived as its utopian coloring. It was not the late Freud who captured their imagination but rather the early Freud, the one emphasizing the corruptive and suppressive power of bourgeois society on the individual's psychic freedom (Berman, 1993).

A second thread, to be found in the local psychoanalytic discourse, concerns Freud's Jewish identity and its relation to his theory. Freud himself was of course anything but Jewish nationalist yet his Jewish self-understanding constitutes one of the chief problems in the history of psychoanalysis. The tendency of some historians to downplay the Jewish dimension in the history of psychoanalysis, and in the biography of its founder, could indeed serve the good purpose of stressing the universal aspirations of a humanistic discipline embedded in the scientific positivist tradition. Yet any kind of ethnic minimalism may risk ignoring part of the context that provided psychoanalysis with both its intellectual roots and theoretical constructions. Whether we agree with either the ethnic minimalists who dispute any ethnic component to Freud's ideas, or with the kind of ethnic maximalism which considers psychoanalysis a "Jewish science", the particular ethnic dimension emerging with scrutiny of Freud's reception in Palestine is once more brought to the fore. (On the significance of Jewish ethnicity within psychoanalysis, see: Yerushalmi, 1991; Gilman, 1993; Oxaal, 1988; Gay, 1987; Klein, 1981; Robert, 1976). Without granting some significance to this ethnic dimension it will not be possible to historicize the reception of psychoanalysis in Jewish Palestine.

A letter of Freud's to the Jewish folklorist Alter Druyanov, written in 1910, is the oldest evidence we have of the interest psychoanalytic theory had begun to hold for Palestine's Jewish intelligentsia. In the letter Freud was replying to Druyanov must have called attention to affinities between themes in *The Interpretation of Dreams* (Freud, 1900) and certain ideas in the Talmud and the Kabbala. Freud's answer reads like a direct rejection of any influence of that sort: "The remarks in the Talmud on the dream-problem have frequently been brought to my attention. It seems to me, however, that the similarities with the ancient Greek understanding of dreams are far more striking" (Freud, 1910).

This was not the only occasion on which Freud used such a pointer to stress his full identification with Greek culture and, at least when it came to psychoanalytic theory, his preference for the Hellenic over the Judaic. This freely involved an implicit expression of preference for universalistic over particularistic values. The Hebrew translator of *Totem and Taboo* (Freud, 1913) went even further then Druyanov in his ambition to move Freud's texts closer to Holy Scripture. He undoubtedly surprised Freud when he told him that he had furnished the Hebrew text with a large number of reference to and citations from the Biblical and Talmudic literature, which served "as a confirmation and strengthening of your book...and here and there [is] designed so as to shed new light on it" (Dwosis, 1938). Several years later, when *The Psychopathology of Everyday Life* (Freud, 1901) was presented to the Hebrew reader it was once again the biblical language and the rendering of the text "as if it was written by one of our biblical ancestors" that won the translation the prestigious Tschernichowsky prize.

When it came to the acceptance of psychoanalysis among mental health professionals the enthusiasm was much milder. Two early analysts were active in Palestine in the early twenties. Montagu David Eder (1866-1936), a founding member of the London psychoanalytic Society, who between 1919 and 1924 was chairman of the Zionist Executive Council, spent part of his time in Palestine as a member of one of the Zionist Commissions but was soon to return to England. Although Eder's activity in Palestine was by and large devoted to Zionist politics he was the first to conduct few analyses in British Mandate Palestine and there is one reference to an attempt he made to present a psychopolitical analysis of some of the Arab leaders of the region (Hobman, 1945).

Dorian Feigenbaum, The first psychoanalyst to settle in Palestine served as director of the *Ezrat-Nashim* Mental Institution. He had planned to deliver three talks on the unconscious, dream theory, and the Freudian theory of neurosis. But the heated protests sparked by his first talk caused the clinic's administration to ban the other two. Shortly after, in March 1923, Feigenbaum was given notice by *Ezrat Nashim*, this marking an abrupt and early end to the first attempt in Jewish Palestine at practically applying psychoanalytic theory in a public hospital (Bergmann, 1923). Feigenbaum then moved to New York City, taking over the editorship of the *Psychoanalytic Quarterly*. When he applied for membership in the New York Psychoanalytic Association in 1925, he made no mention of the years in Palestine (Feigenbaum, 1925).

In 1924, an initial overview of psychoanalytic activity in Palestine was published in the official English-language organ of the psychoanalytic movement, the *International Journal of Psycho-Analysis*. It contains the following observation:

> ...in certain quarters (especially amongst the young immigrants) there is a tendency to introduce so-called 'psychoanalysis' far too carelessly, and in a 'fashionable' and vulgarized form. This, quite obviously, is doing harm, and it is most necessary that psychoanalysis should interfere in the direction of correct exposition and, above all, in checking this injurious growth (*International Journal of Psycho-Analysis*, 1924, p. 414; I assume that this unsigned report was written by either Ernest Jones or Dorian Feigenbaum).

In Jewish Palestine of the time, two very different concepts of psychoanalysis were in fact often manifest alongside each other: One was ideological and political; the other scientific and therapeutic. The instrumentalization of psychoanalysis for purposes of social construction, developing above all in *Hashomer Hazair* and eventually leaving a strong mark on socialist psychoanalysis in general, contained the same internal contradiction that blocked the development of the discipline in the Soviet Union. The conceptual tension at work here clearly marks the encounter between an immigrant society of collectivist-constructionist orientation, its basic tenets emerging primarily from East European socialism, and a theoretical framework deeply rooted in both German positivism and a hermeneutic dialectic. In the decade following Feigenbaum's failed effort to convince his psychiatric colleagues in Jerusalem that psychoanalysis had inherent therapeutic value; it was the *kibbutz* socialist movement that mainly furthered the study of Freud's ideas--to be sure, with the above-mentioned goals of socialist pedagogy and collective child-rearing. With the arrival of psychoanalysts from Central Europe, the circumstances informing this tension would be sharply altered.

5. Berlin in Jerusalem

The catastrophic political developments of 1933 in Germany mark the beginning of a new chapter in the history of psychoanalysis. The migration of psychoanalysis from Central Europe and the formation of a psychoanalytic Diaspora. "The third Diaspora", as Ernest Jones called it, had its repercussion in every psychoanalytic realm, institutional and cultural, as well as theoretical. In the case of some countries outside the German linguistic sphere, it is scarcely possible to describe the development of psychoanalysis without considering the great migration of Central European intellectuals and scientists in the 1930s. Naturally, in the lands of reception, psychoanalysis was often strongly stamped by immigrant psychoanalysts. They played a distinctive role as direct emissaries for the scientific and cultural ferment of fin-de-siècle Vienna, with psychoanalysis being never far from the center of these cultural changes. From the 1930s onward, the history of psychoanalysis was directly or indirectly bound up with the phenomenon of emigration. Every effort to consider psychoanalysis in countries beyond the German cultural sphere from a historical vantage must therefore take account of the mutual influences at play between Central European psychoanalysts and the new environments that received them. In this regard, it is important to keep in mind the key role of emigration for both psychoanalysis as a concrete institutional movement and psychoanalysis as an evolving intellectual enterprise (Gast, 1999; Handlbauer, 1999; Grinberg & Grinberg, 1989; Funke, 1989; Steiner, 1989; Reichmayr, 1987).

Until Max Eitingon's arrival in Palestine, no professional psychoanalyst settled there for a period that exceeded the two years Feigenbaum spent in Jerusalem in the early Twenties. Acting as head of the Berlin Institute and as president of the training committee of the International Psychoanalytic Association, Eitingon's decision to settle in Palestine came as a surprise to just about all of his colleagues. "If you really must leave Berlin", wrote Anna Freud to Eitingon, "where would you go? Not to Vienna? Should we not build a new analytic center here? I believe we will be allowed to work here, where we could get all the assistance we need" (A. Freud, 1933a). From his domicile in London, Ernest Jones had also tried to convince Eitingon not to leave Europe, to at least stay in France, in the hope of helping the local psychoanalytic association overcome its difficulties getting started. In a letter to Anna Freud he wrote: "I fear he [Eitingon] is moved by private considerations to do with his wife, but possibly their visit to Palestine this autumn may convince her of its relative unattractiveness" (Jones, 1933).

Albert Einstein would also try to dissuade Eitingon from immigrating to a place where psychoanalysis "was likely to evoke great resistance from local intellectuals tending to stand in each other's way" (Einstein, 1934).

In fact, both Sigmund Freud and his daughter ascribed great importance to Eitingon's choice of a new home in the case of his forced departure from Berlin. As new conflicts had constantly emerged within the International Psychoanalytic Association, Eitingon's combination of organizational talent and absolute loyalty had rendered him especially valuable to Freud, who had already suffered grave disappointments with gifted students such as Rank and Jung. From Freud's perspective, psychoanalysis thus no longer needed such brilliant thinkers, ready to spread psychoanalytic theory throughout the world, but rather cohesion among the group of its loyal adherents, who would always bear in mind the movement's original nature. In the context of an ever more threatening political reality, many members of the psychoanalytic movement had increasingly come to view it as a besieged fortress. For Eitingon, the struggle to preserve what already existed was a life-long principle. In turn, it expressed the feelings of all those whose faith in psychoanalytic orthodoxy was incarnated by an effort to regain a status that the movement was now being denied. The psychoanalysts' experience of expulsion and emigration was a basic factor in the appeal to an imaginary image of Freud that was to be defended at any price (Grotjahn, 1987).

With the Nazi rise to power, a bitter fight broke out over the future of the Berlin Institute, a fight taking place both within and outside the German Psychoanalytic Association itself. A number of the non-Jewish members wished to preserve the Berlin Institute by adapting it to the sort of psychology being promoted by the new regime. In his correspondence with Freud, Eitingon, a native of Russia who had been living in Germany for forty years, emphasized his boundless identification with the institute he had founded, expressing his determination not to leave Berlin until he was forced to (Eitingon, 1933). On this basis, Eitingon battled to the last possible moment against the "indifferent" members of the Institute, meaning non-Jewish members, who were attempting to gain Freud's consent to the replacement of Jewish by non-Jewish colleagues. This was indeed a most dubious chapter in the history of the German Psychoanalytic Association (Lockot, 1994; Bohleber, 1995).

Mosche Wulff, the Odessa born analyst who fled to Berlin in 1927, was the first member of the Berlin Psychoanalytic Association who emigrated to Palestine (Eitingon, 1933). Two months after his arrival he furnished Eitingon with a report on his unsuccessful efforts to find patients for psychoanalysis, as well as on his first contacts with the health insurance system, which demonstrated no interest in Wulff's services as an analyst: "My fears appear to have been justified," he explained, "neither the cultural nor the material state of the populace appears favorable to psychoanalysis" (Wulff, 1933). The sole development to encourage the otherwise discouraged Wulff was the founding of a small press to publish translations of psychoanalytic literature, or, in Wulff's words, "proper Freud." Wulff named Chaim Nachman Bialik, the Hebrew national poet, as one of those responsible for the project's literary portion. A psychoanalytically oriented study of Bialik was already published in Palestine in 1928. Bialik's name meant something to Freud, who sent off a postcard on the occasion of the holiday for the poet in 1932 (Freud , 1932)

A month later, Wulff reported to Eitingon that while he had given up on the idea of establishing ties between psychoanalysis and the medical community, his two students from Berlin, David Idelson and Shmuel Goldstein (Golan), had enjoyed greater success, since they stood closer to socialist pedagogic circles in the *Yishuv*. But within two additional months, Wulff had two patients, one introduced by David Eder, the other being Idelson himself. The latter was continuing the training analysis he had begun in Berlin. Wulff's comment: "This brings together half of what I need to live" (Wulff, 1933).

In October 1933, Max Eitingon arrived in Palestine with a letter of recommendation from Freud, meant to ease the task of obtaining a work permit (Eitingon, 1933; Department of Health, 1933). He speedily assembled his Berlin colleagues and, a mere month after his arrival, informed Freud of the founding of a Psychoanalytic Association in Palestine (Eitingon, 1933). Against the backdrop of the threatened closure of the movement's two main training institutes, in Vienna and Berlin, Anna Freud remarked laconically to Ernest Jones that

> "My father had a letter from Eitingon today. You will soon hear from him about the formation of a new group in Palestine. The members are mostly or all old Berlin members. New groups used to be a pleasure. They are not just now" (A. Freud, 1933).

During this period, the Viennese professor Martin Pappenheim, who had been a student of Freud's since 1912, joined Eitingon and his colleagues Kilian Bluhm, Ilja Shalit, Anna Smeliansky, and Mosche Wulff at the Psychoanalytic Association. All these individuals were medical doctors. In addition, David Eder in London and Anna Freud in Vienna were made honorary members.

Yet, for those who chose Palestine as their destination, the days in which one fought the wars of psychoanalysis in the scientific and intellectual arena were long gone. Choosing Palestine as a new homeland required the analysts to participate in a new kind of discourse and to adopt a new set of identifications that were foreign to most of them. Even Freud's son, Ernst, was soon to discover that a visa to Palestine was not likely to be granted someone who was not well versed in the basics of Zionism. Martin Freud feared he could not be of great help to his brother, young Ernst, who was trying to get such a visa to Palestine. Writing to worried Eitingon he had to inform him that the boy made a miserable impression on the committee examining his suitability for a Palestine certificate (M. Freud, 1933). It turned out that Freud's son hardly knew anything about Judaism, let alone Zionist problems; and it took a great deal of good will on the part of the examiners to decide he knew who Herzl was.

For those analysts who made it to Palestine the prospects of finding a position were grim. Professor Martin Pappenheim, for instance, was hardly welcomed as the first neurology professor who wished to settle in Palestine once the question was raised as to his real motivation in choosing the country as a place of refuge. To a considerable extent, Pappenheim's effort to establish his place in the Jewish public sphere represents the experience facing a range of Central European immigrant physicians and intellectuals. The contribution of German-Jewish immigrants between 1933 and 1948 to the development of medicine in Palestine cannot be overestimated. But they suffered conflicts with the rigid, collectivistically-oriented health services then in existence (Niederland, 1982, 1988).

In 1933, Martin Pappenheim was being considered for the post of director of the psychiatric clinic then planned to be opened in the town of Bnei Brak (Pappenheim, 1933). But following the receipt by the Tel Aviv city administration of letters warning of the "non-Zionist motives" for Pappenheim's candidacy, the city fathers, steered by Mayor Meir Dizengoff and Vice Mayor Israel Rokach, agreed to end their contacts with the candidate. Pappenheim, the letters asserted, had left the Jewish community in Vienna; certain voices had even suggested he intended to convert. And other voices had suggested that had the Tel Aviv opportunity not came up, his closeness to communism would have led him to try his luck in Russia, sure sign of an absence of genuine Zionist engagement. (Kermensky, 1933; Schnirer, 1933). The national poet Bialik, the distinguished Zionist-religious thinker Rabbi Avraham Yizhak Hacohen Kook, and several other prominent public figures all interceded with Dizengoff on Pappenheim's behalf, without avail. Instead, the city administration committed itself to "maintaining no contact with those considered traitors to our people" (Dizengoff, 1933). Pappenheim's case exemplifies the level of suspicion, which reached a high level when it came to accepting central European Jews as equal partners. The Jewish community of Palestine did not like to think of itself as just a sanctuary for any refugee.

6. "Misguided Piety"

At this point we should pause to consider the actual role ascribed to Freud himself in the reception of psychoanalysis in Palestine. As has been pointed out by many historians, the history of psychoanalysis be it in the conceptual, institutional or cultural level, is intimately linked with the biography of its founder. Freud's extensive correspondence with Jews in Palestine is quite cryptic in any of the many allusions he made to Judaism in general and to his own ethnic identity in particular. However, it does reveal a great deal about the imagery of psychoanalysis active in shaping its reception among the settlers. I would like to concentrate briefly on Freud's attitude towards the Zionist movement, only inasmuch as it was reflected in the reception of his teachings in Palestine. Whereas in the early twenties one could still recruit Freud's name for the purposes of the Zionist endeavor, the older, disillusioned Freud would find it increasingly difficult to sympathize with the Jews of Palestine. Soon after the 1929 Arab riots in Palestine an appeal was made to Freud to express publicly his sympathy with the Jewish national movement. It is not hard to understand why Freud's answer was hidden from the public and was explicitly retrieved from the Jewish National Library and requested to be sent back to Vienna:

> My distaste for the idea of burdening the public with my person is insurmountable; the present critical inducement does not even seem suitable for doing so. Whoever wishes to influence a mass needs to have something sonorous and enthusiastic to say, and my sober assessment of Zionism does not permit this. I certainly have the greatest sympathy for voluntary efforts, am proud of our university in Jerusalem, and am happy about the thriving of our settlements. But on the other hand I do not believe that Palestine can ever be a Jewish state and that either the Christian or Islamic world will ever be ready to place their holy places under Jewish guardianship. It would seem more sensible to me to found a Jewish fatherland on historically untroubled soil--though I realize that such a rational goal would never have gained the enthusiasm of the masses and the collaboration of the wealthy. I also regrettably admit that the fanaticism of our fellow Jews, estranged as it is from reality, bears its share of responsibility for the rise of mistrust among the Arabs. I can conjure up absolutely no sympathy for that misguided piety rendering a piece of Herod's wall a national relic and aggravating the feelings of the native population on its account. Judge for yourself if, possessing such a critical stance, I am the proper person to offer solace to a people shaken in its unfounded hope (Freud, 1930).

I am not sure whether we can see in this letter a final proof to Freud's anti-Zionist convictions. (Nor is it our concern here to draw Freud's name into the restrictive legitimacy discourse of Zionist historiography). The opening lines do however capture Freud's growing dissatisfaction with the interweaving of his personality into the public facet of his work as was increasingly done in Palestine. Behind the harsh yet ambiguous tone (so familiar to every Freud reader) we feel the pulse of an emotional issue that reached deep into Freud's self-understanding. And indeed repeated invitations to come to Palestine were declined for reasons of health until 1933. Only then, in a letter to Magnes, the aging Freud would confess to 'a psychic inhibition' that prevented him from taking the trip to Palestine ("Eine Reise nach Jerusalem ist für mich nicht etwa schwierig, doch mit opfern ausführbar, sondern sie ist psychisch unmöglich" Freud, 1933). Could Jerusalem be placed next to Rome and Athens as a city which represents some crucial landmark in the psychic constitution of Sigmund Freud?

The year was 1933 and the political climate in Germany was beginning to make itself noticeable in the activities of Freud and his disciples. Within a year's time Freud would complete the first draft of the last of his monumental essays. *Moses and monotheism* (Freud, 1939) became the talk of the day in Palestine even before it was actually published in German. If we have to summarize the reactions to the essay, which presented both Moses and monotheism as Egyptian, the word 'betrayal' is the first that comes to mind. As one critic wrote in an open letter to Freud, published in the Hebrew literary Journal *Moznaim*,

> It would have been a better service to your fellow Jews if you devoted your creative powers to the preservation of Judaism and confronted a much worthier question: why is it that Jewish Bible critics are constantly acting against the basic truths of the Bible, instead of siding with this trend of criticism (Perlmann, 1939).

The writer of the letter had an answer of his own to this question: Such a critical approach is the result of an unconscious wish to justify the author's flight from his own Jewish identity and the abandoning of its commandments. By the time the Moses ordeal had shown itself to be as explosive as he feared it would be, Freud grew ever more pessimistic towards the Zionist enterprise. "History", he would write to the desperate Arnold Zweig who could not find peace of mind in Palestine, "has never given the Jewish people cause to develop their faculty for creating a state or a society" (Freud, 1936).

Outraged letters reached both Freud and Eitingon from Jews all over the world and the Hebrew press condemned the celebrated Jew for depriving his people of the one consolation remaining to them in this time of misery. While Zweig found the reception of *Moses* among the Hebrews amusing, Freud felt he was being overestimated: "Can one really believe that my arid treatise would destroy the belief of a single person brought up by heredity and training in the faith, even if it were to come his way?" (Freud, 1938).

What may have surprised Freud, who was not familiar with the kind of Freudianism that had begun to establish itself among the Jews in Palestine, came as no surprise to someone like Hugo Bergmann. This philosopher's critical approach toward psychoanalysis did not prevent him from undergoing analysis (In fact he is the first analytic patient we have on record in Israel), and as much as he could convince himself of the importance of psychoanalysis to the individual, he gradually became concerned about this theory's propensity to be used in an ideological way. "In our land", wrote Bergmann in his diary in March 1935, "I can imagine combating the deductive tendencies bound up with psychoanalysis by offering people Jung instead of Freud" (Bergmann, 1935/1985, p. 385).

The rapid pace with which Eitingon and few of his former Berlin colleagues built up the Palestine Psychoanalytic Institute on the model of the Berlin Institute they left behind was no substitute for the longer adaptation period needed to secure both the legal and the public status of the analyst's profession. Eitingon was the first to notice the constructive-collectivist atmosphere that would tend to undermine the individualist and critical nature of psychoanalysis. Yet he choose to integrate in the public sphere by supporting such organizations as *'Youth Aliya'*, an organization devoted to young immigrants coming without their families, *'Bezalel'*, the Jerusalem art academy, The Hebrew Writers' Association, *'Habima'*, the Hebrew Theater company, and many more.

The activity of the Palestine Psychoanalytic Institute was not only subject to the irregularities accompanying the living conditions in Palestine. It also reflected the political climate and the immediate concerns of the institute's members. Themes such as 'communal child rearing' or the 'Talmudic approach to sexuality and dreams' that were discussed in the institute at the time can convey the special place that psychoanalytic theory occupied in the minds of the newly arrived analysts. In its inaugural period, the Palestinian Psychoanalytic Society hardly succeeded in pleasing all its members. A portion of its internal conflicts appears to have centered, either directly or indirectly, upon the constructivist and Zionist-national nuances accompanying the scientific program. In a letter he sent to Otto Fenichel, Shmuel Goldstein (Golan), one of the new members, complained about what he referred to as the "linkage with Jewish matters, which have been suddenly refurbished on certain sentimental, pseudo-national grounds" (Golan in Reichmayr & Mühlleitner, 1998). Such sentimental grounds were not without practical implications for the popularity of the new discipline among Jews in Palestine. Max Eitingon for instance noted a remarkable increase in the applications for analysis that reached the institute in Jerusalem in the months following the annexation of Austria. He ascribed it to the immense interest shown by the local press in the prominent Viennese Jew who was being so ill treated by the Nazis (Eitingon, 1938a,b).

We cannot delve here into the various ramifications of the personal conflicts at work in the Palestinian psychoanalytic society; Goldstein's words point to the general political-ideological tenor accompanying the society since its founding. To this extent, the political-ideological substance of the *yishuv* appears to have been assimilated quite readily into the local discourse of scientific psychoanalysis. Both Obernik's talk on "Psychoanalytical Observation of Individuals within the Children's Group and its Value for the Construction of Communal Education" and Eitingon's on "Sexuality and Dream in the Talmud" serve as examples of the ethnic-national framework for much psychoanalytic activity of the time. In the association's annual reports, Eitingon would nonetheless designate therapy as the main activity of its members. We thus find him reporting in 1938 that 36 patients had undergone psychoanalysis over the previous year (Eitingon, 1938b). In his communications with various parties, he consistently emphasized that the association was part of an international organization, hence subject to its rules and statutes. This legalistic position is linked to the status he wished to see accorded the psychoanalytic praxis then taking shape. The position is reflected in his negotiations with the Jewish medical association of Palestine over the question of paying a minimum wage; in the course of the negotiations, he indicates

...that in accordance with the traditions of psychoanalytic institutes, conceived as public establishments, I and my colleagues (Dr. Miriam Brandt and Dr. D. Dreyfus) at the Jerusalem Psychoanalytic Institute cannot commit ourselves to a minimum wage, since we go as far as to treat destitute patients at no cost, when the long-term treatments make this necessary. In our private practice we naturally consent to this minimum wage. (Eitingon, 1936)

Doubtlessly, this depiction of the analyst's professional activity as a particularly philanthropic activity was offered in the service of the main point Eitingon is stressing: that the psychoanalytic institute founded in Jerusalem, oriented toward the tradition of continental psychoanalysis, will remain independent; that it will continue to be steered according to precisely the principles Eitingon had established, in his capacity as chairman of the International Psychoanalytic Association. In other words, Eitingon wished to see the organizational framework of psychoanalysis settled in a separate space from that of the medical establishment. This brings to mind the debate over the training of psychoanalysts with or without previous medical education, with Eitingon here taking Freud's side, and arguing against the demands of American psychoanalysts at the time (Bos, 2001). Shmuel Golan, who seldom missed an opportunity to criticize Eitingon's 'Noble Berlin Tradition' (cf. Reichmayr 1998. p. 184), was nonetheless complaining to Fenichel on the restrictions that lay analysts like himself were subjected to (cf. Reichmayr, 1998).

7. Emigration and Neurosis

The writer Arnold Zweig had emigrated to Palestine in 1932. During the period of his largely unsuccessful struggle to find his place in the local literary community, he maintained a lively correspondence with Sigmund Freud (E. Freud, 1968) In his book *Traum ist teuer* ("Dream is Dear"), finished during the last years of his life in East Berlin, he tells the story of a Jewish psychoanalyst who had served in the British army's medical corps. During his Palestinian sojourn, the protagonist in this narrative abandons his Zionist dream, after it has accompanied him in the course of the entire war (Zweig, 1985). For Zweig, psychoanalysis did not simply serve as a personal life buoy. Among the central European immigrants, Freud's doctrine, symbolizing a German cultural identity and intellectual world confronting an abyss, enjoyed a status that was virtually iconic. Once Zweig was forced to see that precisely the main representatives of the new Hebrew culture took no notice of either German culture or his own writings, his strong desire to maintain his cultural identity in Palestine rendered his life ever-more unbearable (Wormann, 1970). During his Palestinian exile, Zweig followed the activities of the psychoanalytic association from its inception, participating in some of them. One evening, he gave a talk to a group of analysts on a subject we can assume was close to all that heard it: "Emigration and Neurosis" (Eitingon, 1937).

As members of a subculture within the community of intellectual emigration from central Europe, the psychoanalysts were confronted with a reality offering them very limited room for maneuver. Unlike fellow intellectuals, whose integration was facilitated by the mediation of academic institutions, and in contrast to colleagues who had emigrated to other countries, Jewish immigrant psychoanalysts in Palestine were forced to start by constructing the same framework in which they had exerted their European influence. It is self-evident that the group of German-speaking psychoanalysts that migrated to Palestine in the 1930s was too small to have any direct influence on the society that received them. It is also doubtful that the immigrants had any strong intention of influencing the society in the same manner as central European lawyers, physicians, architects, or engineers: the activity of such professionals was naturally far more in the public limelight (Gelber & Goldstern, 1988; Jütte, 1991; Niederland, 1988).

Like the majority of those participating in the fifth large wave of Jewish immigration to Palestine, and being aware of the particular character of their vocation, most psychoanalysts were inclined to find their place faraway from the public sphere (Gelber, 1990). Still, neither the lack of a structure for integration nor limited possibilities of employment were decisive factors in the organization of analysts outside the establishment, in the framework of an institute combining education with psychoanalytic treatment. For years, the interest of Palestine's Jewish population in psychoanalysis had been closely linked to ideological and national needs, and had been largely untouched by clinical or therapeutic praxis. For this reason, the analysts were compelled to discover a middle way allowing them to continue their scientific work with the highest possible degree of autonomy, as befitting the nature of their discipline. More than in any other country, psychoanalysis in Palestine was under the influence of an ideological climate essentially opposed to what psychoanalytic theory offered the individual analysand. This climate did not lead to a rejection of Freud's doctrine, but rather to an effort at its appropriation. The shift of emphasis to psychoanalysis as bearer of social-revolutionary ideas, its emergence as a tool for both collective goals and the construction of a new Palestinian Jewish society, as well as for the return of therapy to its proper place, was a laborious process marked by various heights and depths.

When the psychoanalytic association was being started, each émigré psychoanalyst was forced to cope in his own way with one dominant source of tension: that inherent in the existence of a psychoanalytic practice within an environment subordinating the individual and his past to the demands of a socio-historical collective. Our historical evaluation of the immigration of German-speaking psychoanalysts to Palestine is thus linked to our willingness to locate it, using the aid of relatively many coordinates, within the framework of both Jewish and Central European twentieth century history and its scientific-ideological transformations. Given our framework, a critical hermeneutics stood opposed to principles of solidarity and construction; social pessimism stood opposed to social utopianism; the notions of psychotherapy, the individual past, and individualism in general to ameliorative pedagogy, the collective past, and collectivism in general; universalism and scientific scrutiny stood opposed to particularism and ideological syncretism. Whereas the discourse over Freud's ideas hovered between these poles prior to and during the formative years of the psychoanalytic movement in Jewish Palestine, the displacement of psychoanalysis from central Europe to Israel continues to unfold between these contrary axes until this very day. Indeed, these axes may prove pertinent to any future study into the stigmata of Israeli society which seem to have developed a special taste for psychoanalytically informed 'group therapies'. But this last assertion should be the subject of a separate investigation.

* * * *

Sigmund Freud's house, where our conference was held, has a tradition of its own if we consider concepts such as trauma, conflict and identity as part psychological part historical. Each of these psychological concepts entails a notion of both the past and the present and could be deconstructed into historical terms. Each touches on both the individual and the group with which he aligns himself. The concepts have challenged Freud in each of his psychohistorical ventures (as in the case of *Moses and Monotheism*) and they challenge the vocation of both professions ever since.

What distinguishes the disciplines of psychoanalysis and history is surely not an emphasis on the past. Every good historical study is to some degree a history of the present (at least as far as its motivation is concerned). Likewise, every good analysis involves an effort to relate and reconcile things past with present experiences and sensibilities. It is thus not the past as such, in the old positivist sense, that both disciplines are usually concerned with, but rather the traces the past has left on present memory and self-identity. Indeed, among the things that psychoanalysts and historians may share in common is an understanding that human memory takes as much trouble to forget and distort facts as to retain them. It is in this vein that neither psychoanalysts nor historians any longer consider it their task to recover and evoke the past as an objective and distinct reality, a terra incognita, waiting to be discovered. Historical facts, as we establish them, are psychic realities archived on different levels and given a multitude of meanings in the course of time. They are composed of past events (sometimes referred to as trauma) and present experience in a highly condensed and sometimes contradictory form, and are thus no more 'true', or immune to distortions, then any other constructs of memory. Given the special nature of their discipline historians are quite familiar with the complex interaction, at times complementary, at times competitive, between the memory of the individual and that of the group. The same can be said about psychoanalysts who promote the individual's capacity to view the objects around him, as well as past objects of desire, in their entire subjectivity and to treat her own subjective experience more objectively. While historians are striving to acknowledge the "Otherness" of the past, I think it is psychoanalysis to which we owe our recognition that the borders between the scholar and the subject matter of his analysis, between the present and the past, cannot always be sharply delineated. As a historian one can also learn a lot from psychoanalysis on the usefulness of transference-countertransference reactions in the understanding of past events. In other words: whether a clinician or a historian, in the clinical setting or in the archives, we are constantly reminded of the objective-intersubjective dialectics that is in the nature of any interpretative endeavor.

I am reminded here of the philosopher and psychologist William James (incidentally, one of the first Americans to acknowledge the genius of Freud) who seem to have captured the epistemological paradox that is inherent to psychoanalysts and historians alike. "The recesses of feeling", he once wrote, "the darker, blinder strata of character, are the only places in the world in which we catch real fact in the making" (James, 1902/1982, p. 501). For James then objective reality is something we should look for deep within our innermost, subjective, experience. Hence, once we abandon these artificial dichotomies, such as 'narrative truth' vs. 'historical truth' or 'real' as opposed to' fantasized' or 'chosen' traumas, it may be easier for historians and psychoanalysts to develop a language that will facilitate the resolution of the conflict that shaped the many identities of those living in Palestine and Israel (LaCapra, 2001; Volkan, 1996; Spence, 1982).

Freud is properly credited as the originator of psychoanalysis as both a theory of the individual mind and a treatment technique for the disorders of the mind. But, if we take the full corpus of his large scale work on society (*Totem and Taboo, Group Psychology and the Analysis of the Ego, The Future of an Illusion, Civilization and its Discontents, Moses and Monotheism*) into account, he can be said to have paid almost as much attention to the disorders of society as to the disorders of the individual psyche (Wallerstein, 1999).

The observation that painful memories lay at the bottom of most intrapsychic conflicts and hence over-determine their outcome, cannot be irrelevant to the study of political conflicts such as the Arab-Israeli conflict, and even if we refuse to share Freud's ambition that "one day someone will venture to embark upon the pathology of cultural communities", we may still believe that some of the memory-laden conflicts, at work in the historically overburdened land of Israel, are nonetheless amenable to some sort of analysis and to some degree of change. If psychoanalysis is ever to contribute to this task it must first reflect upon its own history. The history of the reception of psychoanalysis in Palestine demonstrates some of the pitfalls that await any attempt to instrumentalize and ideologize Freud's legacy.

References

Beit-Hallahmi, B. (2002). Political and literary answers to 'Jewish Questions': Proust, Joyce, Freud, and Herzl. In this volume.

Bergmann, S.H. (1923) Letter to Robert Weltsch R., 27.3.1923. In S.H. Bergmann, (1985). *Tagebücher und Briefe*. Miriam Sambursky (Ed.). Königstein/Ts.: Jüdischer Verlag bei Athenaum.

Bergmann, S. H. (1985). *Tagebücher und Briefe*. Miriam Sambursky (Ed.). Königstein/Ts.: Jüdischer Verlag bei Athenaum.

Bergmann, M. (1993). Reflections on the History of Psychoanalysis, *Journal of the American Psychoanalytic Association* 41, 929-956.

Berman, E. (1993). Psychoanalysis, Rescue and Utopia. *Utopian Studies*, 1993, 4 44-56.

Bohleber,W.(1995). *Zur romantisch-idealistischen Freudrevision deutscher Psychoanalytiker nach 1933*. In L. Hermanns (Ed.), *Spaltungen in der Geschichte der Psychoanalyse*. Tübingen: Edition Diskord.

Bos, J. (2001). Notes on a controversy: The question of lay analysis. *Psychoanalysis and History*, *3*, 153-169.

Bunzl, M. (1997). Theodor Herzl's Zionism as Gendered Discourse. In R. Robertson & E. Timms (Eds.), *Theodor Herzl and the Origins of Zionism*. Austrian Studies VIII, Edinburgh, 74-87.

Bunzl, J.(1992). Siegfried Bernfeld und der Zionismus. In K. Fallend & J. Reichmayers (Eds.), *Siegfried Bernfeld oder die Grenzen der Psychoanalyse*. Frankfurt/Main: Stroemfeld/Nexus.

Derrida, J. (1998). *Archives Fever: A Freudian Impression*. Chicago:

University of Chicago Press.

Dizengoff, M.(1933). Letter to the editors of *Die Neue Welt*. 04/10/1933 (Tel-Aviv City Archives).

Dwosis, Y. (1938). Letter to Sigmund Freud 30/11/1938 (Courtesy of Mrs. Ora Raphael, Israel)

Einstein, A. (1933). Letter to Max Eitingon, 21/04/1933 (Eitingon Archives, Jerusalem).

Eitingon, M. (1933-8). Letters to Sigmund Freud, 19/03/1933, 21/04/1933, 02/11/1933 24/01/1937. (Freud Collection, Library of Congress).

Eitingon, M. (1936). Letter to the Jewish Medical Association, 5.2.1936 (Eitingon Archives, Jerusalem).

Eitingon, M. (1938a) Report on the Palestinian psychoanalytical Society for August 1936-August 1938. (Eitingon Archives, Jerusalem).

Eitingon, M. (1938b) Bericht des Instituts der Palästinensischen Psychoanalytischen Vereinigung für das Jahr 1937/8, Jerusalem July 1938, (Eitingon Archives, Jerusalem).

Ekstein, R. (1979). Siegfried Bernfeld: Sisyphus or the boundaries of education. In F. Alexander et al., (Eds.), *Psychoanalytic Pioneers*, New York: Basic Books.

Eksteins, M. (1989). *Rites of Spring: The Great War and the Birth of the Modern Age*. London: Bantam Press.

Esman, A.H. (1998). What is 'applied' in 'applied' psychoanalysis. *International Journal of Psychoanalysis, 79*, 741- 756.

Etkind, A. (1994). Trotsky and Psychoanalysis. *Partisan Review, 61*, 303-308.

Etkind, A. (1997). *Eros of the Impossible: The History of Psychoanalysis in Russia*. Boulder, CO: Westview Press.

Even Zohar, I. (1990). The emergence of a native Hebrew culture in Palestine, 1882-1948., *Poetics* Today, *11*, 175-193.

Feigenbaum, D. (1925). Letter to A. Polon, 26/01/1925. (A.A. Brill Library and Archives, New-York).

Forrester, J. (1997). *Dispatches from the Freud Wars: Psychoanalysis and its Passions*. Cambridge, MA: Harvard University Press.

Freud, A. (1933a). Letter to Max Eitingon, 16/04/1933. (Freud Collection, Library of Congress).

Freud, A. (1933b). Letter to Ernest Jones, 07/11/1933. (Archives of the British Psychoanalytic Society).

Freud, A (1934). Letter to Max Eitingon, 11/05/1934. (Eitingon Archives, Jerusalem).

Freud, E. L. (Ed.) (1968). *Sigmund Freud/Arnold Zweig Briefwechsel*, Frankfurt/Main.

Freud, M. (1935). Letter to Max Eitingon, 16/07/1935. (Central Zionist Archives, Jerusalem).

Freud, S. (1901). *The Psychopathology of Everyday Life*. In *The Standard Edition of the Complete Psychological Writings of Sigmund Freud*. Vol. 6. London: Hogarth Press.

Freud, S. (1910). Letter to Alter Druyanov, 03/10/1910. (Freud Museum, London).

Freud, S. (1913). *Totem and taboo*. In *The Standard Edition of the Complete Psychological Writings of Sigmund Freud*. Vol. 13. London: Hogarth Press.

Freud, S. (1914). On narcissism: An introduction. In *The Standard Edition of the Complete Psychological Writings of Sigmund Freud*. Vol. 14. London: Hogarth Press.

Freud, S. (1914). Remembering, repeating and working-through.. In *The Standard Edition of the Complete Psychological Writings of Sigmund Freud*. Vol. 14. London: Hogarth Press.

Freud, S. (1920). Beyond the pleasure principle. In *The Standard Edition of the Complete Psychological Writings of Sigmund Freud*. Vol. 18. London: Hogarth Press.

Freud, S. (1921). Group psychology and the analysis of the ego. In *The Standard Edition of the Complete Psychological Writings of Sigmund Freud*. Vol. 18. London: Hogarth Press.

Freud, S. (1930). Letter to H. Koffler, 26/02/1930. (Schwadron Collection, National Library, Jerusalem).

Freud, S. (1931). Letter to *Histadrut Ivrit*, 18/12/1931. (Bialik Archives, Tel-Aviv).

Freud, S. (1933) Letter to Y.L. Magnes, 05/10/1933. (Freud Collection, Library of Congress).

Freud, S. (1936). Letter to Arnold Zweig, 21/02/1936. In E.L. Freud, (Ed.), (1968). *Sigmund Freud/Arnold Zweig* Briefwechsel. Frankfurt/Main: S. Fischer.

Freud, S. (1938). Letter to Arnold Zweig, 28/06/1938. In E.L Freud (Ed.), (1968). *Sigmund Freud/Arnold Zweig Briefwechsel*. Frankfurt/Main: S. Fischer.

Freud, S. (1939). *Moses and Monotheism*. In *The Standard Edition of the Complete Psychological Writings of Sigmund Freud*. Vol. 23. London: Hogarth Press.

Funke. H. (1989). *Die andere Erinnerung: Gespräche mit jüdischen Wissenschaftlern im Exil*. Frankfurt/Main: Fischer Taschenbuch Verlag.

Gast, L.(1999).Fluchtlinien-Wege ins Exil. Psychoanalyse im Exil.*Forum der Psychoanalyse*, 15, 135-150.

Gay, P. (1987). *A Godless Jew*. New Haven: Yale University Press.

Gelber.Y. & Goldstern,W. (1988).*Emigration deutschsprachiger Ingenieure nach Palestina 1933-1945*. Düsseldorf: VDI.

Gelber,Y. (1990). *New Homeland: Immigration and Absorption of Central European Jews 1933-1948*. Jerusalem: Ben-Zvi Memorial Foundation.

[Hebrew].

Gilman, S. (1993). *The Case of Sigmund Freud: Medicine and Identity at the Fin De Siècle*. Baltimore and London: The John Hopkins University Press.

Gluzman, M. (1997). Longing for Heterosexuality: Zionism and Sexuality in Herzl's *Altneuland*. *Theory and Criticism* 11, 145-162 [Hebrew].

Grinberg, L. & Grinberg, R. (1989). *Psychoanalytic Perspectives on Migration and Exile*. New Haven: Yale University Press.

Grotjahn, M. (1987). *My Favorite Patient: Memoirs of a Psychoanalyst*. Franfurt-am-Main: Peter Lang.

Handlbauer, B. (1999). Über den Einfluss der Emigration auf die Geschichte der Psychoanalyse. *Forum der* Psychoanalyse, *15*, 151-166.

Hobman, J.B. (Ed.)(1945). *David Eder: Memoirs of a Modern Pioneer*. London: Victor Gollancz.

Hobsbawm, E. (1990). *Nations and Nationalism since 1780: Programme, Myth, Reality*. Cambridge: Cambridge University Press.

Hobsbawm, E. (1997*). On History*. New York: The New Press.

Hoffer, W. (1981) *Early Development and Education of the Child*. London: Hogarth Press.

Jaffe, R. (1966). Moshe Wulff: Pioneering in Russia and Israel. In F. Alexander, S. Einstenstein, & M. Grotjhan (Eds.) *Psychoanalytic Pioneers*. New York: Basic Books.

James,W. (1902/1982). *The Varieties of Religious Experience*. Harmondsworth, Middlesex: Penguin Books.

Jones, E.(1933). Letter to Anna Freud, 19/09/1933. (Archives of the British Psychoanalytic Society).

Jütte, R. (1991). *Die Emigration der deutschsprachigen "Wissenschaft des Judentums*. Stuttgart: Steiner.

Kermensky, J (1933).Letter to Meir Dizengoff, 28/09/1933. (Tel-Aviv City Archives)

Klein, D.B. (1981). *Jewish Origins of the Psychoanalytic Movement*. New York: Praeger.

Kloocke, R. (1995). Mosche Wulff (1878-1971), Leben und Werk des russisch-jüdischen Psychoanalytikers. *Luzifer-Amor: Zeitschrift zur Geschichte der Psychoanalyse, 16,* 87-102.

Knei-Paz, B. (1978). *The Social and Political Thought of Leon Trotsky*. Oxford: Oxford University Press.

LaCapra, D. (2001) *Writing history, writing trauma*. Baltimore & London: The John Hopkins University Press.

Liban, A. & Goldman, D. (2000). Freud comes to Palestine: A study of psychoanalysis in a cultural context. *International Journal of Psychoanalysis, 81,* 893-906.

Lockot, R. (1994). *Die Reinigung der Psychoanalyse: Die deutsche psychoanalytische Gesellschaft im Spiegel von Dokumenten und Zeitungen*. Tübingen: Edition Diskord.

Luria, A. (1978). Psychoanalysis as a system of monistic psychology. In M. Cole (Ed.), *The Selected Writings of A.R. Luria*. New York: M.E. Sharpe.

Margalit, E. (1971). *Hashomer Hazair: From Youth Community to Revolutionary Marxism (1913-1936)*. Tel-Aviv: Tel Aviv University [Hebrew].

Miller, M. A. (1990). The reception of psychoanalysis and the problem of the unconscious in Russia. *Social Research, 47,* 875-888.

Miller, M.A. (1998). *Freud and the Bolsheviks: Psychoanalysis in imperial Russia and the Soviet Union*. New Haven: Yale University Press.

Department of Health, Jerusalem (1933). Letter to Max Eitingon, 23.11.33 (Eitingon Archives, Jerusalem).

Mintz, M. (1995). *Pangs of Youth: Hashomer Hazair 1911-1921*. Jerusalem: World Zionist Organization: The Zionist Library. [Hebrew].

Niederland, D. (1982). *The Influence of Doctors from the Ger₃ an Immigration on the Development of Medicine in Palestine.* Unpublished Ph.D. Thesis, The Hebrew University, Jerusalem [Hebrew].

Niederland, D. (1988). The emigration of Jewish academics and professionals from Germany in the first years of Nazi rule. *Leo Baeck Institute Year Book* XXXIII, 285-300.

Niederland, D.(1988). Der Einflucht der Ärzte der deutschen Immigration;I. Heinze-Grinberg, Erich Mendelsohn und die Einwanderung deutscsh-jüdischer Architekten nach Palästina (1918-1948). *Bulletin Leo Baeck Institute*, 80, 3-12.

Oxaal, I., (1988) The Jewish origins of psychoanalysis reconsidered. In E. Timms & N. Segal (Eds.), *Freud in Exile: Psychoanalysis and its Vicissitudes.* New Heaven: Yale University Press.

Pappenheim, M. (1933). Letter to Israel Rokach, 09/08/1933. (Tel-Aviv City Archives).

Perlmann, N. (1939). Letter to Sigmund. Freud, 02/07/1939 (Gnazim Archives, Tel-Aviv).

Rapaport, D. (1958) The study of kibbutz education and its bearing on the theory of development. *The American Journal of Orthopsychiatry.* 28, 587-597.

Reichmayr, J. (1987). Anschluss und Ausschluss- Die Vertreibung der Psychoanalytiker aus Wien. In J. Reichmayr & E. Mühlleitner (Eds), (1998) *Otto Fenichel 119 Rundbriefe.* Frankfurt am Main: Stroemfeld Verlag.

Rice, J. (1993). Freud's Russia: National Identity in the Evolution of Psychoanalysis. New Brunswick and London: Transaction Publishers

Rieff, P. (1979*). Freud, The Mind of the Moralist.* Chicago: University of Chicago Press.

Robert, M. (1976). *From Oedipus to Moses: Freud's Jewish Identity.* Garden City, NY: Doubleday.

Rolnik, E.J. (2001a). Between Memory and Desire: From History to Psychoanalysis and back. *Psychoanalysis and History*, 3, 129-151.

Rolnik, E.J. (2001b) Between technique and ethic, between hermeneutics and science: Freud and the right guess. *Sihot: Israel Journal of Psychotherapy.* In press. [Hebrew].

Sagan, E. (1999). Some reflections on the failure to develop an adequate psychoanalytic sociology. In N. Ginsburg & R. Ginsburg (Eds.), *Psychoanalysis and Culture at the Millennium.* New Haven: Yale University Press.

Schnirer, M.T. (1933). Letter to Meir Dizengoff, 02/10/1933. (Tel-Aviv City Archives).

Solms, M. (2000). Freud, Luria and the clinical method. *Psychoanalysis and History. 2,* 76-109.

Spence, D. (1982). *Narrative Truth and Historical Truth: Meaning and Interpretation in Psychoanalysis.* New York: W.W. Norton.

Stadler, F. (Ed.) (1987) *Vertriebe Vernunft: Emigration und Exil Oesterreichischr Wissenschaftler 1930-1940.* Wien: Jugend und Volk.

Steiner, R. (1989). 'It is a New Kind of Diaspora...'. *International Review of Psycho-Analysis, 16,* 35-78.

Sternhell, Z. (1986). *Nation-Building or a New Society: The Zionist Labor Movement (1904-1940) and the Origins of Israel.* Tel Aviv: Am Oved. [Hebrew].

Toews, J. (1999). Historicizing the psyche of psychohistory. In N.Ginsburg & R. Ginsburg (Eds.), *Psychoanalysis and Culture at the Millennium.* New Haven: Yale University Press.

Volkan, V. (1996). Intergenerational transmission and "chosen" traumas: A link between the psychology of the individual and that of the ethnic group. In L. Rangell and R. Moses-Hrushovski, *Psychoanalysis at the Political Border: Essays in Honor of Rafael Moses.* Madison, CT: International Universities Press.

Wallerstein, R. (1999). Freud and culture in our fin de siècle revisited. In. N. Ginsburg & R. Ginsburg (Eds.). *Psychoanalysis and Culture at the Millenium.* New-Haven, CT: Yale University Press.

Wistrich, R. & Ohana D. (1995). The shaping of Israeli identity: myth, memory, and trauma, *Israel Affairs* I/3.

Wormann, K. (1970). German Jews in Israel: Their cultural situation since 1933. In *Leo Baeck Institute Year Book*, *15*, 73-103.

Wulff, M. (1928). Bemerkungen über einige Ergebnisse bei einer psychiatrisch-neurologischen Untersuchung von Chauffeuren. *Internationale Zeitschrift für Psychoanalyse, 14*, 27-242.

Wulff, M. (1933) Letter to Max Eitingon, 31/05/1933 (Eitingon Archives, Jerusalem).

Yerushalmi, Y.H. (1991). *Freud's Moses: Judaism Terminable and Interminable*. New Haven: Yale University Press.

Zohar, Z. (1930). Letter to Ernst Federn.(Hashomer Hatzair Archives).

Zweig, A. (1985). *Traum ist Teuer*. Frankfurt-am-Main: Fischer Taschenbuch Verlag.

Chapter 8

Beyond Analytic Anonymity: On the Political Involvement of Psychoanalysts and Psychotherapists in Israel

Emanuel Berman
University of Haifa

This chapter is unique in combining several levels of discussion. One is the technical-theoretical discourse of psychoanalysis, aimed at therapeutic effectiveness, which, according to older models, recently challenged, will be hampered or eliminated by the analyst's disclosing any real information about personal opinions and preferences. Another is autobiographical, as Emanuel Berman frankly discusses, and reflects on, his life history, including both early family and later political opinions and actions. A third is a well-informed brief history of political activities by mental health professionals in Israel wishing to take a role in unfolding historical developments around them. An interesting ethical and political question is raised: Should mental health professionals take a public stand on political issues *qua* mental health professionals? The writing in this chapter is marked by an uncommon degree of self-disclosure, self-analysis, and self-criticism, of the kind that has always been the ideal, if not the reality, in the history of psychoanalysis. One wonders how many of us could live up to that ideal in the way Emanuel Berman does.

1. Introduction

The question of political involvement has baffled psychoanalysts, as clinicians and intellectuals, for many decades. A well-known example is the history of the Third Reich. The reaction of the international psychoanalytic community to the rise of Hitler was, from our present viewpoint, cowardly. It is amazing, when looking in the old volumes of *The International Journal of Psycho-Analysis*, to find the brief factual announcement informing the readers that the German Psychoanalytic Society was disbanded, without one word of commentary, not to mention protest. Ernest Jones (1879-1958), Freud's later biographer, and the editor of the *Journal*, was apparently determined not to provoke the new German authorities, and so were some "Aryan" German analysts who stayed in Berlin and worked in the Goering Institute (Cocks, 1997).

In retrospect, we may say that a belief in 'neutrality' allowed these analysts to collaborate with a most destructive and fanatical force, to disregard the danger that such collaboration will let its toxic effects penetrate their work and their lives, and to give up even the slim chance of reducing its murderous impact through honest critical examination. In their illusory 'neutrality', which really was their avoidance of the issues, they actually helped Hitler in gaining legitimacy, and in creating a semblance of 'normal life' in Nazi Germany.

Some of these issues came up around the first post-war psychoanalytic congress in Germany, held in Hamburg in 1985. I assume the willingness of analysts from around the world to attend that congress was aided by the capacity of certain leaders of German psychoanalysis to discuss that horrible era in the history of their nation, and its implications for psychoanalysis, in an honest and straightforward manner. But the experiences of many participants were ambivalent, and Moses & Hrushovski-Moses (1986) suggested that aspects of denial could be noticed in the congress itself.

But the issues are far from being limited to Nazi Germany. *International Psychoanalysis*, the bulletin of the International Psychoanalytic Association, has recently become the arena of a stormy debate regarding Chile under the Pinochet military regime. In preparation for the international psychoanalytic congress held in Santiago in 1999, the bulletin published a note by a Chilean analyst, Omar Arrue (1998a), about the recent history of Chile. This note treated the Pinochet years in a very cavalier way, emphasizing Pinochet's popularity and achievements, while totally avoiding terms such as dictatorship, assassination, torture, disappearance or the like.

Several analysts from around the world (Gampel, Canestri, Diatkine, Braun and Puget, 1998) protested angrily, and Arrue published an answer, which aroused bitter disappointment. Arrue (1998b) did not seem to genuinely grasp the outrage felt by his critics, or to reconsider his position with any thoughtfulness. Some of his new glib formulations ("The avoidance of unnecessary detail is also a form of respect for people's memory") aroused again the intense malaise and distress caused by his original contribution.

Arrue's claim for a consensus in Chile regarding the dictatorship years was formulated before Pinochet's arrest in Britain and the subsequent developments in Chile itself. From the stormy and divided reactions in Chile to the possibility of bringing Pinochet to trial, one could learn that the wish to forgive all atrocities in the name of 'national reconciliation' is not shared by all Chileans, and many of them are not willing to forgive Augusto Pinochet and his henchmen. Those in Chile, like Arrue, who see this issue as 'an internal Chilean affair' must realize that their view is not shared by the international community. Towards the end of the 20th century many individuals around the world would come to see the issues of assassination, torture, abduction, and brutal political persecution as problems involving all of humanity, so that no country has a mandate to 'forgive and forget' such actions.

As psychoanalysts, we have our own unique reasons to object to such 'forgetfulness'. Our work with trauma, both individual and collective, has taught us the crucial role of bringing the pain, and the rage, into full consciousness, and of their honest verbalization, if a recovery is to be eventually reached. Denial, affective isolation, rationalization, and identification with the aggressor (abundantly used by Arrue) are major obstacles to insight and to recovery.

The lessons from Germany under (and after) Hitler and from Chile under (and after) Pinochet are not limited to dictatorships. They point, I believe, to the need for analysts in all countries to confront openly major issues in their country's history, when these issues have unavoidable psychological implications for their analysands and for their society. Israeli society, and more specifically the Israeli-Palestinian conflict in which it is engulfed, is a case in point. The impact of this still unresolved national conflict on the mental health of Israelis and Arabs alike is, as I will discuss, an unavoidable topic for Israeli analysts.

2. Fathers and Sons

Let me start my exploration of the Israeli scene with a clinical vignette.

Some time ago, the Israeli daily Ha'aretz published an interview with a woman dedicated to teaching about the Holocaust in Israeli schools. Among other points, she protested the fact that the memory of Holocaust victims is commemorated in ways resembling those of soldiers who died in battle. As an example, she used the Holocaust memorial sculpture at *Yad Vashem* (the Holocaust commemoration center) in Jerusalem, created by Nathan Rapaport. "Those Tarzan-like figures bear no resemblance to actual Holocaust victims", she said.

I was quite upset about the comment, and wrote a letter to the editor, which was then published. The sculpture at *Yad Vashem*, I pointed out, is but a replica. The original sculpture was erected on the ruins of the Warsaw Ghetto, in the late forties. It had been planned by the Central Committee of the Jews in Poland, chaired by my late father, before the State of Israel was established in 1948. Therefore it represented, besides the sculptor's personal style, the esthetic values of European Holocaust survivors of that generation, and not any Israeli images. Can there be, I wondered, a 'true' representation of the Holocaust, beyond the values and tastes of a particular culture?

The day after my letter was published, one of my analysands, as he was lying on the couch, started talking about it. He was particularly intrigued by the figure of my father, and by my identification with him. He noticed I refer to my father as "Dr. Abraham Berman" (which I did out of loyalty, as that was the way my father presented himself), and asked me in what field this doctoral degree was. I told him it was in psychology, though since the war years my father abandoned psychology in favor of political activity. My patient made the comment that this explains a lot about me, as a politically involved psychologist. (He was right).

His subsequent associations turned to his own father. His father's family left Europe shortly before the Holocaust, and only recently he found out about some of his uncles who were killed by the Nazis, a topic his father avoided. He thought about his impression that while the rupture caused by the Third Reich apparently made my father struggle and develop, it made his own father constrict himself, limiting his ambitions and goals. One expression of that constriction was a disinclination to influence his children in vocational or ideological matters. During elections, he recollected, he used to ask his father for what party he voted, and the father would answer that the ballot is secret. Eventually, the influence went in the other direction: when the patient became politically involved in the Israeli peace movement, his father started voting for lists his son favored.

His associations now turned to his aging father's recent suggestion, that he could take into his possession a beautiful antique desk the father owns, and with it all the old family documents stored in it for decades. This possibility intrigued the patient, but also scared him. How will he decipher those documents, in a language he only barely reads; will he have the energy to do that?

In my subsequent interpretation, I referred to a recent trip my patient made to Europe, in which he discovered his grandfather's grave, and other milestones in his family's history. His father declined his invitation to join (he had consistently avoided visiting his native land again), but was helpful in planning the trip. I pointed out that regardless of how much more energy he will invest, the analysand already built a bridge to the family past, a bridge which was also constructed on his father's behalf, although the father was unable to erect it on his own.

There were many additional associations later on (the issue of soldiers who die in battle, and of the patient's own traumatic military experience, came up in the very next session), but I feel the present material is sufficient to introduce my point.

When writing now about that moving session, it becomes clear to me there were two additional levels to our dialogue, which were not spelled out by either of us, but I believe were on our minds. On one level, while our fathers indeed responded very differently to the rupture in their lives caused by the Nazi regime and by their migration from Europe, the two of us responded similarly vis-a-vis our fathers: my letter to the editor, and my analysand's trip to Europe (or his contemplated reading of the documents in the antique desk), were acts of filial loyalty, of seeking links, of trying to restore the rupture and to create intergenerational continuity.

The second level, which has been actually spelled out on other occasions, is the nature of our own transferential-countertransferential relationship, and the way it differs from the patient's relationship with his father. While his father emphasized that the ballot was secret, my "ballot" was never secret to the analysand. My left-wing views are well known in Israel, and so are my critical opinions about psychology, psychoanalysis, training and related topics. I often write or lecture about political issues, both of the national and the professional variety. (Some of these papers I will quote below).

Moreover, with this particular analysand-colleague (Berman, 1995a), our superficial acquaintance started years before analysis was ever contemplated, and one of our first contacts was in the context of an initiative to organize a conference on the psychological aspects of the Israeli-Arab conflict. He actually chose me as an analyst, to some extent, on the basis of this known affinity. And in the particular session I described, I chose to answer in a brief factual manner his question about my father, maybe on the basis of an intuitive feeling that my willingness will serve the intrinsic goals of analysis (goals such as free association, open exploration, direct emotional expression) better than silence, or a stereotypical "turning the question back".

Some of the questions this material brings up are universal, and I will return to them later on, in the context of discussing relational and inter-subjective models in psychoanalysis, and their implications for the issues of anonymity, abstinence, self disclosure and so on.

At the same time, I believe the session described is a very Israeli session, because the issues it raises, the Holocaust, migration, the 1933-1945 rupture, intergenerational transmission, war and peace, and political activism, are central preoccupations of Israeli culture, typical of a society in which history and politics have visibly affected the life of so many individuals, and in which analytic and therapeutic involvement often activates questions of national, ethnic, religious and ideological identity.

We cannot understand our patients, I suggest, if we are not attentive to the way history and politics shape their destiny, in subtle and complex interaction with intrapsychic factors. We cannot understand ourselves without similar self scrutiny, and this has implications for counter-transference, and for being clinically effective. Does such insight about the social roots of individual experience lead to a broader social understanding? And can such understanding lead to effective influence on political processes?

3. Denial and Reality

Political and historical reality, including the Israeli-Arab conflict, forms an omnipresent layer in the mind of any Israeli. Doing apolitical, ahistorical, analysis in such a society implies a degree of denial. Naturally, the particular form and intensity in which this 'external' reality is represented differ enormously from individual to individual. I consider it a trademark of the psychoanalytic approach that it rejects generalizations, and is attuned to the minute nuances of individual uniqueness. Over-inclusive statements, be they about PTSD or about 'second generation' Holocaust influences, are out of place in psychoanalytic discourse.

I do not share the opinion that psychoanalysis deals exclusively with inner, psychic, reality. Quite the contrary, in my view. Sigmund Freud paid attention all along to the impact of 'civilization and its discontents', and his theories often gave rise to ideas about potential social change (Berman, 1993). In my view, "[t]he capacity to explore 'external' reality undefensively may be conceived as facilitating a greater acceptance of psychic reality, rather than as competing with, and taking away from, the importance of psychic reality" (Berman, 1995a). I fully agree with Winnicott (1945, p. 153) when he states: "fantasy is only tolerable at full blast when objective reality is appreciated well". In discussing Winnicott's notion of transitional space, which is for me a central attribute of the analytic process, Phillips (1988, p. 119) suggests: "Transitional space breaks down when either inner or outer reality begins to dominate the scene, just as conversation stops if one of the participants takes over".

The history of psychoanalysis in Israel (starting before the state of Israel was established; see Rolnik, 2002) is characterized by two opposing trends: strong attention to the unique characteristics of the evolving new society, at times culminating in mobilizing psychoanalysis for societal goals while sacrificing some of its radical, critical nature; and at the other extreme an attempt to keep its universal intrapsychic purity, at the risk of turning a deaf ear to the historical and social context.

The first trend appears more dominant from the 1920s to the 1950s, and is expressed for example in the idealistic (but at times naive) involvement of psychoanalysts in molding educational systems, in the *kibbutz* movement and elsewhere, in the Siegfried Bernfeld tradition (Berman, 1988a).

The second trend is more dominant in recent decades, as part of the shift of Israeli society in general away from idealistic pioneering concerns, and as an aspect of the wish for 'normalization'. Most Israeli analysts, and many of the more experienced clinical psychologists and psychotherapists, work nowadays mostly in private practice, and avoid involvement in the deteriorating mental health system or in the problem-ridden school system. Still, they are often forced to realize that private patients, even if they are relatively affluent, are social creatures too, and are not exempt from the influence of historical and political forces.

This growing (though conflictual) realization accounts, I believe, for the repeated attempts of Israeli analysts and therapists to express their political concerns; but the conflicts aroused, and possibly the introverted style of many analysts, their greater comfort in the privacy of their consulting rooms and embarrassment about exposure, may account for a certain instability and discontinuity in these attempts.

Overall, the distribution of political opinions among Israeli analysts, therapists, clinical psychologists etc. is quite consistent. Over 70% identify with left-wing groups and with secular, democratic, socialist or liberal values; with the wish to achieve an Israeli-Arab accommodation, including a territorial compromise; and, in recent years, with the goal of establishing a Palestinian state, side by side with Israel. Less than 10% side with the right wing, with nationalistic and anti-Arab sentiments, or with the wish to transform Israel into a religious state (Rubinstein, 1994). Mental health professionals who are Orthodox Jews usually identify with moderate religious groups, and the few who live in settlements in the West Bank usually support the more pragmatic and compromise-seeking line among the settlers. Several of them are active in an organization, "Besod Siah" (literally translated as "in intimate discourse"), which seeks dialogue with colleagues on the Left, in spite of ideological disputes.

When, as a notable exception, an extreme right wing psychologist, Neta Dor-Shav, published a hostile pseudo-diagnostic character assassination of Itzhak Rabin (a prelude to his actual assassination later on), her article aroused enormous anger among most psychologists. The widespread rejection of the paper as unethical, was combined for many with a dismissal of Dor-Shav's fanatical political agenda as well (Berman, 1996a).

This distribution, let me add parenthetically, while radically different from the one in the general population (which is closer to 50:50), is characteristic of most Israeli professional groups with higher education in the humanities and the social sciences. Tempting as it may be, it need not be necessarily interpreted as a unique outcome of psychological knowledge or of psychoanalytic values, though these may have some impact.

But should these views be expressed, and if so, how? Can our psychological insights contribute or lead to political understanding, even to political influence? The dilemmas of Israeli analysts and therapists in expressing their political thought can be traced through a long sequence of events. Let me list a few of them chronologically. To some extent, this is also a history of my own personal odyssey in this terrain.

4. Entering the Public Arena

When Israeli analysts, together with American colleagues (and at the latter's initiative), met in the 1960s to discuss the psychological bases of war, their concerns were great. "At first the Israelis demurred, feeling their views about war were suspect because they themselves are involved in one" (Ostow, 1973, p. 9); "Could we be purely objective and our thinking abstract enough, no matter how hard we tried?" (Bental, 1973, p. 17). Eventually the discussions took place and a book was published, but the attempt to keep the exploration apolitical is evident throughout (Winnik, Moses & Ostow, 1973).

Before the elections in 1981 a group of psychologists considered issuing a public statement about Prime Minister Begin's shaky mental condition. Others, including myself, objected on ethical grounds; and the compromise was to issue instead a statement about the manipulative propaganda of Begin's party, the Likud, which we all feared will lead us towards another war. Although today we have an even clearer impression that Begin was probably manic-depressive, I am still glad we avoided this particular form of political involvement, which may shift attention from substantial political matters to the personality traits of leaders, utilizing amateur diagnosis of non-patients as a political weapon. Years later, when several of us made complaints to the ethics committee about Dor-Shav's public diagnosis of Rabin as "borderline", we could do so with a clear conscience.

Even that petition, dealing with issues of principle (psychological manipulation by politicians), came under attack from within the profession. You should express your political views as citizens, and not to tie them to your professional identity, we were told. Rebutting this criticism, we argued that as psychologists we have unique expertise, which is relevant to interpreting political processes as well, and can be legitimately utilized.

In 1982, several psychologists planned a conference about the impact of the occupation of the Palestinian territories on individuals and society in Israel. It was cancelled due to the war that indeed erupted in Lebanon. Although fruitless, this initiative is noteworthy due to its timing: long before the First *Intifada* (1987-1993), when the destructive consequences of the occupation was generally denied by Israelis. Later on, an organization of "Psychologists for Social Responsibility" was established, emphasizing educational goals, supporting democracy and condemning racism; it was active only for a brief period. Another initiative in the 1980s was a public call by numerous psychoanalysts supporting the suggestion for an international conference on the Israeli-Arab conflict (an idea which eventually materialized in the Madrid international meeting of 1991).

I should also mention the pioneering theoretical attempt by Rafael Moses to clarify the emotional dynamics of the Israeli-Arab conflict, through the notion of the group self and its pathology (Moses, 1982, 2002).

The heavy emotional impact of the Lebanon war led me to present, in 1985, a paper entitled "From war to war: Cumulative trauma", at a conference of the Israel Association for Psychotherapy. The Mental Health Division of the Israeli Army (in which I was involved at the time, in my capacity as a member of the Army reserves) would not allow me to use the painful data and case material regarding severe battle reactions of soldiers, so I had to present a fictionalized version. I spoke of three soldiers: Abraham, who went through traumatic experiences in the 1967 and 1973 wars, suppressed his panic and nightmares, and collapsed in 1982 when his past undiagnosed reactions were reactivated; Isaac, who went through parallel traumata but was never diagnosed, and his agony was only discovered when interviewed as part of a control group in a PTSD study; and Jacob, who was seemingly unharmed, but became cynical and emotionally aloof. (I was asked later on whether I deliberately chose the names of the patriarchs. I did not. Consciously, at least, I was looking for a Hebrew equivalent of 'Tom, Dick and Harry').

Later on in that paper I raised the issue of the defense mechanisms developed by Israeli mental health professionals, and which have led to a conspiracy of silence regarding the impact of cumulative war trauma, on soldiers, on their spouses, and on their children, in shaping psychopathological aspects in the lives of many Israeli patients. An awareness of this rising psychological cost could create moral dilemmas for Israeli psychotherapists, threatening their attempt to remain politically neutral on issues of war and peace.

Similar defense mechanisms, I suspect, made it very difficult to publish that paper itself. It was censored (almost mutilated) when reluctantly published in the bulletin of the Israel Psychological Association, and only when *Sihot: Israel Journal of Psychotherapy* was started I managed to have a full version published (Berman, 1987). My views were then criticized by one of the editors, who suggested that I disregard the main source of trauma: "Our inability to give the traumatic experience of prolonged war a clear, coherent and optimistic meaning" (Shalev & Berman, 1988, p. 147). In my rejoinder to his rebuttal I expressed the concern, that the belief, on both sides of a national conflict, in the clear and coherent meaning of wars, and the illusory optimism as to their outcome, prolong wars; maybe only a pessimistic view of wars' meaninglessness could push enemies to seek compromise?

Sihot: Israel Journal of Psychotherapy also published an intriguing series of papers about the history of battle reactions in Israel, their initial denial and the phases in their treatment (Witztum et al., 1989-91); as well as empirical studies on PTSD in Israeli soldiers (e.g., Solomon et al., 1987). Nevertheless, to my mind, the silence about the broader social implications of these issues is still persistent.

The next meaningful milestone in our chronology appeared in 1988. With the outburst of the First *Intifada*, the denial of the destructive impact of a continued occupation of Palestinian territories broke down (Berman, 1988b). A group of Israeli mental health workers visited Gaza, meeting with local colleagues, and I recall this visit as particularly meaningful in making Palestinian needs and concerns much more vivid and clear to us.

Two petitions by mental health workers about the psychological price of occupation appeared in the press, and they soon gave rise to the foundation of *Imut* [Hebrew for "verification"]: Mental health workers for the advancement of peace". This organization had at its peak hundreds of active members. It organized several successful conferences, on topics such as "The psychology of occupation", "Psychological obstacles to peace", "Nationality, nationalism and chauvinism" and "Imagining peace". It established ties with Palestinian mental health workers, participated in joint conferences in various countries, and initiated fruitful educational programs (Gampel, 2002).

In one of the *Imut* conferences I presented a paper which aroused stormy reactions, this time from the Left. While rejecting once more the sterility of 'reclusive psychology', I suggested that some of the political discourse of psychologists runs the risk of becoming a 'mobilized psychology'; namely, of seeking psychological rationales for pre-conceived ideological conclusions. This I contrasted with 'committed psychology', where the psychological (and specifically, psychoanalytic) tools are utilized creatively to re-think political reality, and contribute to fresh insights.

Such a re-examination, I suggested, should be directed towards the Israeli Left itself, towards what has been known as the Israeli "peace movement". (The equation of the two terms is inexact, but I will follow here this Israeli custom). One factor in the failure of the Left in the 1980s, I suggested, was its rationalistic attitude, its advocacy of principled solutions, while disregarding or even condemning as 'irrational' the emotional obstacles to their acceptance (the deep-rooted national identifications on both sides, the annihilation anxieties of many Israelis, and so on). Greater empathy with the emotional experience of the individuals involved in the conflict, rather than a hostile labeling of their motives, could pave the way to a more effective detoxification of hostility and fear by a new leadership which can be more easily identified with (Berman, 1989).

I am not sure myself why the activity of *Imut* declined in recent years. Is it a result of personal burnout, which made several leaders step down? Is it an expression of the depressive pessimism in the Israeli peace movement during the bleak Netanyahu years? Is it a reaction to complications in the collaboration with Palestinians, related to internal issues of the Palestinian Authority? Is it a retreat by psychologists to their familiar introverted style? Possibly a combination of all these and other factors. With the resumed outburst of violence in 2000, an initiative was taken to resume this activity of concerned mental health professionals, Jews and Arabs.

The First *Intifada* (1987-1993) aroused heated debates in the Israeli army, about the impact of military service in the occupied territories on the soldiers. I participated in one meeting, where the participants were visibly divided. Most practicing mental health officers present described severe post-traumatic stress reactions of soldiers after they participated in violent clashes with demonstrators, shot demonstrators or harshly beat them up, and conducted brutal searches in Palestinian homes. Many of their descriptions indicated intense experiences of anxiety, conflict and guilt. In contrast, their superior officers, heads of psychiatry and behavioral sciences in the army, made many efforts to trivialize these accounts, dismiss them or rationalize them away, and kept warning of risky political influences. (The army prevented empirical PTSD research during the First *Intifada*, after it was legitimized during the Lebanon war). Only those of us who came from outside army ranks, and participated in the discussion as consultants, kept encouraging the field officers to describe their experiences openly, and not to allow them to be silenced.

The trumatic experiences of soldiers fighting against a civilian population were explored in a documentary film, "Testimonies", in which the soldiers were interviewed by a clinical psychologist in psychoanalytic training. The emotional impact of the violent attempts to suppress the *Intifada*, (in addition, of course, to the emotional impact on Palestinian victims of violence, an important topic in itself), and its contribution to violence in Israeli society in general, is still an open issue. Such possible influences came up in a number of murder trials in recent years.

Bar-On (1999) asks:

> Was there emotional injury to the soldiers? How does an *Intifada* injury (moral trauma) differ from usual battle reactions (mental trauma)? How can it be treated? Why is it difficult to diagnose in a situation of social conflict, when its recognition has political significance too? (p. 174).

Bar-On suggests that the free exploration of these silenced questions may become possible only when peace with the Palestinians progresses, and gains broader public support.

Let me mention a few other turning points when political events captured the attention of Israeli analysts and therapists. One was the Gulf War of 1991, when Israeli cities were attacked by Iraqi missiles; many families left their city homes and moved to the countryside; and citizens were ordered to wear gas masks and enter gas-proof rooms when the air-raid sirens sounded (what does one do if it's the middle of a psychotherapy session, analysts and therapists debated ; what happens to boundaries?).

An analytic issue I recall as characteristic of that period was an analysand's anger at me for moving with my family outside of Tel Aviv (I came by train to see the patients who could continue, but had to change their hours). We gradually came to understand her anger at me in the context of her mother's Holocaust experiences: the mother's father and older brothers escaped from the ghetto, leaving her and her mother behind.

A special meeting of the Israel Psychoanalytic Society was dedicated to discussing the implications of these unusual situations for the practice of analysis; one analyst described the reactions of patients to the destruction of her home and office by a missile. Some of these issues were further explored by Keinan-Kon (1998).

Sihot: Israel Journal of Psychotherapy urgently published a special issue, with 15 brief papers on these dilemmas. In my own contribution, "So far only questions", I asked:

> How can we still be attentive to subtle nuances, when the exploding missiles are so noisy? Can we give full credit to the massive influence of this external reality, and at the same time keep the door open to the expression of inner reality? How can we take into account the collective experience we all undergo, and yet notice its completely individual translations? How can we avoid projecting our own interpretations on our patients, and help them reject the banal uniformity of experience offered by the mass media? (Berman, 1991).

The election of Itzhak Rabin as Prime Minister in 1992, and the Oslo process initiated by the new government in 1993, introduced greater optimism into the Israeli peace movement, including the mental health professionals involved in it. Personally,

I felt that Rabin offered the kind of leadership I hoped for a few years before; namely, a leadership which is experienced by many people as close enough to their national identifications, to their resentments and fears, as to allow it the power of detoxifying the darker, more paranoid and violent expressions of these fears and angry affects, transforming them into more pragmatic concerns. His military background was helpful in this respect. When Rabin said his stomach ached when he shook Arafat's hand, this made the handshake more acceptable to many Israelis, who until then saw the PLO as a demonic archenemy, and would have rejected a more enthusiastic handshake.

Still, this effectiveness was far from complete, and the presence of a vocal minority fighting the budding peace process tooth and nail culminated in Rabin's assassination, at the end of a moving mass rally celebrating the growing Palestinian-Israeli understanding.

In an editorial in *Sihot: Israel Journal of Psychotherapy,* a few days after the assassination, I said:

> It is no coincidence that psychotherapy has developed in a democratic, pluralistic culture. Many of its basic assumptions are close to those of democracy: the complex and paradoxical nature of human reality, which

cannot be explained by an overriding single principle; the uniqueness of the experience of different individuals and different groups, which precludes the possibility of absolute truth; the power of words and verbal communication in clarifying reality and solving conflicts; the value of free choice, and the difficulty in making it possible; the importance of attempting 'to step into the other's shoes' and take his needs into account; the effort to avoid black-and-white thinking, drastic polarizations of good and evil, and paranoid perceptions demonizing the other, individually or collectively.

The assassination, I suggested, proved that there are groups in Israeli society which reject these values completely. Psychotherapists cannot be indifferent to such trends, which threaten the foundations of their work; they must struggle against them thoughtfully, within ethical boundaries and within democratic structure (Berman, 1995b).

Many of my patients cried in the sessions following the assassination, and could barely return to discussing their private lives. Some analysands chose to sit up, needing face to face contact. I tried to seek with all of them the links between the collective trauma and its personal echoes, but I made no attempt to hide my own turmoil.

The further political upheavals of recent years in the Israeli-Palestinian arena again left their mark on every aspects of our lives, including analytic work. The basic tensions of Israeli society, as well as the fundamental difficulties at the core of the Israeli-Arab conflict (including its psychological aspects, such as mutual fear and rage, feelings of victimization and entitlement) will take many decades to resolve.

*

There are, of course, many additional conflicts in Israeli society, which have psychological implications. I will not approach here major issues such as conflicts about the place of religion, or *Sephardi-Ashkenazi* tensions, in which Israeli analysts and therapists were not particularly active. Israeli psychoanalysis has always been characterized by a secular *Ashkenazi* domination (in its early years, meetings of the Israel Psychoanalytic Society were held in German), and some of the few analysts of oriental origin speak today in retrospect of an abandonment of their ethnic identity ('*Ashkenazation*', or specifically '*Yekkization*', namely adopting German Jewish identity) as an implicit and unspoken aspect of their professional socialization. In future psychoanalytic discussions of Israeli identity, I hope the place of ethnicity will be explored much more thoroughly.

Another rarely discussed issue is the fact that there are no Arab analysts in Israel, no Arab analysands, and Arabs are underrepresented among clinical psychologists and psychotherapists. A committee sponsored by *Imut* tried to explore this situation and offer remedies, a few years ago, with little success.

I recall discussing this issue with a highly talented Arab undergraduate psychology student, who told me he will pursue graduate studies in another discipline, because clinical psychology may remove him too far away from the values and interests of his milieu. As there are few Arab therapists and few Arab patients in psychotherapy, there is barely any Israeli literature on issues of nationality in transference and countertransference.

The only additional issue I will mention are the social implications of recent changes in the mental health system in Israel. In the early years of the state, as part of an idealistic atmosphere influenced by socialist values, psychotherapy in the public domain flourished. Mental health clinics operated by the Ministry of Health, and of the General Sick Fund affiliated at the time with the trade unions, offered free psychotherapy to people who could not afford private treatment. Many Israeli analysts were active in this system, often in leadership roles. Side by side with the withdrawal of most analysts into their private offices, which I mentioned, the whole system is in a state of decline in recent years.

The growing privatization of the health system in general, under the influence of Thatcherist-Reaganite values, has been particularly damaging to psychiatry and clinical psychology. Cost-effectiveness considerations, usually calculated on a short-term basis (within the current year's budget) only, have led to massive cuts in many services, and to a heavy pressure to prefer pharmacological treatment and short term therapies, irrespective of the needs of individual patients. These issues came up in 1997 during a long strike by clinical psychologists, whose worsening work conditions are an aspect of the overall crisis. The Israel Psychoanalytic Society supported the psychologists' struggle. Clearly, the continuation of these destructive processes will damage the settings in which all future psychotherapists are being trained, and will limit psychotherapy mostly to the affluent parts of society, casting aside the emotional needs of the poor and the uneducated, of Arabs and of new immigrants, of the unemployed and of foreign laborers (Berman,

1997a, 1998a).

In a recent attempt to arouse interest in the political implications of psychology, Dan Bar-On (1999) raises the question: Why is there no 'new Israeli psychology'? Using the example of the Israeli 'new historians', who rebelled in recent years against the traditional Zionist narrative, offering new interpretations of the Israeli-Arab conflict, Bar-On expresses his disappointment with the meager contribution of Israeli psychologists to the evolving critical discourse regarding our society and its ideological foundations. He explains this, in part, by pointing out there is no 'old psychology' either; namely, that unlike history or sociology, which a few decades ago were intensely mobilized to support the Zionist ethos, Israeli psychology tended from the start to be individualistic and universalistic.

One of the issues Bar-On hopes a future Israeli 'new psychology' could deal with, is the acknowledgment of a unique Palestinian voice, substantially different from our own collective voice. Both Palestinian children and Israeli children (many of the soldiers who were sent to suppress the *Intifada* were only 18 or 19...) paid a heavy price for our inability to change our social perceptions, of ourselves and of the other (Bar-On, 1999).

5. Conclusion

In conclusion, let me return to a broader perspective on these issues.

First, I feel it is quite clear that attention to historical, social and political processes can help Israeli psychoanalysts and psychotherapists in better understanding their own lives, the lives of their patients, and the juncture in which they and they patients meet, namely the transferential relationship in its broadest sense.

Second, I feel that as concerned citizens, as professional experts, and as critical intellectuals, Israeli analysts often find themselves forced to form and express an opinion about central political issues, which have a major impact on the emotional lives and emotional well-being of many Israelis. Not to do so would be morally reprehensible.

How does such a political involvement of analysts influence their clinical work?

From the point of view of classical theory of technique, such self-exposure is clearly disastrous. The blank screen is soiled, and can no longer serve as a background for the analysand's projections.

Anonymity and neutrality are compromised, and the analyst becomes present as an actual person, disturbing the development of transference.

This view probably contributed to the determination of psychoanalysts in the past to keep their political views hidden, even to the point of not taking for several years a public position against the Nazi movement, and condemning and expelling Wilhelm Reich when he did (Scharf, 1983).

The earliest critique of the classical position was offered by Ferenczi (1932), who suggested that the patient often perceives the psychoanalyst's emotional reactions in spite of the attempt to maintain anonymity; and that the psychoanalyst's denial of such perceptions, while interpreting them as displacements or projections, may become 'professional hypocrisy', mystifying and re-traumatizing the patient (Berman, 1996).

Paraphrasing Ferenczi, I would suggest that withholding the analyst's political views and reactions, in a society which experiences political issues with great intensity (especially at times of crisis, war, crucial elections, etc.), may also be experienced by some patients as professional hypocrisy, and become destructive for the analytic process.

The growing trend towards relational and intersubjective re-formulations of psychoanalysis (Berman, 1997b) supplies us a new framework for these issues. If we take the personal and subjective nature of the analyst's presence for granted, the political aspects of this presence are not necessarily disruptive. If we come to suspect that "anonymity for the analyst is impossible", because "every intervention hides some things about the analyst and reveals others... [and] any way an analyst decides to deal with his or her emotional response is consequential" (Renik, 1995, p. 468), the anxiety and need to be constantly on guard are reduced. A conception that assumes that transference is constantly influenced by countertransference, and self-disclosures and enactments naturally happen in most sessions, implies that what is crucial is not the avoidance of contamination (the image of the sterile test tube, which Freud imported from the natural sciences), but the free exploration of this unavoidable reciprocal influence, and its utilization for the development of insight and of a deeper and richer analytic relationship.

When an analysand of mine became saddened (back in 1981) by my public statement against Begin's propaganda during the election campaign, this proved a fruitful starting point for exploration, which unearthed his deep transferential feelings towards Begin as a father figure. He could have guessed my views about Begin to begin with (they were shared by most analysts and therapists), but as long as I did not express them the issue remained dormant. Similarly, my open positions on various controversial issues in Israeli psychoanalysis (Berman, 1998b) allowed my analysands who were in psychoanalytic training to voice their reactions, both approving and disapproving, and join in exploring their deeper implications, more, I believe, than would have been possible had I attempted to hide them.

Much, I believe, depends on the psychoanalytic atmosphere. "[A]n analyst who regards his or her own constructions of reality as no more than personal views to be offered for a patient's consideration has no reason to avoid stating them explicitly" (Renik, 1995, p. 478). In this respect, what is destructive is authoritarian certainty, whether in interpreting the patient's unconscious, or in interpreting the political situation. If the analyst is not experienced as an omniscient authority, if discourse is free and flowing, a transitional space can evolve. Both external and internal reality, and their frequent interactions, may be noticed and contemplated, and one can work fruitfully with the analysand's reactions and associations.

Certainly, there can be painful moments in such a process. A realization that one's analyst is 'on the other side of the barricade' can be upsetting (just as being together 'on the same side of the barricade' may lead to defensive solidarity which whitewashes other areas of conflict). But this may happen with personal issues as well, such as when a vocational or romantic choice the analysand is excited about is interpreted by the analyst as destructive. (In my experience, analysands notice very fast the analyst's disapproval, even if expressed through a supposedly 'purely intrapsychic' interpretation). A lot depends on the analyst's tact, on her or his ability to maintain empathic listening in spite of different opinions, without putting down or dismissing the analysand's views, without hurting the analysand's feelings.

The last major issue I want to discuss is the nature of analysts' and therapists' contribution to political discourse. As I mentioned earlier on, this contribution may be at times shallow and limited, when psychological concepts are used in the service of preconceived political opinions. Whether one offers psychiatric diagnoses to a resented leader, or derogatory generalized interpretations about resented political groups ("the right wing is prone to projection and splitting", as if such trends never appeared in left wing movements), these uses of psychology are barren intellectually. Being visibly manipulative, they lack credibility, and may easily backfire.

The kind of involvement I believe we should strive for is based on utilizing our expertise in listening for a fresh examination of political reality. To give one example, I would suggest that a major weaknesses of many peace movements is their pacifism; namely, their utopian tendency to deny group loyalties and aggression as basic human realities, and to appeal to an idealized peace-loving humanity free of any dividing forces (Berman, 1993). Such idealizations, based on a narrative of progress ('from national or religious loyalties towards internationalism'), which postmodern thinking has exposed for its wishful thinking, may become an obstacle to realistic peace-making, which in my mind necessitates full awareness of the power of national, ethnic and religious belonging, and of the universal tendencies to fear and distrust the other.

For me, fighting chauvinism is aided by fully understanding its emotional dynamics; and only empathy towards national sentiments can facilitate their detoxification from destructive hostilities, so that pragmatic compromises can be reached. This is parallel, to some extent, to the way an analyst can absorb toxic projective identifications, and return them to the analysand in a detoxified version, a process Bion (1977) and Ogden (1997) have described as crucial for achieving change.

A rationalistic, condescending or judgmental attitude, rejecting common human feelings as base, primitive and 'irrational', does not allow such healing processes to evolve. Empathic listening, even to a violent patient, may eventually calm down the violence more than moral condemnation.

Listening empathically to the individuals on both sides of a bloody dispute does not imply agreeing with their opinions, which may be extreme and rigid, especially when historical rights are at issue, and each side has an experience of victimization based on a frightful accumulation of well-remembered past atrocities. It implies, however, a realization that unless the yearnings and anxieties on both sides are not sufficiently attended to, no lasting peace is possible. Analysts are equipped to offer a model of such patient and insightful listening.

*

In the long run, I personally conclude, social responsibility, leading to an attempt to contribute to the understanding and resolution of crucial political issues, and the responsibility to help a particular individual in need of treatment, while they may be in tension and at some moments in conflict, do not necessarily exclude each other.

The analyst's political involvement, if it is thoughtful and non-manipulative, and if it is expressed in non-authoritarian terms and remains open for candid critical discussion, can become a stimulus for fruitful intersubjective analytic exploration with each analysand. A straightforward and serious political involvement of analysts may then acquire a positive significance, of broad-minded innovative thinking about our historical destiny, both collective and individual; of willingness to take risks, and step out of one's self-centered interests and concerns.

References

Arrue, O. (1998a). Brief note on the history of Chile in the last thirty years. *International Psychoanalysis*, 7(1).

Arrue, O. (1998b). Omar Arrue answers his critics. *International Psychoanalysis*, 7(2), 5.

Bar-On, D. (1999). The silence of the psychologists; or, why is there no 'new' Israeli psychology? *Sihot: Israel Journal of Psychotherapy*, 13, 172-175.[Hebrew]

Bental, V. The subjectivity of Israeli psychoanalysts in discussing war. In H.Z Winnik, R Moses, & M. Ostow (Eds.). *Psychological Bases of War*. New York: Quadrangle.

Berman, E. (1987). From war to war: Cumulative trauma. *Sihot: Israel Journal of Psychotherapy*, 2, 37-40.[Hebrew]

Berman, E. (1988a). Communal upbringing in the kibbutz: The allure and risk of psychoanalytic utopianism. *Psychoanalytic Study of the Child*, 43, 319-335.

Berman, E. (1988b). The silence of the psychologists. *Politika*, 19, 23-25 [Hebrew].

Berman, E. (1989). Mobilized psychology and involved psychology. Presentation at the *Imut* annual conference, Jerusalem.[Hebrew]

Berman, E. (1991). So far only questions. *Sihot: Israel Journal of Psychotherapy*, *5*, 3, [Hebrew]

Berman, E (1993). Psychoanalysis, rescue and utopia. *Utopian Studies*, *4*, 44-56.

Berman, E. (1995a). On analyzing colleagues. *Contemporary Psychoanalysis*, *31*, 521-539.

Berman, E. (1995b). The day after [unsigned editorial]. *Sihot: Israel Journal of Psychotherapy*, *10*, [Hebrew].

Berman, E. (1996a). Psychologists who slandered Rabin. *Sihot: Israel Journal of Psychotherapy*, *10*, 154. [Hebrew]

Berman, E. (1996b). The Ferenczi renaissance. *Psychoanalytic Dialogues*, *6*, 391-411

Berman, E. (1997a). Psychology for the rich and psychology for the poor? *Ha'aretz,* June 1, 1997 [Hebrew].

Berman, E. (1997b). Relational psychoanalysis: A historical perspective. *American Journal of Psychotherapy*, *51*, 185-203.

Berman, E. (1998a). Evil winds are blowing: Mental health services in Israel. *Sihot: Israel Journal of Psychotherapy*, *12*, 140-141 [Hebrew].

Berman, E. (1998b). Structure and individuality in psychoanalytic training: The Israeli controversial discussions. *American Journal* of Psychoanalysis, *58*, 117-133.

Bion, W.R. (1977). *Seven Servants: Four Works*. New York: Jason Aronson..

Cocks, G. (1997). *Psychotherapy in the Third Reich: The Goering Institute*. 2nd ed. New Brunswick: Transaction.

Ferenczi, S. (1932/1980). Confusion of tongues between adults and the child. In *Final Contributions*. New York: Brunner/Mazel.

Gampel, Y. (2002). The unavoidability of links and violable links: Israelis and Palestinians in psychoanalytic psychotherapy training. In this volume.

Gampel, Y., Canestri, J., Diatkine, D., Braun, J., & Puget, J. (1998). The history of Chile? (letters to the editor). *International Psychoanalysis, 7*, 4-5.

Keinan-Kon, N. (1998). Internal reality, external reality, and denial in the Gulf War. *Journal of the American Academy of Psychoanalysis, 26*, 417-442.

Moses, R. (1982). The group self and the Israeli-Arab conflict. *International Review of Psycho-Analysis, 9*, 55-65.

Moses, R & Hrushovski-Moses, R. (1986). A form of denial at the Hamburg Congress. *International Review of Psycho-Analysis, 13*, 175-180.

Ogden, T.H. (1982). *Projective Identification and Psychotherapeutic Technique.* New York: Jason Aronson.

Ostow, M. (1973). Preface. In H.Z Winnik, R Moses, & M. Ostow (Eds.). *Psychological Bases of War.* New York: Quadrangle.

Phillips, A. (1988). *Winnicott.* London: Fontana.

Renik, O. (1995). The ideal of the anonymous analyst and the problem of self-disclosure. *Psychoanalytic Quarterly, 64*, 466-495.

Rolnik, E.J. (2002). Psychoanalysis moves to Palestine: Immigration, integration, and reception. In this volume.

Rubinsrtein, G. (1994). Political attitudes and religiosity levels of Israeli psychotherapy practitioners and students. *American Journal of Psychotherapy, 48*, 441-454.

Scharf, M. (1983). *Fury on Earth: A Biography of Wilhelm Reich.* New York: St. Martin's Press.

Shalev, A. & Berman, E. (1988). Exchange on "From war to war: Cumulative trauma". *Sihot: Israel Journal of Psychotherapy, 2*, 147-148.[Hebrew]

Solomon, Z., Garb, R., Bleich, A., & Gropper, D. (1987). Reactivation of battle reactions among Israeli soldiers during the Lebanon war. *Sihot: Israel Journal of Psychotherapy, 2*, 31-36. [Hebrew].

Winnicott, D.W. (1945/1975). Primitive emotional development. In *Through Pediatrics to Psycho-analysis.* New York: Basic Books, 1975.

Winnik, H.Z., Moses, R. & Ostow, M. (1973). *Psychological Bases of War.* New York: Quadrangle.

Witztum, E., Levey, A., Kotler, M., Granek, M., & Solomon, Z. (1989-91). Battle reactions in Israel's wars, 1948-1982. Series of papers, ? *Sihot: Israel Journal of Psychotherapy, 4-5* [Hebrew].

Chapter 9

Unavoidable Links and Violable Links: Israelis and Palestinians in Psychoanalytic Psychotherapy Training

Yolanda Gampel
Tel-Aviv University

In this chapter we reach an area which may strike some readers as risky and impractical: An attempt to use psychotherapy as a bridge between Israelis and Palestinians. Such attempts may lead to charges of naiveté, as well as other criticisms, but what we find here is a unique combination of theoretical ideas about violence at many levels, together with a story of real courage. The theoretical sections offer an abstract level of conceptualization which may strike the reader as too abstract at times, but they offer a rich, original world of interpretations and sensitivities. Our common fears and hopes are translated into the language of depth analysis, and we are forever reminded of their origins in our childhood, our parents, our developing ego and its attempts at finding safety. We also find here a factual report on the history of one practical attempt at creating links and cooperation.

1. Introduction

In response to the escalating violence and the intensifying conflict between Israelis and Palestinians at the onset of the First *Intifada* (1987-1993), a group of Jewish and Palestinian mental health professionals began meeting in connection with the organization known as *Imut* [Hebrew for "verification"] (Berman, 2002). The members of *Imut* believed in serving as professional change agents, using their understanding of social and psychological processes to work towards greater democracy, mutual and egalitarian recognition of the rights of individuals and national groups, and non-violent solutions to the conflict, through the creation of dialogue. Despite the political situation, numerous acts of terrorism and the increasing escalation of the *Intifada*, we searched for a working link that would foster a space for dialogue and thinking. We believed that the creation of a working link is part of a gradual maturation process which requires the establishment of discussion groups comprised of both parties.

Our purpose was to create, if only temporarily, a medium with which to explore common professional concerns and to enable a working alliance. A dialogue creates choices and possibilities which both groups can consider and accept. While our encounters made possible a dialogue between Israeli and Palestinian mental health professionals, the process was extremely arduous and lengthy. Perhaps even more significant was the sense of impotence felt by all participants, and our inability, as a group made up of professionals, to bringing about change on a political level. However, all the conferences and encounters that we held were acts of courage on both sides in that all participants dared to face cruel political realities, without running away or ignoring it.

To discuss the inviolable and violation would put me on a different conceptual register than if I were to discuss the possible and impossible. Violation is linked to profanity. One profanes something protected by the law, something holy. The act of profanity breaks a taboo. The act of violation is contradictory to the life drive; it is contrary to the construction of a link. It is contrary to the psychic function of representation and symbolization. Symbolization is the nurturance of psychic life. Violation destroys the symbol and turns it into raw and fragmented stuff which is ineffective for encouraging thoughtfulness. On the other hand, inviolability means accepting the symbolization and the link that extends "Beyond any conflict". In this way, the link is grounded in the roots of being and becoming, the future, the law, and a human ethical consensus.

During our work together, the "possible" seemed to me to be related to social responsibility, courage, and the acceptance of objective limits, those of time and space. These "possibles" were realized to some extent, until there was a terrorist attack which blew apart both body and mind as well as the capacity to think. It seemed to me that I had forgotten my experience of the "impossible" at these moments, and when facing this "violation" there was no possibility for thought. We were left with only an overwhelming feeling of pain, suffering, and despair. We would ask ourselves whether there was any point in continuing the struggle to create a link. In these moments it seemed impossible. The ambivalent feelings that existed in all of us at certain times, combined with the belief in the possibility of the restoration of links, and their apparent impossibility at times. When acts of terrorism on the part of Palestinian terrorists or acts of oppression and violence on the part of the Israeli Defense Forces occurred, limits were violated and this resulted in the destruction of a consensus that allows being and becoming. Faced with this violence there is an emergence of sadness, anger which at times is transformed into hatred and other destructive elements inherent in the human fantasy which manifests itself in its fullest intensity in the Biblical prescription of "An Eye for an Eye".

The Israeli-Palestinian conflict is ongoing. When faced with this reality, our memory forces us to affiliate with a "father". The father transmits ideals, culture, religion and in the name of the ideals that he represents, we agree to make sacrifices. We love this father figure, this homeland, the landscape of our national identity. Inherent in these "fatherly transmissions" is the expectation that we fulfill our obligations to our ancestors no matter what personal sacrifice is required.

Implicit in the efforts of Palestinians and Israelis who worked together to give birth to something new was the sense of transgression or violation of transmitted ancestral ideals. We were betraying the "father". Freud noted in his work on the ego and the id: What assures the security of the ego is the maintenance of the security of the object (Freud, 1923). At certain moments in our dialogue we were conflicted between the transmitted legacy of our ancestors and our desire to create a new legacy where we would ensure the security of the other. This brought about feelings of hope and despair. There were many times that we felt that we could not change the transmitted ancestral order (represented by the extremists on both sides). This was our despair. Nonetheless, stopping the dialogue would be to lose all hope. Our only option was our faith, in the value of exploring the irrational factors that lead to war and terrorism with the knowledge that perhaps we could not find a rational solution.

When we began to organize the training of Palestinian

psychotherapists the First *Intifada* was at its height. It was during the summer of 1992, one of the most intense periods of violence and tension. There was a sense of hopelessness, of not seeing any possible solution to the conflict. Despite this, some members of *Imut* on both sides of the political spectrum had developed close and reciprocal relationships. We were interested in promoting the professional development of Palestinian mental health workers and in improving the health services rendered. Dr. Eyad El Sarrajj, the director of the clinic in Gaza, and a member of *Imut*, then agreed to allow his staff to be the first participants in this training program. A small group of Israeli *Imut* members decided to contribute to this training program, which was an act of faith towards the links that had been forged long ago. Our working group (members of the steering committee included Tamar Zelniker, Rachel Hertz-Lazarowitz, Yolanda Gampel, Gabi Mann, and Yossi Hadar) believed that this project was feasible and this act was the right one.

However, when we spoke with our friends, colleagues and relatives in Israel, we were surprised by the violent resistance that this project evoked. Rarely did we find individuals or organizations that were willing to assist us in this project. The Department of Psychology at Tel Aviv University, the Embassy of Canada, and the Embassy of the United States in Tel Aviv were the only bodies that agreed to support this project. The most painful encounters were experienced with those who were closest to us. As far as our friends and dear ones were concerned, this project was in the realms of the forbidden, and for some, we were in the process of violating the sacred; we were traitors. These responses were encountered by Israelis and Palestinians alike. Because of the many obstacles and the disapproval we encountered, we decided that rather than stop the project we would have to stop discussing our plans with even those closest to us.

The training of the Palestinian psychotherapists began in the spring of 1993 and the meetings took place at Tel Aviv University. We met on Fridays, from 10 a.m. until 4 p.m. For the Palestinian participants it was their free day. For us it was half a day of work. There are usually no activities at the university on Fridays. The themes that we worked on initially were "The Theory and Clinic of Post Traumatic Reactions", "An Introduction to Psychotherapy" and a seminar on the supervision of clinical cases.

Initially, relations between the two sides were very sensitive especially during supervisory sessions. We, the Israelis, represented "the occupiers" and they "the people who were in revolt". We possessed the knowledge base of psychotherapy and psychoanalysis and they had to submit themselves to our expertise. We, the instructors, were in the position of strength and they were in a position of submission.

The first cases presented in supervision dealt with children that suffered from post-traumatic reactions related to violent interactions with Israeli soldiers. Together we were to grapple with some dilemmas: How to find a way to accept the differences that exist between us without ignoring the similarities. How to respect the identity and space of the other side, as well as the wide variety of reactions determined by socio-cultural ideals. How to transmit knowledge while taking into account the big difference between fantasies, intention, and the accomplished action. How to refrain from clinging to a metaphor of violence but to allude to and to denote the repressed in our emotional links and in the personal history of each patient. In this lay the attempt to expand one's understanding and to search for the beginning of a cure. The Palestinian colleagues had an additional "mission", to denounce and condemn, and we the Israelis were there to hear their testimony. However, the great challenge lay in going beyond the social political testimony and creating a professional working alliance which could focus on the psychic reality. The great fear of both sides lay here, the fear of betraying the "sacredness of the subject".

Many of our difficulties were on a practical level, such as obtaining permits for the Palestinians who traveled from Gaza to Israel. Tamar Zelniker was the driving force that allowed this coming together. Without her insistence and stubbornness this work would not have been possible. Every week we had to work very hard to convince the Israeli and Palestinian administration of the "innocence" of our project. Not to mention what would happen when there was a terrorist attack and the border was closed. One small anecdote will help you visualize the kind of obstacles we struggled with. One Friday, after many trials and tribulations at the border, the Palestinian group arrived in a car that we had put at their disposal. They arrived at the gates of the university and the Jewish guard, who was a descendent of immigrants from an Arab country, asked them what they were doing there on a day when everything was closed at the university. The guard refused to telephone the Department of Psychology and to check whether we were there, while we were sitting there and waiting. The group had no option but to return to Gaza. We waited for them, knowing that they had managed to cross the border, but not knowing what had happened to them. Upon their return to Gaza they called and told us what had happened. An unpredictable obstacle? Frustrated and with great discomfort, we felt that others were undermining our efforts.

Let me share some of the thoughts that crossed my mind during the process. They are the notes scribbled in a copybook that I found recently.

(1) written during the preparation of the course......

> The reality of the Israeli/Palestinian conflict, two opposing communities, two traditions, two cultural affiliations. This conflict can be and cannot be resolved. There is a desire to know who is right and who is in the wrong. Each side is fighting in the name of what it believes is right. Violence is a way of reclaiming one's rights. A blind will to fight to the death in the name of these rights, to defend these rights. The sense of the defiance of justice. Can the recollection of the memories of each people and community help us in the dialogue that we try to initiate? (cf. Gampel, 1997, 1999).

(2) The following notes were written during the first supervisory sessions:

> Identity and belonging are difficult notions...in order to be one over time, we need to belong to a particular context. Belonging creates identity. Identity is created from the moment of conception through the parental unconscious. What a difficult game it is to play where we must accept and obey the rules are imposed beforehand. Sometimes it does not give us the opportunity to express the ethics and rigor of our deepest being. What an impossible illusion. What comes to mind is that we should give ourselves up to the world of meditation, to stop the struggle and let things happen on their own. Taking a position of waiting, a centered and attentive rigorous expectation that is far from the events...the sky, the sea, how marvelous they are, the world is so beautiful, how can we live in it?

(3) And just after the incident at the university that I recounted earlier

> ....What despair, what disillusionment, such an unhappy coincidence, what more has to happen...nothing is working, what should we do, ...stop struggling, do nothing as if we are in an absurd movie? We are ready to communicate, we are willing, but it is impossible. All these efforts in vain. We think that we have a link, a communication, but is this true, is it real? What an invasive sadness, hopelessness and

frustration, where will all this take us? This work has connected us to the psycho-soma and the conscious and unconscious fantasy, and its origins in the history of this culture.

Despite all the difficulties and resistance, we tried to transform the impossible into the possible and to continue the training program. One of the difficulties surrounding research on the phenomenon of fanaticism is that rarely does it appear as a characteristic of the mind. In general, it is a "use" that adheres to each enunciation, that is to say, the fanatic characteristic can be related to any emotion, idea, feeling, or theory, that has the potential of acquiring a fanatic quality.

The fanatic quality is acquired very quickly, because it does not require the collaboration of the other parts of the personality. It can give up all the structures being developed, and for a time nurture itself. This is related with the difficulty in abandoning autocratic thinking, because thinking that leads to tolerance is self-realized very slowly, accompanied by psychic pain. To achieve tolerance is an arduous task. While the acquisition of fanaticism is immediate. Sometimes fanaticism is similar to a virus, which seeks a place to harbor itself in order to survive; it has no independent life. Fanaticism prefers to install itself in mental cells rich in thought, because the matrix in which it establishes itself is vital for its survival. Fanaticism inculcates itself in all the openings where doubt resides, spreads quickly, and is therefore contagious. Fanaticism invades the cells of thought little by little, and no one knows a priori where it will lead to (one may speak of radioactive identification). When it installs itself in the mind it requires that an idea installs itself in isolation from other ideas, transformed into a doctrine. Fanaticism is a unique idea that does not permit living side by side with other ideas. It is possible that the fanatic structure does not tolerate catastrophic change without violent destruction. It may be characterized as an attack on knowledge, which refuses any union with divergent ideas. Sometimes fanaticism reaches pseudo-articulation, and so passes unnoticed into the closed realms of science, mysticism, and art. Fanaticism calms us just as does the rereading of a story calms a child; a new idea is painful, since it evokes emotions of fear, loneliness, and emptiness. Fanaticism is always present, intolerant of absence, doubt, change. Fanaticism hates the unique and the diversity of emotion, but most of all, it is intolerant of impotence, need, and doubt. It offers itself in order to fill the soldiers, offering solace in the form of salvation, relief, and false patronage. Basically, fanaticism is closed and causes closure. Fanatic youth hides behind it the phenomena of continuous adherence, and the conglomeration of ideas, without admitting contradiction, asymmetry and asynchronicity.

2. A Jewish Israeli Perspective

From a psychological point of view, the influences of the Holocaust went far beyond the individual, affecting and coloring the social-political situation within the Jewish state. The *Shoah* scarred not only those people who were the direct victims but also those who lived at the same period as well as the generations that followed. Everyone living in the twentieth century was exposed to its destructive radiation. This is especially evident in Israel, where almost all the aspects of life are permeated with this massive trauma.

While all individuals harbor within themselves this silent and hidden legacy of aggression, it is very important to underline that the individuals who went through the *Shoah* were forced into acquaintance with terrible aggression by a brutal, external world and not because of their own hidden aggression. At times, however, the violence which they experienced was swallowed up in their fantasy world and the aggressor became internalized in their psychic apparatus in some manner. These horrifying experiences were not allowed the opportunity to be worked through; they were not transformed through the working through of a mourning process. At the same time, the country's repeated wars created a situation of violence, death, and loss, and the need for an additional mourning process.

3. Clinical vignettes

3.1 *On radioactive social historical identification*

The constant search by humans for a safe place and a secure identity leads us to question the continuous existence of war that destroys, exiles, divides, and confuses. This struggle for a secure identity and a safe place in which to live was poignantly expressed in a psychoanalytic session with an adult patient.

a. Mrs. A spoke of the lack of security which is a basic part of life in Israel, and expressed her concern about the economic and security conditions. She said: "I remember the fifties. I was a child, we had very little, but we were united, we had hopes; today the future threatens us with war and catastrophe." She was referring to a criminal event in which Arabs were involved. "What is going to happen? In my associations the Arabs are linked with the Germans. I understand that that is an internalized interpretation of the history of my parents who went through the *Shoah*. From that standpoint I should be in favor of *Gush Emunim* (the religious-nationalist movement that believes in settling Greater Israel), but that is the neurotic approach of the past, that everybody is persecuting us and that everybody is against us. In general, I don't hate Arabs, but towards the murderers in the bus attack I would implement the rule of 'an eye for an eye'. I grew up with a sick mother and father knowing it was all because of the War; it wasn't talked about but it was clear, their longing for their childhood and their parents. Afterwards came the Sixties, with the awareness of the consequences of the atomic bomb. I thought that children should not be brought into the world when danger is so concrete. Who can guarantee that the *Shoah* won't happen again?"

Later, after referring to another event, Mrs. A said:

> I asked myself who is more important, me or my children? I do not know. Smadar Haran, the woman in Nahariya whose house was broken into by terrorists, was no worse a mother than anyone else, when she had to silence her daughter, when she was so scared that she smothered her to death. My three-year-old son can't understand what I ask him to do. How do you live with it afterwards.

b. In a group of *Shoah* survivors I have been meeting with for several years, the unpalatable role Israeli soldiers are being forced to play has been a constantly recurring motif since the First *Intifada* began in December 1987. Being able to talk about it has added special shadings to the participants' understanding of the social violence that took place at the time of the *Shoah* and to which they, the survivors, bear living witness. The group is composed of *Shoah* survivors who were children at the time of World War II, and who meet regularly to share their past and ongoing experiences (Gampel, 1988, 1990, 1992; Kestenberg & Gampel, 1983). The topic was first broached by a couple who have been in the group since its inception. The husband, Mr. S, was released from Auschwitz when he was twelve and a half years old after having been there for a long time. The wife, Mrs. S, had been a child in a different camp, and was subjected to many traumatic experiences and displacements before entering the camp.

Mrs. S. opened the discussion by saying she wanted to raise the issue of the occupation and hear how everybody in the group felt about it. It made her feel very bad and restless when she thought about her own son, in particular, but also about the other young Israeli soldiers having to enter homes in the middle of the night, wake up families, and at times take away the father of frightened, anxious children. The whole scene was impossible for her to deal with, because it reminded her of what was done to her as a child. In her words: "How can a Jewish soldier do that? We who suffered from persecutions, we can't allow ourselves to do that.

I will not try to reproduce all the reverberations her words generated over the next two years, but will only mention that part of the group identified with Mrs. S. and expressed great sadness, while others were outraged by the comparison. The latter viewed the occupation as one more necessary form of self-protection for the purpose of survival, given the lack of other alternatives. Their chief concern was that the *Shoah* should never recur, and they were convinced it would recur if Jews allowed themselves to be wishy-washy. But it was evident that they, too, were experiencing great pain.

I perceived Mrs. S. and the other members of this group of *Shoah* survivors as crying out to the world and to Israel, the country to which they had come to collect themselves and to try to go on living. I heard them pleading to be freed from the telescoping of generations, from transgenerational transmission (Gampel, 1988, 1990, 1992), and from the transposition of trauma. To me they seemed to be crying out against being taken back into a reversed mirror of their past, in which their children enact the role that others had once played towards them, to be pleading for disidentification from that role, if any identification ever existed in them. And above all, I heard them crying for a background of safety. Through the above vignette, we can see how the *Intifada* arouses feelings of uncanniness in survivors in response to their children's behavior. Through the military roles which their children are forced to play, the survivor/parent comes into contact with aggression and brutality, and with certain cleaved, undifferentiated and ambiguous aspects of himself which had been repressed (Gampel, 1990).

We reached September 1993, the moment when Yitzhak Rabin and Yasser Arafat signed the first peace agreement. *Imut* then initiated a meeting to reflect upon ways of organizing ourselves to live in a state of peace. At this meeting, I presented a certain conceptualization, a way of looking at the impact of the quality of social violence on psychic reality. The impact of social violence and its vicissitudes over an extended period was discussed. In previous papers, I have defined two types of background which I believe co-exist: the background of safety and the background of the uncanny. The hypothesis put forward is that people who have experienced extreme traumatic and violent elements need to split off or dissociate the two backgrounds and maintain it in order to continue living without being overwhelmed or engulfed by their traumatic past.

What sometimes emerges later, not through screen memories or dreams but through recollections that are raw and real, are concrete memories of a terrible reality once suffered. At certain moments, these traumatized people are unable to disguise, differentiate, or integrate their memories within the psychic reality of their daily life. A theoretical analysis followed on the consequences of a psychic reality where the two backgrounds come into contact, and what is more extreme, a situation that manifests itself when the uncanny seeps into or engulfs the background of safety. These different modes were illustrated with clinical material and the technical difficulties that arise in psychoanalytic practice were taken into consideration.

The participants in the meeting examined the concepts of the background of safety and the background of the uncanny from the perspective of the Israeli-Palestinian conflict. From a discussion with the participants it transpired that what is the background of safety for a Palestinian is a background of the uncanny for an Israeli and visa versa. As the discussion unfolded, participants began to look at their own national identity and could see that such a polarization exists within Palestinian and Israeli society. Thus, what is a background of safety for a left wing Israeli is actually a background of the uncanny for a right-wing Israeli. The same applies to different factions in Palestinian society. It was agreed that there is not only one Palestinian or Israeli psychic reality but that a number of different psychic realities exist within each people.

An underlying theme of the discussion related to identity, identification, the vicissitudes of belonging to a nation, affiliation to a party or an ideology, a religion, and a family. An important conclusion was that there was work to be done not only to bridge the two peoples but to create a link between the two backgrounds within each nation in order to facilitate the possibility of living in peace.

During the second year of our training program, we had reached a stage of thinking constructively and objectively together about the psychotherapeutic processes. At the beginning of the year, the patient was the figurative term in a three-way relation. The patient served to objectify the conflict in the inter-subjective relationship which could not be stated by either Palestinian or Israeli. Little by little the possibility of discussion allowed an awakening of different aspects of knowledge that existed in the Palestinians and Israelis. Although it was also an overture to an unknowable future, at this point nothing could prevent the continuation of the dialogue. The symptoms of the patient were not just something that we had to find a quick solution for. Rather they were related to a lack that had to be understood and solved through a process. The conflict that in certain individuals became a symptom or illness could now be thought as something that unlatched/unbridled a history of frustrations, of trauma and lacking that had become inscribed in the structure of the personality. If in the beginning of our training program, it was impossible to create genetic-historical-social links, by now we were on the path to finding the way to symbolize the birth, the structure, the current situation and all that has been repressed. All this rendered possible the restoration of links and perhaps even a new genesis.

By the third year, the training program was already officially made part of the psychotherapy program in the school of medicine at Tel Aviv University (participating teachers in this phase included Michel Granek, Hanna Biran, Na'ama Havkin, and other members of the faculty in the psychotherapy diploma program). Graduates were now trying to transmit their knowledge and know-how to their colleagues in Gaza. An ongoing contact was maintained on several levels, including a supervision program, special seminars, and the establishment of a similar training program at Gaza University.

References

Freud, S. (1923/1961). The ego and the id. In *The Standard Edition of the Complete Psychological Writings of Sigmund Freud.* Vol. 19, 1-66. London: The Hogarth Press

Gampel, Y. (1988). Facing war, murder, torture and death in latency. *Psychoanalytic Review, 75,* 500-509.

Gampel, Y. (1990). A daughter of silence. In M.S. Bergmann & M.E. Jucovy (Eds.), *Generations of the Holocaust.* New York: Columbia University Press.

Gampel, Y. (1992). I was a Shoah Child. *British Journal of Psychotherapy, 8,* 391-400.

Gampel, Y. (1997). The role of social violence in psychic reality. In J. Ahumada, J. Olagaray, A.K. Richards, & A. Richards (Eds.) *The Perverse Transference & Other Matters.* Northvale, NJ: Jason Aronson.

Gampel, Y. (1999). Between the background of safety and the background of the uncanny in the context of social violence. In P. Fonagy, A. Cooper, & R.S.Wallerstein (Eds.) *Psychoanalysis on the Move. The Work of Joseph Sandle.* London and New York: Routledge.

Kestenberg, J. and Gampel, Y. (1983). Growing Up in the Holocaust Culture. *Israel Journal of Psychiatry, 20,* 129-146.

Epilogue

Looking Forward

John Bunzl
University of Vienna

Reading this book again with the crucial hindsight learned since 1999, some key words come to mind: originality, complexity, and pessimism. Some of the chapters may look overly optimistic, while others may appear overly pessimistic. It is impossible to keep updating our interpretations so that they remain consistent with the unfolding and changing historical events. The ideas presented in our nine chapters, even with the absence of any updating, remain vivid, provocative, and insightful.

It has often been said that the Israeli-Palestinian drama was the most over-analyzed conflict in the world and the same thing could be said about Israeli society itself. Still, I think this volume has contributed new dimensions and has opened new perspectives. It is one of the rare attempts to bring together sophisticated political and psychological observations covering two major fields: Jewish and Zionist identity and history on the one hand, and conflict and conflict-transcending strategies in West Asia on the other.

Although we were not sure if a focus on psychoanalysis would be helpful in this endeavor, now we can claim that a non-dogmatic application of Freud's ideas was indeed stimulating and thought provoking. I believe this has something to do with the structure and function of psychoanalysis itself. Being at the same time a conceptual tool for analysis of human behavior and a psychotherapy technique, always oriented towards the past and committed to overcome the past, this method seems appropriate for individual and collective questions of identity and conflict which have their still burning roots in both more distant and more recent history.

But, as the contributors to this book have reminded us, not all determining factors are unconscious, and a major role is assigned to the conscious intentions of individuals, especially those in positions of leadership.

Looking forward at this tragic juncture of events in the West Asia seems a bit preposterous. In view of the political impasse that led to the Second Palestinian *Intifada* (starting in October of 2000), I would like to focus on Zionist-Israeli behavior and rationalizations, which have become a pattern of long duration: I have in mind the persistent inability to link intentions and consequences. It is by no means accidental that "old" historians focus on the self-emancipatory features of Zionism, while "new" historians focus on the price Palestinians had to pay for the realization of the Zionist dream. We find an extension of this pattern, and its logical conclusion, in an elaborate system of blaming the victims. In some stages of the negotiations the Zionist narrative became an obstacle on the diplomatic level as well. Although Prime Minster Ehud Barak in the year 2000 was forced to concede that the fate of the Palestinians in 1948 was tragic, he refused to link this tragedy to any Israeli wrongdoing. His idea of "ending" the conflict without a process of re-examination of narratives proved short-sighted and can be seen as a reflection of considerable anxiety and an attempt at desperate coping. Israeli-Palestinian sociologist Nadim Rouhana (2001) notes that for genuine reconciliation ("end of the conflict") to take place four key issues should be addressed:

+ justice
+ truth
+ historical responsibility
+ restructuring social and political relationship between the parties

He believes that, as a starting point, Israelis should recognize the simple historical truth that the realization of Zionism and the establishment of Israel were incompatible with justice and/or equality for the Palestinians.

> In order to avoid the moral implications, Israel developed a massive and sophisticated system of denial mechanisms and multilevel justifications to come to term with its own history. Israel, inevitably, denies both the means by which the establishment of a Jewish state in another people's homeland was achieved and its consequences for the Palestinian people (p. 21).

In other words: a painful working-through of history appears to have become an essential pre-condition for any durable peace perspective. This process does concern the "self" and the "Other" as a matter of equal urgency. While our volume offers many insights into the Israeli-Jewish side of the equation and opens new field of research, we still hope to raise similar questions concerning Palestinian society. Such an enterprise would have to consider the almost non-existent reception of psychoanalytic thought within Arab-Islamic culture, although there is no lack of mental health concerns especially in a society as traumatized as the Palestinian one. In a vicious circle being traumatized by the consequences of Zionist colonization blocks any consideration of intentions resulting from Jewish suffering. We have here, as so often, a reverse version of the Zionist mindset. The practical implications of this state of affairs should not be under-estimated.

Politically speaking the Palestinian difficulties in choosing between strategic and tactical attitudes towards co-existence with Israel result from the dilemma of being confronted with the demand of recognizing the Zionist state not only as a fact, but also as a "legitimate" one (cf. Beit-Hallahmi, 1993). Nadim Rouhana offers an insight into, and perhaps a way out of, this dilemma, by pointing to a distinction between the state and its people :"The most difficult prerequisite is the acknowledgement of the right of the Israeli Jewish people – an acquired right. Palestinians will have to make a distinction between their refusal to accept Zionism (that is, the claim that Jews have a right to establish a state in Palestine) and the acquired right of the Jewish Israelis – not the Jewish people – for self-determination" (p. 23).

Even this distinction, which would not satisfy most Jewish Israelis, would require a de-mystification and a de-demonization of Zionism, hardly imaginable under conditions of occupation and humiliation. The enormous task ahead therefore includes not only overcoming the present cycle of victimization, but also the creation of conditions which would allow for the (conceptual) humanization of the (former) victimizer. Can psychoanalysis contribute to such a process? I believe that it can. This volume is one piece of evidence. But what we have done so far pales in comparison with the tasks lying ahead.

References

Beit-Hallahmi, B. (1993*). Original Sins: Reflections on the History of Zionism and Israel.* Brooklyn, N. Y.: Interlink.

Rouhana, N. (in press). Reconciliation in protracted national conflict: Identity and power in the Israeli-Palestinian case. In A. Eagly L. Hamilton, L. & R. Baron, (Eds.). *The Social Psychology of Group Identity and Social Conflict: Theory, Application, and Practice*. Washington, DC: American Psychological Association.

Index